Dependency Approaches to International Political Economy
A Cross-National Study

DEPENDENCY APPROACHES TO INTERNATIONAL POLITICAL ECONOMY

A Cross-National Study

VINCENT A. MAHLER

Columbia University Press   New York   1980

Library of Congress Cataloging in Publication Data

Mahler, Vincent A
Dependency approaches to international political
economy.

Bibliography: p.
Includes index.
1. Underdeveloped areas.   2. International
economic relations.   I. Title.
HC59.7.M247   382.1′09172′4   79-26200
ISBN 0-231-04836-X

Columbia University Press
New York   Guildford, Surrey
Copyright © 1980 Columbia University Press
Printed in the United States of America

To Mary

Contents

Acknowledgments

ACKNOWLEDGING THE CONTRIBU-
tions of the people who have helped along the way is one of the
most pleasant parts of bringing a book to completion. I would like
especially to express my thanks to Gerald Finch, Joan Spero, Stuart
Fagan, Philip Oldenburg, Clyde Weed, and Bruce Russett, all of
whom read complete drafts of this work and offered many valuable
comments and criticisms; and to James Mittelman, Andrew Bev-
eridge, Walter Bourne, Stanley Heginbotham, Alice Amsden, Patrick
McGowan, James Caporaso, Terrance Gough, and Joseph Galas-
kiewicz, whose assistance of various kinds over several years is much
appreciated.

The computing time used in this study was provided by a grant
from the Columbia University Center for Computing Activities, and
data storage space was made available by Columbia's Center for the
Social Sciences; I am grateful to both.

Finally, and above all, I wish to thank my wife, Mary, to whom
this work is dedicated; my debt to her is profound, and I am proud to
acknowledge it publicly.

Dependency Approaches to International Political Economy
A Cross-National Study

CHAPTER ONE

What This Book Is About

IT IS EMINENTLY CLEAR TO ANY-
one familiar with the literature that *dependency,* like *gravity, cancer,* or *intelligence,* does not refer to a single unambiguous phenomenon, concept or set of traits. Indeed, the term itself does little more than direct attention to a group of related issues, and the "theory" of international political-economic dependence is really more a paradigm or framework of analysis than a body of commonly accepted relational propositions. Although most dependency theorists share a common outlook on North-South relations in general, they disagree on a wide range of particular issues, many of them important. Moreover, within the dependency tradition there are entire avenues of approach that are simply at such different levels of analysis that they render synthesis not only difficult but also largely irrelevant.

Despite these difficulties it is useful to begin this study by briefly proposing several very broad themes that are common to almost all formulations of dependency theory and by providing some indication of how they will be dealt with here. Later, closer attention can be given to more subtle points and disagreements among dependency theorists, but for now the intention is only to set the scene for future discussion by offering the reader some notion of where and how this study will proceed.

One of the most distinctive contributions of dependency theory is that it considers political and economic underdevelopment in the Third World not a residual condition that stems from a paucity of interaction with more advanced countries, but rather the product of extensive but asymmetrical contact with just such countries. For dependency theorists interaction among nations or social groups at very different levels of development tends to operate within a structure that is biased in favor of more developed participants. A high level of participation within a framework of this kind is viewed as likely to result in the solidification of patterns of relationship, both between less developed and developed countries (LDCs and DCs) and within LDCs themselves, that retard meaningful development.

Among the external linkages most often cited by dependency theorists as characteristic of such a process are private direct investment, trade, economic assistance, debt, educational and military ties. To the extent that a less developed country engages in a relatively intensive relationship with very much more developed and powerful nations in some or all of these areas, and to the extent that these ties are concentrated among relatively few economically and politically dominant partners, we might say that it is *externally dependent* as the literature usually defines the term.

But while a careful examination of the nature and extent of linkages between industrialized and Third World countries itself merits attention, it is of equal interest to consider the consequences of these linkages for domestic political systems in underdeveloped countries. Perhaps the most frequently cited consequence of a high level of external dependence is the emergence of a co-opted elite within an LDC which uses leverage achieved from its internationally reinforced position to prevent meaningful distributive and social welfare policies that might threaten its dominance at home. This elite can be expected to be antidemocratic in political orientation, to require or to prefer a relatively large military and internal security establishment and to emphasize the production or import of "luxury" consumption goods at the expense of more substantive development. A larger proportion of the population in a highly dependent country is likely, other things being equal, to receive a small share of the country's wealth, to be poorly educated and unfairly taxed and to experience a low level of social welfare than in a country which is less dependent.

The central purpose of this book is to restate some of these very broad propositions as formal hypotheses, and then to test these hypotheses by means of a cross-national study of seventy underdeveloped countries. While the details of this process will emerge in the following chapters, it may be useful at this point to pose some of the major questions that will govern the organization of the study that follows and to give some preliminary indications of the methods that will be used in answering them.

Question 1   Does external dependence constitute a syndrome which, while it may consist of distinct subsyndromes, contains no serious inconsistencies? What are some of the broad mechanisms through which external dependence operates?

Although the derivation of the specific indicators used in this study will be discussed at length, it can be stated here that, while different theorists emphasize different mechanisms of dependence, most would agree that an LDC can be considered externally dependent to the extent that some or all of the following are true:

It is host to a relatively large stock of private direct foreign investment from corporations based in developed countries, and this investment is highly concentrated by source.

Its economy is strongly oriented to external trade, which is concentrated by partner and by commodity and which is characterized by the exchange of exports at low levels of processing for imports at higher levels.

It receives a large amount of foreign economic assistance relative to the size of its own economy, and this assistance is highly concentrated by donor.

It devotes considerable resources to the servicing of foreign debts, and it has a relatively poor reserves position.

It trains a large proportion of its university students in a relatively few advanced countries.

It maintains close military ties with more advanced nations and devotes considerable resources to the purchase of arms from abroad.

The first task of this study is to collect data for seventy less developed countries on a number of indicators that attempt to tap these dimensions and then to perform principal component R-factor analysis on these variables. This technique will allow us to identify distinct subsyndromes within a broader syndrome of external dependence by isolating composite variables that embody most of the variance of a wider range of individual indicators. From this exercise we should also receive some indication whether the single broad rubric, external dependence, masks serious internal inconsistencies.

Question II   Are high levels of external dependence in less developed countries related to basic internal structural distortions in these countries, resulting in a relatively disadvantaged position for nonelites? Are they related to economic stagnation? Do relationships continue to hold when important outside variables are taken into account?

The study will next discuss predictions from the dependency litera-ture regarding the consequences for LDCs of high levels of external dependence. The main theme is that a global center–periphery in-teraction structure is paralleled in dependent LDCs by an internal structure in which elites are co-opted into a broader international "center" which serves to reinforce their domestic dominance, while nonelites are drawn into the same system in a manner whereby they tend increasingly to be marginalized and their relative position to de-teriorate.

A series of multiple regression analyses will be used to relate levels of external dependence to a wide range of internal character-istics with which they are hypothesized to be associated, among them equity of income distribution, level of general social welfare, extent of government efforts in the areas of education and social in-surance, level of unemployment, progressivity of national taxation systems, pervasiveness of mechanisms of political coercion and (more controversially among dependency theorists) rate of economic growth. The analysis will also take into account a series of control variables, the most important of which are gross national product per capita and natural resource endowment; the multiple regression for-mat will allow us to compare countries with these variables, in effect, held constant.

Question III   What is the regional dimension of the external interac-tions of LDCs? Do there exist regional subgroupings of countries that share a common pattern of external linkages? Are these structured according to a "feudal interaction structure" linking groups of LDC "satellites" with major DC partners?

Very few studies of international political-economic dependency have gone beyond studying relationships among variables and exam-ined patterns of similarity on these variables among groups of LDCs. This study will address this gap in the literature by attempting to de-termine whether there exist coherent groups of LDCs which demon-strate a common pattern of external dependence. The method that will be used is *Q*-factor analysis, a multivariate technique which explores relationships not among variables but among cases (in this instance individual LDCs) on those variables. If there emerge from this analysis clusters of LDCs sharing a common configuration on the various modes of external dependence, the often broad and abstract body of dependency theory will be given a spatial dimension that should add greatly to its usefulness in understanding specific characteristics of individual countries.

We must also ask whether individual industrial nations maintain particularly intensive networks of interaction with identifiable groups of LDC satellites, as would be predicted by theorists who posit an international system characterized by feudal ties between industrial nations and LDCs. Although sufficient data are not available for a comprehensive study of dyadic relationships, it is possible to construct matrices for many of the variables of most interest to dependency theorists, including private direct foreign investment, international trade, arms transfers, official development assistance and educational ties; principal relationships within these matrices will be displayed in a series of detailed tables which will summarize their most important characteristics.

SOME PROBLEMS

A study of this sort raises numerous issues, several of the most important of which are discussed in this section.

A first problem stems from the fact that this study stands at the intersection of two very different approaches to scientific validation. It is almost a truism that dependency theory is rarely posed in the form of a series of clearly falsifiable hypotheses, and because of this one detects among many scholars an impatience to specify and to test, once and for all, this "theory" in the same manner as has been attempted for other social science theories. Tyler and Wogart, for example, suggest that

> the theory of dependency has become something of a cause célèbre. It is either eagerly accepted or scornfully rejected as a matter of faith—primarily because of its political implications. . . . As a result of the politicization of the dependency thesis there so far has been a dearth of objective and scholarly research attempt[ing] to examine its validity.[1]

The point is well taken. But, unfortunately, the task of distilling falsifiable hypotheses from the dependency literature is not an easy or straightforward one. For one thing dependency arguments are often very complex and subtle, and any attempt to subsume them in explicit hypotheses is almost doomed to appear in some respects painfully shallow by comparison. But, beyond this, when we attempt to test dependency theory using standard social science techniques, we are operating at the border of two very different approaches to the problem of scientific validation, one generally embraced by the formulators of dependency theory and the other by its testers. As put by James Caporaso,

> it is easy to see how this controversy might escalate along a number of lines, with positivists arguing that if dependency theory is not testable it is worthless (at least as theory) and dependencia theorists retorting that theory-testing is not limited to quantitative statistical assessments and that ideas are also confirmed or disconfirmed by the success or failure of political practice.[2]

It must be clearly stated from the outset that this study is predicated on the first approach to scientific validation. I have, however, tried to be sensitive to the sorts of variables (such as indicators of marginality and income distribution) that the formulators of dependency theory consider most relevant, and to be as faithful as possible to the subtleties of the dependency approach. Obviously, cross-national quantitative analysis is not the only way of studying dependency, even within the positivist tradition, but it is hoped that this study will provide a body of evidence that will complement rather than compete with other forms of inquiry, and will make, in its own terms, a useful contribution to the ultimate objective of a fuller understanding of the relationship between poor and rich countries.

A second issue is that this study analyzes for a monochronic cross section what is (as is almost always the case in social science) a fundamentally dynamic theory. The reason for this is obvious: for many of the variables of most concern to dependency theorists, especially in the areas of private direct investment and income distribution, data covering periods before the late 1960s are simply unavailable for more than a handful of LDCs.

The assumption of the cross-sectional approach used here is, of course, that if an objective condition of external dependence has explanatory relevance, the most externally dependent of a given group of countries at a given time (controlling for differences among countries that would invalidate meaningful comparison) will also exhibit the strongest manifestation of the various internal characteristics—marginality, inequitable income distribution and so on—with which this condition is hypothesized to be related. It is important to note that variation within the cross section of countries analyzed is not assumed to represent any particular historical progression (the most developed countries, for example, to represent the future of the less developed); on the contrary, level of development and several other such characteristics are introduced at every stage of the analysis as control variables in order to determine whether variation in internal characteristics owes more to these than to variation in levels of external dependence.

It is clear that, while there are certain advantages to time-series analysis of this and similar topics, there are also certain disadvantages, particularly for the short-term time series that are all that are available for most LDCs. One of these is expressed by Douglas Hibbs, citing two other studies, in reference to a cross-sectional analysis of the causes of political violence:

> There is no reason . . . to be apologetic about having used cross-sectional data in this research. In many ways cross-section-based models are superior to those estimated against time-series data, since typical time series, especially those available to social scientists, are of relatively short duration. Short-duration time series simply cannot pick up the effects of [a wide range of variables that] have important effects . . . [but] do not change much in the short run; and without variance, estimation precision and causal inference are not feasible. This is why careful studies of the utility of cross-sectional versus time-series analysis in economics indicate that ". . . cross-section data tend to measure long run and other effects that are not observable, for a number of reasons, in short period . . . time series variations . . ." [Kuh and Meyer]. And ". . . cross-sections typically will reflect long run adjustments whereas annual time series will tend to reflect shorter run reaction" [Kuh].[3]

We must remember that longitudinal analysis does not in itself offer assurance of causality or even of causal direction; one need only recall the *post hoc, propter hoc* fallacy to agree with one commentator that although "many scholars seem to feel that the use of a longitudinal research design . . . is sufficient to prove the hypothesized causal ordering of the model," there are ". . . innumerable . . . misspecifications that will 'fit' any set of longitudinal data just as there are . . . innumerable [misspecifications] which will 'fit' any set of cross-sectional data."[4] In the end, as put by the same scholar,

a unit of analysis . . . is simply an instance of the replication of a process. Therefore, to test the relationship between [two variables] one can
use any instance in which these two variables occur, providing the
scope conditions of the theory are met. A set of valid units for comparison, then, may be found in time (a time-series analysis), in space (a
cross-sectional analysis), or in both time and space (a panel analysis).
Any theory can be tested in any or all of these ways, because what is
being compared is the relationship among variables. There is no one
proper or improper unit of analysis.[5]

All of this is not to say that time-series analysis, other things being
equal, is not to be preferred to cross-sectional analysis. It is only to
say that longitudinal analysis is not a panacea and that its use should
not be bought at any cost. For the purposes of this exploratory study
the costs of time-series analysis seemed too high: an analysis that
went back in time even ten years would risk either drastically reducing the sample size, with the result that findings would represent only
a handful of semideveloped countries, mostly from Latin America; or
omitting (or very imperfectly measuring) many of the variables of
most interest to dependency theorists, especially in the areas of income distribution and private direct foreign investment. And even at
these costs we would have no way of knowing whether ten years was
a meaningful period in terms of dependency predictions, which are
often very long-term in character; a meaningful test might as easily
require a lag of twenty, fifty or a hundred years.

Even given these difficulties, time-series analysis might prove most
useful in examining some of the issues raised in this study (I make
some suggestions as to how this might be done in chapter 8), but I
would maintain that until longer time series are available for many
of the variables of interest to dependency theorists, time-series analysis will be able to complement, but not wholly supersede, analysis of
the sort reported here.

A third issue concerns the choice of countries examined in this
study.[6] Table 1.1 lists the countries of the sample, which, as can be
seen, include a large proportion of all less developed countries with
populations greater than one million. Although some such countries
are omitted, this sample is one of the largest to date in a cross-national test of dependency hypotheses.

It is evident, however, that an analysis based only on less developed countries allows us to explore but one set of interactions among
the full range of interactions that comprise world politics. The scope

of relationships that might have been considered is suggested by table 1.2, which rests on the very rough division of the world into four categories of countries.

Table 1.1 Countries of the Sample

Black Africa

Cameroun	Liberia	Sierra Leone
Central African Empire	Madagascar	Somalia
Chad	Malawi	Sudan
Congo	Mali	Tanzania
Benin	Mauritania	Togo
Ethiopia	Mauritius	Uganda
Gambia	Niger	Upper Volta
Ghana	Nigeria	Zaire
Ivory Coast	Rwanda	Zambia
Kenya	Senegal	

Middle East

Egypt	Lebanon	Syria
Jordan	Morocco	Tunisia

Latin America and Caribbean

Argentina	El Salvador	Mexico
Bolivia	Guatemala	Nicaragua
Brazil	Ecuador	Panama
Chile	Guyana	Peru
Colombia	Haiti	Paraguay
Costa Rica	Honduras	Uruguay
Dominican Republic	Jamaica	

Asia

Afghanistan	Republic of Korea	Singapore
Burma	Malaysia	Sri Lanka
India	Pakistan	Thailand
Indonesia	Philippines	

Southern Europe

Greece	Turkey	Yugoslavia
Spain		

Table 1.2 Interactions in World Politics

Categories	*DCs*	*SocCs*	*OilCs*	*LDCs*
Developed capitalist countries	A			
Socialist countries	B	C		
Oil-producing countries	D	E	F	
Less developed countries	**G**	**H**	**I**	J

Of the ten broad areas of contact indicated in the table, this study concentrates upon categories G, H and I (and especially upon category G, within which most of the external contacts of LDCs take place). This seems a not unreasonable basis for limiting the scope of the study, since it is on relationships between developed capitalist countries and Third World countries (LDCs) that most dependency theorists have focused their attention.

But, although other relationships are not directly considered in this study, it might nevertheless be of use briefly to mention a few that have been the subject of comment by dependency theorists and their critics. First there is category A, relationships among developed capitalist states. Since there is no question that developed capitalist countries do differ in absolute power and wealth (although by definition they do not differ fundamentally in the *level* of development), it is possible that countries like Canada, which exist in the shadow of a much more powerful neighbor and suffer serious, if not entirely nonreciprocal, constraints on their autonomy as a result, experience internal effects similar to those that are hypothesized to characterize highly dependent LDCs. The same might be said of countries such as Australia and New Zealand, which specialize heavily in the production of primary products for export and thus maintain what dependency theorists consider very unfavorable degree-of-processing trade ratios. On the other hand, it is possible (indeed, it seems likely) that differences in level of development, as well as in absolute power or wealth, are a precondition of the sorts of internal consequences predicted by dependency theorists.

Exploration of these competing possibilities is, quite simply, beyond the scope of this study, and would probably be most profitably addressed in a separate study: the few cross-national tests of dependency hypotheses that have included both DCs and LDCs have resulted in findings that have tended to reflect more clearly the enormous differences between DCs and LDCs within the sample than relationships that were of substantive interest.[7]

A second major omission from consideration in this study is category C, relations among socialist countries. This topic has been the subject of considerable debate, particularly concerning the question whether relations between the Soviet Union and Eastern Europe or Cuba might as accurately be characterized by the dependency syndrome as relationships among capitalist countries.

Many dependency theorists simply limit dependency theory by def-

inition to the study of intercapitalist relations; as put by Bodenheimer,

> if imperialism is dissociated from capitalism then it must be regarded as
> little more than a policy; in this respect the logical conclusions of many
> non-Marxist theories of imperialism almost converge with those of in-
> ternational relations theory. And if imperialism is dissociated from the
> global expansion of capitalism at the international level, the concept
> loses its potential as an explanation of dependency in Latin America.[8]

Other scholars within the dependency perspective do not remove in-
tersocialist relations from consideration by definition, but instead
deny that these have, in practice, the same characteristics as do
Western–Third World relations. As put by Guy Gilbert, Soviet relations with Eastern Europe offer "no Soviet advantage . . . in normal
economic relations," while "trade imbalances between the USSR
and Cuba are a matter of bookkeeping entries, unlike the multilateral
trade between capitalist states which requires a 'real' medium of
exchange."[9]

A good many scholars, however, maintain that a general theory of
dependency or imperialism must go beyond exclusive emphasis on
relationships among capitalist countries. George Lichtheim, for example, suggests that attempts to "make imperialism rhyme with capitalism" limit the concept along ideological lines in a manner that is
essentially arbitrary.[10] David Ray concurs, suggesting that

> Soviet economic imperialism has been no less a reality than the capital-
> ist variety. Indeed, there is a striking similarity between the economic
> dependence which has been imposed upon Latin America by the United
> States and the economic dependence which has been imposed upon
> Eastern Europe by the Soviet Union.[11]

The position governing this study is that the question whether relationships between weak and strong socialist states have consequences
similar to those between developed capitalist states and Third World
countries is an issue worthy of much more sustained and serious analysis than it has received from dependency theorists, but that this
study is not the place to attempt such analysis.[12] In fact, the practical
problems of creating indicators valid across groups of countries for
which even basic concepts like national product and foreign investment have very different meanings might best be attempted in a separate study of its own, rather than in a study which integrates socialist

and nonsocialist countries in a single analysis. About what such a study would find, no predictions are offered but, by the same token, whatever the findings were they would not in themselves invalidate the findings of this study.

A final omission from the sample examined in this study is of countries that were in 1970 major oil producers (except for a few moderate-scale producers with very large populations). This restriction was made primarily for practical reasons: basic statistics for major oil producers, especially those with small populations, are not readily compared with those for Third World countries, and if the two are indiscriminately grouped together, findings can be very misleading.

This is substantively unfortunate, since it eliminates from the study a group of nations which, while in some ways highly *externally dependent* as the term is defined by dependency theorists, have prospered as countries rarely have prospered. But, then, oil is a unique primary commodity in terms of the extent and stability of demand pressure and the ease and rapidity with which supply can be regulated; clearly the oil producers' experience has not been repeated for the producers of any other primary commodity, nor is it likely to be in the near future.

In any case the posture of this study toward categories D, E and F is again an agnostic one, and no assertions are made as to whether dependency operates in these spheres, and if so in what direction. Once again, this omission does not detract from the findings of this study, but merely limits their generality.[13]

A fourth issue concerns the assumption of this study that the level of external dependence does vary meaningfully among LDCs. The issue arises from the fact that "dependency" is often characterized as if it were a dichotomous variable: a country is deemed dependent if it meets certain criteria and nondependent if it does not. In the most extreme case this approach tends toward circularity: in a rephrasing of Santos' familiar definition by one scholar, "dependent countries are those which lack the capacity for autonomous growth, and they lack this because their structures are dependent ones."[14]

The central assumption of this study is that while all of the seventy countries included are potentially dependent—they were chosen, after all, because they are "less developed" than are others of the world's countries—they do differ significantly in the degree and nature of that dependence. This assumption can be supported on several grounds. One is the conceptual ground that if "dependent" is exactly identified with "underdeveloped, but living in a world dominated by rich countries," the term loses much of its utility: such a concept tells us little that we did not already know. (As put by O'Brien, "Was it really necessary to write so many millions of words to establish just this perspective?")[15] A second ground is the empirically verifiable fact that LDCs do vary considerably on a wide range of the external ties that dependency theorists identify with "external dependence."

In the words of John S. Odell

> a theory should be made to account for variations in behavior as well as its central tendencies. . . . Any theory which is in the position of discounting the relevance of interesting differences could be made even stronger and more comprehensive by research that focuses directly on variation.[16]

We need not, of course, assume that variation among LDCs ranges from "total" to "non-" dependence, but only that it is meaningful.

THE CHAPTERS TO COME: A PREVIEW
This chapter, the first, has attempted to provide a general overview of the study to come. A chapter by chapter preview will now be presented.

The next chapter, the second, offers a discussion of the academic literature most immediately relevant to the study. In this chapter seven previous cross-national quantitative tests of dependency hypotheses are examined in an effort to illustrate ways in which the problems of operationalization and testing faced in this study have been dealt with in the past, and a number of suggestions are made as to how these studies will be supplemented or improved upon in this analysis.

The third chapter focuses directly on the operationalization of *external dependence*. After two brief introductory sections proposing various ways in which dependency theorists have conceived of contact between developed and underdeveloped countries, thirteen indicators of external dependence, as the term is usually used in the literature, are presented. These indicators are then submitted to correlational and *R*-factor analysis in an effort to determine whether they demonstrate inconsistencies which would cast doubt upon their coherence even as a process which can operate through distinct modes, and to explore the possibility of distilling from these narrow indicators a smaller number of composite dimensions. This chapter conveys a notion of the dimensionality of at least the most important North-South linkages and offers an operational means of determining whether one LDC is more externally dependent than others and in which areas.

The fourth chapter assesses the dependency literature dealing with the consequences of high levels of external dependence for the internal distribution of power and wealth in underdeveloped countries. A first section delves briefly into the intellectual antecedents of dependency approaches: it explores the contribution to dependency theory of two earlier and related approaches to North-South relations, the traditions of imperialism and structuralism, and highlights similarities and differences between these approaches and the dependency tradition. The next sections deal directly with several major strands of the dependency literature: one describes the main lines of the center–periphery imagery commonly employed by dependency theorists; another focuses on the "internationalized bourgeoisie" or "comprador elite" in LDCs which is said to constitute the means of transmission of external influences into domestic politics; a third deals with dependency arguments concerning the hypothesized consequences of high levels of external dependence on nonelites in LDCs; and a fourth focuses on the narrow question, controversial among dependency theorists, whether high levels of external dependence are inevitably associated with economic stagnation in LDCs, or whether aggregate economic growth can and does occur within dependency structures.

The fifth chapter attempts to operationalize and test some of the broad hypotheses that have been summarized in the previous chapter. It first proposes eleven indicators dealing with distribution and marginalization in LDCs—including indicators of income distribution, social policy, tax progressivity, unemployment and internal security efforts—and also an indicator of aggregate economic growth. It then attempts to explain variance in these indicators using the indicators of external dependence developed in chapter 3 as explanatory variables within a series of multiple regression analyses. Also accounted for are a number of control variables, the most important of which, gross national product per capita and natural resource endowment, are included as competing explanatory variables at every stage of the analysis. Supplementing the basic series of multiple regressions are several analyses that deal with particular questions that arise, and an analysis of residuals that identifies individual cases not well explained by the regression generalizations and proposes reasons for their deviance.

Chapters 4 and 5 might be thought of as pursuing one line of inquiry from chapter 3, in which the indicators of external dependence were introduced: these chapters have posed the question of what the consequences are of high levels of external dependence for the internal distribution of power and wealth within LDCs. The next two chapters, 6 and 7, might be seen as pursuing another line of inquiry: they address the question of what the regional and subregional dimensions are of the external relations of less developed countries. Chapter 6 reports the findings of a Q-factor analysis of the indicators of external dependence in an attempt to determine whether there exist regional clusters of LDCs sharing a common pattern of external dependence. Chapter 7 then examines a series of matrices linking particular LDCs with particular DC partners in an effort to determine whether there appear to be, as dependency theorists have hypothesized, "feudal interaction structures" linking industrial countries with groups of LDC "satellites." It is hoped that these two chapters will contribute to an understanding of the regional dimension of external dependence, an element which has been neglected in most previous cross-national studies in this area.

Chapter 8, the last, briefly summarizes the major findings of the study and makes a few suggestions as to directions in which future research might most profitably be directed.

Finally, four appendixes address matters that will be of interest to many readers, but in a treatment that is too detailed for inclusions in the body of the text: the first explores the appropriateness of applying "rigorous empiricist" methods to the analysis of dependency theory, concentrating on arguments of Raymond Duvall; the second examines responses to dependency theory from a Marxist perspective, focusing on the work of Robert Brenner; and the third and fourth discuss the methodology and indicators of the study in more technical detail than would be appropriate in the body of the text.

CHAPTER TWO

Some Previous Cross-National Quantitative Tests of Dependency Theory

MOST DEPENDENCY THEORISTS HAVE either analyzed, in very broad and general terms, the global political economy as a whole or have concentrated narrowly on the external relations of one or a few particular countries. But however effective these authors may have been in distinguishing broad themes of interaction between developed countries and LDCs or in explaining particular sets of circumstances, few have consciously attempted to pose a set of falsifiable hypotheses and then to test these hypotheses for a relatively large sample of Third World countries.

Yet, while dependency theorists themselves have seldom attempted analysis in this mode, their hypotheses have in recent years excited much interest among quantitatively oriented social scientists and have been the subject of a number of cross-national statistical assessments.[1] It is hoped that close examination of the work of scholars dealing with problems of operationalization and testing similar to those faced in this study will prove instructive in suggesting promising avenues that might be further explored as well as in illustrating less useful approaches that might be avoided or improved upon.

One of the earliest cross-national quantitative tests of dependency hypotheses is reported by William G. Tyler and J. Peter Wogart in a 1973 article in the *Journal of Interamerican Studies and World Affairs*.[2] The central hypothesis of these authors is that high levels of external dependence are related to national disintegration in LDCs, and they suggest that, according to the dependency perspective, the crucial feature of "internal colonialism" which occurs during the process of international integration is the transfer of resources from the exploited backward sectors to that sector linked to the international economy. Domestically, such a transfer implies a further skewing in the internal distribution of income.[3]

The authors develop a series of indicators of external dependence which includes a ratio of total exports to gross national product, a ratio of exports to the two principal trade partners to total exports and a ratio of the two principal export commodities to total exports. In providing an indication of marginalization and national disintegration, they offer share data on household income distribution. They then employ multiple regression analysis to determine the relationship between external dependence and internal inequality for a cross section of thirty-nine less developed countries for 1964–1966. The authors' findings are generally weak, but are without exception in the expected direction, and they conclude that "there is not sufficient evidence to reject the dependency hypothesis."[4] They end their article by suggesting that "the task to more closely examine the empirical validity of the dependency argument will be left to future, more thorough, researchers."[5]

What might a "future, more thorough, researcher" learn from this study? How might the researcher best expand upon it? A first priority would be to extend the operationalization of external dependence beyond Tyler and Wogart's reliance on a single mode, trade relations; a more comprehensive test of dependency hypotheses must surely take into consideration the direct investment, debt, economic assistance, military and cultural ties that are the subject of so much of the literature. A second priority would be to increase the range of hypotheses tested; it seems evident that the operationalization of "national disintegration" would be improved by the inclusion of indicators of unemployment, social policy, economic growth, internal security efforts and other variables along with the indicators of income distribution. A third priority would be to increase the range of countries examined and to pay closer attention to the regional dimension of ties of external dependence. Above all, this study is weakened by the absence of any control variables: as the authors themselves admit, "It may well be that the demonstrated relationship between distributional inequality and economic dependence is spurious,"[6] and the complex reality that undoubtedly lies behind these weak but confirmatory findings may have been better specified if such factors as per capita national income or resource endowment had been accounted for.

A second cross-national test of dependency theory, by Christopher Chase-Dunn, is reported in a 1975 issue of *The American Sociological Review.*[7] Here the author uses a panel multiple regression model to test hypotheses relating modes of external dependence to economic growth and income distribution in a worldwide sample of LDCs. In operationalizing external dependence, Chase-Dunn concentrates upon two particular modes of the several that will be examined in this study: a first mode, *investment dependence,* is based on an average for 1950–1955 of the item "debits on investment income" in the International Monetary Fund's *Balance of Payments Yearbook;* and a second mode, *debt dependence,* is indicated by the total external public debt of a country in 1965, as reported by the International Bank for Reconstruction and Development (IBRD). As dependent variables the author also proposes two sets of indicators: a first is comprised of three standard indicators of economic development, each for two points in time, and is intended to measure "aggregate economic development";[8] a second, the Gini index of household income distribution, is intended to measure the overall pattern of income distribution in a country. The author introduces into each set of equations two control variables, domestic capital formation and specialization in mining for the first set of dependent variables and specialization in mining and economic development level for the second.[9]

Chase-Dunn's basic hypothesis is that a high level of external dependence has two major consequences for LDCs. First, economic growth is negatively affected because

> (a) exploitation by the core drains resources from the periphery which are needed for its development . . .
> (b) externally oriented production and penetration by transnational corporations distort the economic structure of the periphery . . . [and]
> (c) links between elites in the core and the dependent periphery act to suppress autonomous mobilization of national development.

And, second, income inequalities are reinforced because "in peripheral countries penetrated by external control structures, the ruling groups are able to obtain a large share of the national income and to prevent income redistribution because their power is backed up by alliances with the core." [10]

Chase-Dunn concludes from his analysis that both investment and debt dependence have negative effects on economic development and positive effects on income inequality, although the latter findings are weak. Both of these findings are, of course, as the theoretical dependency literature would predict.

What can be learned from this study that will be of use in further study of the topic? The feature that might most be emulated is Chase-Dunn's careful consideration of several control variables; that he takes these into account strengthens his findings considerably. Many of the other weaknesses of Tyler and Wogart's study still hold, however: the study focuses on only two indicators of external dependence, debt and investment dependence, and gives no indication of the concentration (as opposed to the extent) of ties in these areas; [11] the number of countries examined ranges only from 24 to 46; and the range of dependent variables, although wider than in the Tyler and Wogart study, is still rather narrow, focusing only upon economic growth and income distribution.

More specifically, a future study might make use of much improved data for several key variables, some of which have only recently become available. Investment dependence, for example, is clearly better measured by estimated book values of foreign investment stocks than by several years' investment income flow, as reported in balance of payments data, and debt dependence is better measured by a ratio that concentrates upon projected debt service than by one which simply measures debt outstanding regardless of the terms or duration of the loans.

A third cross-national test of dependency theory is reported in an article by Lawrence R. Alschuler in a 1976 issue of the *International Studies Quarterly*. [12] The author's hypothesis is that a high level of participation by LDCs in an international political-economic structure dominated by industrial nations produces not development but stagnation, a similar hypothesis to that for which Chase-Dunn provided some confirmation. Alschuler's indicators of external dependence combine features of the capital flow indicators emphasized by Chase-Dunn and the trade indicators employed by Tyler and Wogart: he has collected data on export commodity concentration, on trade partner concentration and on the relative level of processing of foreign trade, as well as on what he calls "capital penetration," the percentage of national income paid as factor income to the rest of the world. He proposes three indicators of the "growth-stagnation" dimension: growth rate of GNP per capita, growth rate of the population in urban areas and growth rate of the percentage of school-aged population enrolled in primary and secondary schools.

Alschuler uses canonical correlation analysis to relate the four indicators of external dependence to these three indicators of growth and stagnation. His findings are generally moderately strong and in the expected direction, and they lead him to state that "as a general conclusion I can say with confidence that satellization is a determinant of stagnation in Latin America." [13]

What does this study demonstrate that will be of use for the "further explorations in the future" that the author recommends? To begin, we might broaden somewhat the hypotheses being tested. While the narrow question whether dependence results in growth or stagnation in LDCs is of interest and has been much debated, it does not by any means exhaust the hypotheses proposed by dependency theorists. For example, it is quite possible that even in countries in which aggregate national income is increasing rapidly, the relative and even the absolute position of the bulk of the population is stagnating or deteriorating. Similarly, the urbanization rate is not necessarily associated with improvement in the distribution of a society's resources; in fact some scholars have suggested exactly the opposite, including at least one prominent dependency theorist. [14] Alschuler's index of educational enrollment is probably more appropriate to a broader concept of development that is sensitive to matters of distribution and welfare, and future studies would do well to explore further indicators of this sort.

A second observation is that the variable "capital penetration," the only one of Alschuler's variables that does not in some way deal with trade, is derived from the item "net factor income paid to the rest of the world," from balance of payments data, and does not distinguish between income from direct foreign investment and that from debt liabilities. Alschuler suggests that this measure "combines the effects due to both the MNCs [multinational corporations] and international aid agencies," but it is clearly preferable to disaggregate the effects of these presumably very different agents. [15] Fortunately, recent studies by the Organisation for Economic Co-operation and Development

(OECD) provide data that allow these effects not only to be disaggregated but also to be more effectively measured.[16]

A third point is that several of Alschuler's cases have extreme values that seem unduly to influence his findings. For example, from the regression plot of the first canonical variate, which the author reproduces, it seems apparent that the results of the study would have been considerably weaker without the inclusion of Venezuela. Since Venezuela is a major oil producer, and thus certainly a special case in many respects, it seems that this country and other major oil producers might in the future best be examined separately from other LDCs.[17]

An interesting effort to specify and to test dependency hypotheses, this time with reference to sub-Saharan Africa, is described in two related studies, one by Patrick J. McGowan in a 1976 issue of *The Journal of Modern African Studies*, a second by McGowan and Dale L. Smith in a 1978 issue of *International Organization*.[18]

For the first study McGowan has collected data for thirty African countries covering several aspects of trade and aid linkages and has related these data by means of bivariate correlation to twenty-three indicators tapping various aspects of economic performance. McGowan reports only occasional strong relationships between his indicators of external contact and his twenty-three dependent variables, and more often than not these relationships are in the opposite direction from that which dependency theorists would predict. His findings lead him to conclude that "the proposition that economic dependence is associated with underdevelopment, and hence with poor economic performance, is simply not supported by the evidence."[19]

McGowan's generally negative findings are, however, the product of an exclusively bivariate research design. This shortcoming has led him, along with Dale L. Smith, to address the issue again, this time giving direct attention to the possibility that unaccounted for third variables may have affected the earlier results. The authors focus on "economic development potential" as a possible variable of this sort, and they consider whether its absence from the first study may have served to suppress the negative relationship between external linkages and economic performance predicted by dependency theorists. They model possible relationships and perform partial correlation and stepwise regression analyses, only to conclude that "not only have we found for a second time that dependency theory does not fit the continent as an explanation of African political economy, but we have also demonstrated that a competing theory, quite compatible with neo-classical doctrines of comparative advantage or with Marxist analyses of the spread of capitalism, fits quite well."[20]

Where might we proceed in building upon these findings, at variance as they are with those of the first three studies discussed? The authors' most important contribution is clearly their careful attention to some of the background variables that must be considered in any analysis linking external ties to internal political-economic patterns in Third World countries, and their efforts in this area will be emulated.

We might also note that this is the only study discussed that concentrates exclusively upon the countries of Black Africa. Certainly these findings suggest that more attention should be paid to the regional dimension of a process that is all too often depicted as if it were worldwide and unitary; if McGowan and Smith's findings are the result of genuine differences between sub-Saharan Africa and the countries of Asia or Latin America, only regional analysis will allow these differences to be effectively addressed.

We might observe, however, that while McGowan and Smith's indicators of North-South linkages are more inclusive than those of most previous studies, there are still some difficulties: their indicator of vertical trade, for example, is a rough ordinal indicator drawn from an early study by Adelman and Morris; they include no indicator of debt ties or of the relative extent (as opposed to concentration) of economic assistance ties; and they include no noneconomic linkages at all.[21]

Their eleven ordinal indicators of "economic development potential" also cause some problems, this time conceptual. The indicators are based on geographer William Hance's ranking of African states' potential for such economic sectors as agriculture, manufacturing, mining and tourism, for such infrastructural capabilities as irrigation and hydroelectric power and for such developments as the expansion of a cash economy and growth in the income of the "average man." The difficulty is that "potential" in these areas is often based as much on human factors as physical geography, and is in part the product of both internal political interplay and external factors. This makes economic development potential very difficult to separate, even in principle, from either the independent or the dependent variables of the study, rendering the implicit assumption of causal priority demanded by the authors' methodology somewhat questionable.

Finally, while the twenty-three dependent variables of the study—the indicators of economic performance—are many in number, they address only that part of dependency theory that posits that external dependence leads to economic stagnation in LDC's, largely failing to deal with the more important tradition that emphasizes the effect of external ties on the *distribution* of power and wealth within LDCs.

A sixth study of interest is reported in an article by Robert LeRoy West published in 1973 in a collection edited by C. Fred Bergsten and William G. Tyler.[22] In this article West employs four indicators of external dependence that are commonly used and have already been discussed: a ratio of exports and imports to gross national product, export commodity and partner concentration ratios and an indicator of "the relative importance of foreign-owned assets in the total productive assets of the nation"—the ratio of GNP to investment income earned by foreigners (from balance of payments data).[23] But West's study differs from the studies previously discussed in that he does not use these indicators to explain growth, distribution or policy in LDCs but, rather, creates a Spearman rank-order scale from them and then attempts to explain scores on this index using what might be called "control" variables relative to the studies that have been previously discussed (whether or not they were actually incorporated into those studies.). Among the variables included are "combined resource endowment," "status as an oil country" and "mode of political style."[24]

After analyzing his full sample of twenty-eight countries, West repeats the analysis for two subsamples divided according to population size. While he recognizes that with so few cases his conclusions "must be cautious and tentative," his multiple regressions result in findings that are almost uniformly moderately powerful factors in explaining the level of external dependence.

Clearly, given these findings, we must take into account as many as possible of these "background" factors if any model using external dependence to explain variance in policy, distribution or growth in LDCs is to be of use. We might go a step further than West by substituting for his single Spearman rank-order scale a series of composite indexes based on factor scores and then including these in a multiple regression framework along with several of the most important control variables: the regression coefficients would then be adjusted for the effects of the control variables. Further control could be achieved by physically subdividing a full sample according to characteristics of interest as West did when he divided his sample into large- and small-population subgroups.

One of the most interesting recent quantitative cross-national tests of dependency theory is presented in an article by Robert R. Kaufman, Harry I. Chernotsky and Daniel S. Geller in a 1975 issue of *Comparative Politics*.[25] These authors operationalize external dependence by concentrating on trade and investment linkages between Latin American countries and the United States. Trade linkages are indicated by four variables: value of trade to the largest trading partner as a percent of GNP, 1967; value of trade to the largest partner as a percent of total trade, 1967 and 1929; and value of the two leading exports as a percent of total exports, 1967–1968. Investment linkages are also indicated by four variables: inflows of foreign public and private investment, per capita and as a percent of GNP, 1967; and book value of accumulated United States private investment, per capita, 1959 and 1929.[26]

The authors speculate that these two linkages might be viewed as more or less independent modes of external dependence, the "trade" indicators representing the more traditional forms of Latin American contact with a dominant world economy and the "investment" indicators representing the more recent penetration of multinational corporations into Latin American countries, and they submit their variables to bivariate correlation analysis and factor analysis to see if these speculations are justified. The results suggest that it "makes sense to retain, in a general way, the trade/capital distinction for purposes of analysis," but that "there are some rather clear exceptions" to these patterns.[27] They thus return to their original variables for further analysis.

The dependent variables of the study are categorized into four groups: a first set deals with income and land distribution in LDCs, a second with political infrastructure, a third with economic performance and a fourth with constitutional stability and militarism.[28] These variables are related to the independent variables, first in a bivariate correlation matrix and then in a series of multiple regression equations which allow the inclusion of various control variables. The findings are many and interesting, but overall they can only be termed mixed, with some confirming dependency expectations and others disconfirming them. The authors conclude their study by surmising that in the case of at least some hypotheses their findings might have been clearer had their sample been divided into subregional components that distinguished South American countries from those of Central America.

What lessons does this study teach that might be useful for further empirical analysis? Perhaps the most important aspect that might be emulated is the authors' wide range of carefully drawn hypotheses, in which they go beyond the narrow focus on economic growth and/or income inequality that characterizes most other studies, allowing for a more subtle operationalization of some of the most important dependency hypotheses. A second useful contribution is the authors' suggestion that future studies pay conscious attention to the identification of subregions which may have special characteristics within a broader regional or world order.

We might, however, agree with the authors that their indicators "do not come close to tapping the many ways that the international environment can impinge upon the socio-political system of 'satellite' countries,"[29] and heed their call for further specification of the nature and terms of trade and investment dependence as well as the inclusion of such noneconomic factors as cultural or military ties.

SUMMARY

It is hoped that this chapter has given some indication of how previous scholars have attempted to operationalize and test dependency hypotheses. It is now necessary to summarize the work of these scholars and the manner in which their experience has been drawn upon in this study.

A first characteristic of these studies is the nature and size of the sample they employ. Of the studies discussed three draw upon a worldwide sample of LDCs, two concentrate exclusively upon Latin America, and two deal only with the countries of sub-Saharan Africa. While the regional samples are more or less complete, the worldwide samples are rather limited in scope, ranging from twenty-eight countries for West to forty-six for certain of Chase-Dunn's variables. In addition several samples include countries with extreme characteristics that may have tended unduly to have influenced the findings:

McGowan and Smith, for example, include Gabon, and Alschuler, as has been noted, Venuzuela, while Tyler and Wogart, and West include both of these as well as such countries as Iraq, Saudi Arabia, Trinidad and Tobago, Israel and Libya. (Several studies do not specify the countries examined.)

The intention of this study is to extend these previous studies by drawing a sample that: (1) eliminates cases that might result in misleading findings, particularly countries with very small populations, very extensive oil production, or both; (2) draws from all of the world's major regions while retaining region as a characteristic that may be used in further analysis; and (3) examines a large sample of LDCs (seventy for most variables) which includes most LDCs with populations greater than one million which are not major oil producers.

A second characteristic of these studies is their operationalization of the independent variable, external dependence.[30] As has been shown, every study draws a list of indicators of this dimension, but few of them are very comprehensive; indeed, every study fails to consider at least one indicator that others include. In this study an attempt will be made to draw upon a wider range of manifestations of external dependence and to choose indicators that measure its underlying dimensions more effectively than has previously been done. Among the indicators that will be included are: (1) A measure of the amount and concentration by source of the accumulated stock of private direct investment in LDCs; with one exception the studies discussed either have not distinguished between private and public flows or have concentrated only upon annual investment income flows, and have failed to consider concentration by source. (2) Measures which indicate both the amount of development assistance and its concentration by donor; previous studies have generally not included such variables, or have included one or the other but not both. (3) Several indicators of trade dependence, including measures of the relative amount of foreign trade, of the concentration of exports by commodity and by state of destination and of the verticality of trade ties between less developed countries and industrial nations; most of the studies discussed have included some of these, but none has included all. (4) An effective measure of projected debt service payments from less developed countries to lenders in developed countries and a measure of the level of reserves holdings; none of the studies discussed has included the latter and only one dealt with the former, using an indicator that did not differentiate among loans of different interest rates or terms. (5) Several noneconomic variables, particularly in the areas of military and cultural ties; several of the studies discussed have indicated the need for variables of this sort, but none has included data for any such ties at all.[31]

A third characteristic of these studies is the range of hypotheses they have tested. As has been seen, several of the studies have concentrated largely upon the relationship between external dependence and economic performance, while a few have emphasized the narrow relationship between dependence and income distribution; none of the studies has given much attention to relationships between external dependence and social policy or the general level of living of the masses in LDCs. In this study the former hypotheses are retested in what it is hoped is a more detailed and subtle manner while the range of hypotheses is extended to include the latter.

A fourth characteristic of these studies is that none has systematically descended to the level of the individual LDC: while individual LDCs are occasionally mentioned, they frequently lie buried under a mountain of aggregate statistics and never see the light of direct examination. This problem will not be completely rectified in his study, but the Q-factor analysis to be done in chapter 6 should be of interest in examining groups of LDCs with common patterns of external dependence; the dyadic analysis of chapter 7 should be of help in highlighting clusters of LDCs sharing a developed metropolis; and the analysis of regression residuals should allow the identification of individual countries that do not fit common patterns. It is hoped that by use of these methods the cross-national analysis of this study will become better grounded in a reality which consists, after all, not of cases "1" through "n" but rather of seventy individual countries, each with both a regional and an individual identity.

CHAPTER THREE

Operationalizing External Dependence

IT IS NOW NECESSARY TO EXPLORE systematically how such notions as "foreign aid," "private direct investment" and "vertical trade ties" can be operationalized in a manner which effectively taps the dimensions referred to in the dependency literature without going beyond the constraints of data availability. Seven previous approaches to this problem have been discussed and some suggestions made as to how indicators that have been used in the past might be extended or improved upon. Table 3.1 provides a summary of the indicators of external dependence used in these seven and several other recent studies.

This chapter will focus on the manner in which external dependence will be operationalized in *this* study. It will be structured in this manner: First, a very brief discussion will be offered of a few of the ways in which dependency theorists have characterized trade, aid, investment, debt, military and cultural ties between developed and less developed countries. Second, two basic dimensions will be proposed along which ties in these areas might be measured. Third, the particular indicators of external dependence to be used in this study will be introduced. And, finally, findings will be reported of an *R*-factor analysis that explores interrelationships among these indicators and attempts to draw from them a set of composite dimensions that can be used in further analysis.

MODES OF EXTERNAL DEPENDENCE: A BRIEF ORIENTATION

This section offers a brief summary of dependency theorists' appraisal of a number of the most important North-South, political-economic linkages. The intention is not to provide a comprehensive

Table 3.1 Indicators of External Dependence: Thirteen Representative Studies

	Kaufman et al. (1975)	McGowan (1976)	Vengroff (1975)	West (1973)	Tyler and Wogart (1973)	Alschuler (1976)	Chase-Dunn (1975)	Rubinson (1977)	Richardson (1976)	Gidengil (1978)	Szymanski (1976)	Walleri (1978)	McGowan and Smith (1978)
Foreign trade													
Extent	X	X		X	X	X		X	X*a*			X	X
Partner concent.	X	X	X	X	X	X		X	X*a*	X		X	X
Commodity concent.	X	X	X	X	X	X		X	X*a*	X		X	X
Verticality						X				X		X	X*e*
Foreign investment													
Extent													
Current	X			X		X	X	X			X*d*		
Accumulated	X*ab*										X*ac*		X
Number of enter-prises			X										
Concentration													X
Foreign assistance													
Concent.	X	X											X
Extent											X		
Foreign debt													
Extent							X	X					

a From the United States only.
b As of 1959, for Latin America only, both public and private investment.
c As of 1960, for Latin America only.
d Net repatriated profits less new direct investments, five-year average.
e Ordinal indicator for 1961–1963.

survey of dependency approaches in these areas, but only to offer some background to the particular indicators of external dependence used in this study. A more general discussion of the hypothesized *effects* of high levels of external dependence will be offered in chapter 4.

International Trade

Dependency theorists generally agree that foreign trade, especially trade highly concentrated by export commodity and trading partner and characterized by the exchange of exports at low levels of processing for imports at higher levels, is one of the most important mechanisms of external dependence. One contention is that trade relations of this sort tend to offer LDCs ever less value for their exports relative to the prices they must pay for goods they import, an assertion based on the familiar structuralist argument that world trade, at least since the 1950s, has been marked by a secular tendency for the prices of primary products to decline relative to those of manufactured goods.

As will be seen, many (but not all) dependency theorists accept the broad outlines of this argument, but most have been inclined to carry it somewhat further. They argue that the basic problem of vertical trade is not so much one of the relative prices of products exchanged as of the nature of the products themselves and of the conditions under which they are produced. Galtung, for example, speaks of sociological, technological, cultural and other "spin-offs" derived from manufacturing activities that stand in stark contrast to the figurative "hole in the ground" that is all that remains after a primary product is extracted (or harvested) and exported.[1] A typical spin-off is in the area of manpower development; as put by Karl Deutsch, "if you work in an aircraft factory, you learn a number of skills that are also useful for other industries . . . but if you learn to shovel asphalt . . . the skills you acquire are almost useless for anything else."[2] Another spin-off is economic; Green and Seidman are only two among many authors who propose that specialization in the export of primary products usually results in only a limited economic multiplier effect, since it tends to be confined to a narrow enclave and because any demand generated is usually directed not toward the domestic economy but outward, toward foreign producers of manufactured goods.[3]

Moreover, many dependency theorists argue, primary product production is not amenable to diversification and is thus often marked by a high concentration of exports in a small number of commodities. This concentration renders trade-dependent countries vulnerable to the vicissitudes of world commodity markets and offers them little leeway in the event either of a disruption of production because of a bad harvest or other disturbance or, on the other hand, the collapse of commodity prices because of overproduction.[4] In addition a high level of trade dependence is said to make integration both within and among LDCs difficult: dependency theorists often speak of situations in which infrastructural improvements have done little to facilitate internal or regional integration, but instead have been directed toward the port of exit and foreign markets.[5]

Private Direct Investment

Perhaps no single mode of international contact has generated as much recent interest as have ties of private direct investment; the number of individual sources from the dependency perspective alone probably runs into the thousands. It is impossible even to summarize this body of work here, and all that will be done is to introduce a few of the more important arguments. (In chapter 4 a somewhat closer look will be given to the hypotheses in this area of one particular author, Osvaldo Sunkel.)

A first argument is that foreign investment in LDCs, far from serving as a conduit for the transmission of capital from developed to underdeveloped countries, actually results in a net drain of capital from host to investor. Theorists making this argument usually cite the facts that investments in LDCs tend to offer higher profits than do similar investments in developed countries, and that annual outflows of investment income from LDCs to developed countries often exceed inflows of new investment; based on this and other evidence they argue that LDCs are actually "decapitalized" by direct investments and that any economic surplus these investments generate is expropriated by DC-based interests.[6]

A second line of argument is that the emergence of the multinational corporation as an important international actor has fostered the development of an integrated global hierarchy in which executive decision making and advanced technology are largely confined to a "center" based in the industrial nations, with "co-opted" LDC elites serving as agents of transmission and LDC nonelites largely excluded from influence. The result is, in the words of Stephen Hymer, "a hierarchical division of labor between geographical regions corresponding to the vertical division of labor within the firm," in which nonelites in LDCs are "confined to lower levels of activity and income."[7] In many ways this division of labor parallels that of the vertical trade structures discussed above; in fact the two often reinforce one another directly, since trade in many cases represents no more than transactions within or among multinational corporations.

A third argument is that foreign investors play an important and negative role in conditioning internal political structures and policies in LDCs. In the narrowest sense extensive foreign investment means that important sectors of an LDC's economy are subject to the priorities of an outside actor whose interests and objectives may be very different from those of the host country. More generally, it is seen as likely that the influence of external interests will serve consistently to reinforce the position of some political actors at the expense of others; the elites whose position is so solidified will, of course, then tend to act more in the interest of the multinational actor with which they are identified than of non-elites of their own countries.

A fourth argument is that domestic investment patterns in LDCs tend to be distorted by large-scale foreign investment. A frequent dependency contention is that extensive foreign investment tends to "interrupt . . . the formation of a local entrepreneurial class"[8] by undercutting local enterprises and by attracting local capital at the expense of domestic efforts at capital formation.

Economic Assistance

Dependency theorists often suggest that negative consequences are suffered by LDCs which are the recipients of large amounts of external economic assistance, particularly when this aid is received from a relatively small number of donors. In some ways this would seem a rather dubious proposition, since economic assistance does, after all, represent a transfer of resources without direct reciprocation. But a number of scholars within the dependency tradition, notably Hayter, Hart, Mende, Goulet and Hudson and Bodenheimer, have argued that, while economic assistance does provide certain genuine resources to LDCs, the conditions on which it has been offered and the development strategy that it has furthered have done more harm than good, if not necessarily to LDC elites, at least to the populations of LDCs as a whole. In the words of one commentator, foreign aid is used "to prop up political systems which resist the kind of social changes which would enable the people to build up independent economies and overcome their underdevelopment."[9]

Aid, then, is seen as one part of a seamless web of dependence, as a tie that reinforces the other linkages that have been discussed: in particular it is seen as deepening trade dependence, especially when it is "tied" to purchases in the donor country; and as providing an entry for investment from firms based in the donor country, by improving the general investment climate and creating advantages for these firms over those based in other developed countries or the LDC itself.[10]

Debt

Debt service burdens of LDCs have been cited by many dependency theorists as an example of "reverse flows" of resources from LDCs to DCs.[11] The general argument is that debt service on past loans has done a great deal to cancel out incoming flows of resources for many underdeveloped countries and has often resulted in considerable external influence, either formal or informal, on internal policymaking. Much the same might be said for a related factor, the level of reserves holdings; when these are low, an LDC will find it difficult to pursue an independent economic policy and will be highly sensitive to trade fluctuations and other short-term economic disturbances, either domestic or foreign.

Military and Educational Ties

Many dependency theorists emphasize that the dependency syndrome is not narrowly confined to economic linkages, but encompasses a wide range of contacts in the political, military, cultural and other spheres. In this study two particular areas of noneconomic contact will be focused upon: military ties, which will be indicated by the relative value of arms transfers; and educational ties, which will be indicated by the proportion of total university students studying abroad.

The literature on the first of these topics, military ties between developed countries and LDCs, is very extensive and cannot be adequately summarized here. Nonetheless, several key points relevant to the concerns of this study will be briefly raised. A first argument (which this study only tangentially addresses) is that LDC arms receipts contribute significantly to the overall level of violence both within and among Third World countries; in many cases, it is argued, tensions and conflicts arise that might have been avoided, or at least mitigated, had the principals not been heavily armed from abroad.[12] A second argument is that political competition within LDCs is strongly influenced by the leverage that high levels of arms transfers offer certain actors but not others; as put by one author, in reference to Chile, "the military in a dependent state is partially dependent on the imperialist state for its capacity to maintain a monopoly of force in society . . . and gains from this relationship resources which, for the most part, are beyond the control of [other actors in] the dependent state.''[13] A third argument is simply that, whatever the effect of arms transfers on regional tensions or on political repression and the distribution of power within LDCs, weapons are very expensive to purchase and maintain, and thus consume resources that might otherwise have been devoted to social programs or other uses of a more distributive nature.[14]

Ties of higher education, for which data have been collected, are one manifestation of the cultural ties that are often considered part of a broader syndrome of dominance-dependence: the general notion is that ties in this area reinforce other, more concrete, ties and serve as an important instrument in ensuring that subordinate countries accept the "rules of the game" made by and in the interest of dominant countries.[15] Eventually, cultural ties might be examined for a wider range of manifestations, including, perhaps, indicators of expenditures on advertising by foreign corporations and press service, radio and television ties; but, for the present, data deficiencies render direct analysis in these areas difficult.[16] Ties of higher education do, however, seem a particularly appropriate manifestation of cultural ties since they imply a strong measure of linguistic and attitudinal contact that is, moreover, experienced disproportionately by groups likely to be part of a country's dominant elite.

DIMENSIONS ALONG WHICH "EXTERNAL DEPENDENCE" WILL BE MEASURED

The preceding section has introduced, in the very briefest fashion, the major modes of contact between DCs and LDCs that will be examined in this study. This section will begin the process of operationalization by suggesting two basic dimensions along which ties in these areas might be measured and indicating a few issues that each raises. The dimensions are the *extent* to which an LDC participates in a relationship with countries more powerful or wealthy than itself; and the degree to which external linkages are *concentrated* among relatively few partners.

The first dimension, as was seen in chapter 2, has been the most commonly addressed in cross-national tests of dependency hypotheses: the principle is simply that a nation which engages in relatively extensive contact with more developed countries in certain key areas is more dependent than one less externally oriented.

But a problem arises: should the amount of contact be measured in absolute terms or should it be standardized to account for the size of the country for which it is being measured? As has been seen, most previous studies in this area have used ratio indicators, most often standardizing for GNP or population. But at least one author of a cross-national study of bilateral economic assistance has made use of absolute receipts of economic assistance. His rationale is as follows:

> There is little a priori justification for adjusting the aid receipts of developing nations for their population size. In fact, . . . there are theoretical reasons for *not* making such a transformation: The context in which questions of foreign aid allotments are discussed; the legislative appropriations for foreign aid; and the resources made available to governing elites in recipient nations all tend to focus attention on the absolute dollar amounts of foreign aid disbursed by aid donors.[17]

These are strong arguments:[18] certainly it is only by using absolute amounts of aid, trade or investment that we will be able to recognize the relative importance of a given LDC in a worldwide context. But for most purposes the intention of this study is not to compare the absolute position of LDCs relative to outside actors but rather to compare LDCs with one another. If this is to be done meaningfully, it is necessary to discount the effects of differences among LDCs which are not directly relevant to the issues at hand but which would invalidate comparison if they were not brought into consideration. The most important of these are differences of size, and some measure of absolute size usually forms the denominator of the ratio indicators that are formulated.[19] The standardization factor varies—in many cases it is the GNP of the country in question, in some cases it is based on imports or total trade, in some cases it is a noneconomic factor like total university enrollment—but in every instance it attempts to ensure that the resultant ratio variables are comparable from one LDC to another.[20]

The relative extent to which LDCs are linked to more powerful and developed countries is not the only dimension of interest. Of equal importance is a second dimension, the *partner concentration* of the contact. Even on the face of it, it is evident that an LDC which maintains linkages with many DC partners is in a position more likely to allow preservation of its autonomy than is one whose external linkages are similar in extent but are confined to one or a few partners. At the least a relatively large number of partners encourages flexibility; at the most it may directly increase LDC bargaining power by making it possible for partners consciously to be played off against one another in order to obtain concessions.

These commonsense propositions form the basis for a key hypothesis of dependency theory. To summarize, it is maintained by many theorists that one of the central characteristics of a dominance-dependence system of interaction is that it permanently relegates LDCs to the "periphery" of a global system marked by "feudal" ties between dominant actors and their "satellites": as the concentration of linkages with a single DC partner increases, relationships with other DCs or with fellow LDCs decrease in importance and the peripheral status of an LDC becomes more pronounced. Developed countries, on the other hand, are held to maintain ties with both their own multiple satellites and with other nations of the "center"; their only limitation is that they do not interfere with the satellites of other developed nations.

A more extensive nonstatistical examination of North-South ties in these terms will be conducted in chapter 7. But for purposes of the cross-national statistical analysis that comprises the bulk of this study, it is useful to construct a single summary measure that taps the degree to which an LDC's external ties fit a feudal or satellite pattern. The most direct indication of such a pattern is the extent to which external ties of an LDC are concentrated among one or a few DC partners. For many purposes concentration is most effectively measured by the Hirschman concentration ratio, and this ratio will be used in another context in this study. But partner concentration will be measured by a simpler and more traditional ratio, the proportion of the total magnitude of a given external interaction conducted with the principal partner.[21] The rationale for using the latter formulation is that since satellization is usually depicted as a relationship between a single developed country and a group of LDC satellites, we would prefer an index not affected (as the Hirschman index is) by different configurations of secondary linkages that might easily be determined by geographic or other factors entirely divorced from the relationship of primary interest.

These, then, are two basic dimensions along which DC-LDC ties will be measured. In the next section these areas of contact and dimensions of measurement will be drawn upon in creating a series of indicators of external dependence.

INDICATORS OF EXTERNAL DEPENDENCE

At this point the indicators representing external dependence are introduced. For ease of exposition only capsule definitions and explanations are offered here. A more comprehensive discussion of sources and definitions is offered in appendix IV.

Exports   Exports as a proportion of GNP, 1970

This indicator attempts to measure the extent to which the economy of an LDC is export oriented. Most previous quantitative studies of dependency have employed a variable of this sort, and its computation is straightforward.

Export Concentration   Proportion of exports directed toward the two most important trading partners, 1970

The purpose of this indicator is to measure the degree to which an LDC's trade is concentrated by partner and, thus, the extent to which it can be considered a "satellite" in the structure of international trade. This indicator, too, has frequently been used.

Commodity Concentration   Modified Hirschman export commodity concentration index, 1972

This indicator taps the degree to which exports of LDCs are concentrated among a relatively few commodities. Most previous quantitative studies of dependency theory have included a measure of commodity concentration among their trade indicators, but most often this has been a ratio based on the top two or three commodities differentiated to the two-digit Standard International Trade Classification level. In this study commodity concentration is indicated by a modified Hirschman index of commodities differentiated at the three-digit SITC level; the data used here are thus more finely gradated than are those used in most previous studies.

Level of Processing   Trade Composition Index, 1970

The purpose of this indicator, used by Galtung and others, is to measure the extent to which trade linkages of LDCs indicate participation in a "vertical division of labor," that is, are characterized by the exchange of raw materials for processed goods.[22] The index used here is constructed as follows:

$$\frac{(a+d)-(b+c)}{a+b+c+d}$$

Where a = value of raw materials imported
b = value of raw materials exported
c = value of processed goods imported
d = value of processed goods exported

The direction of the resultant scale has been reversed in order that all indicators of external dependence operate in the same direction.

Terms of Trade   Terms of trade, 1968–1971

This indicator measures the extent to which LDCs have over the period indicated received decreased value for their exports relative to the prices they have paid for their imports. The direction of this scale, like the last, has been reversed.

Investment   Estimated book value of private direct investment from firms based in OECD-DAC countries as a proportion of GNP, end-1971

Private direct investment is a factor of central importance for dependency theorists. Unfortunately, however, detailed data on this subject for a large number of countries have until recently been unavailable, and researchers have been forced to rely (on the host country side) on data from balance of payments figures or from certain United Nations documents dealing with external resource flows, none of which were available for more than a handful of countries outside Latin America; or (on the investor side) on data from the United States Department of Commerce, which for reasons of confidentiality often combines investments in individual LDCs into regional aggregates and in any case covers only United States investments; or on various, often incomparable, figures published by other Western countries.[23]

In 1972, however, a major Organisation for Economic Co-operation and Development (OECD) survey of Development Assistance Committee (DAC) investments was declassified (and has been annually revised) which provides reliable data on foreign investments for a very wide range of LDCs. These are the data that are used in this study.[24]

Even in this brief discussion several observations must be made about these data. First, it should be noted that the figures include only private investment; this is useful in that it discriminates private from public investments, a distinction which, as has been seen, not all previous tests of dependency theory have made.[25] Second, these figures represent estimated book values of private direct investment stocks in a country rather than inflows of new investments for one or more years; this, too, is desirable given the purposes of this study.[26] Third, these figures include only direct investment; portfolio investments obviously have very different implications from direct investments, and it is desirable that their magnitude be excluded. Finally, these figures do not account for reciprocal investments in OECD-DAC countries by LDC firms; we would expect, however (and the limited evidence available confirms these expectations),[27] that such reverse flows would be limited in volume and mostly in the form of portfolio investments.

Investment Concentration   Proportion of total private direct investment stocks from firms based in OECD-DAC countries from firms of the principal investor country, end-1967

The purpose of this indicator is similar to that of the export concentration indicator; it measures the degree to which investment linkages are concentrated by partner. The countries covered are the sixteen members of the OECD-DAC and investments from all sectors are considered.

Aid Official Development Assistance from OECD-DAC countries as a proportion of GNP, 1969–1971 average

"Official Developmental Assistance" is a term used by the OECD to refer to "all contributions from [its] members which are administered with the promotion of economic development and the welfare of developing countries as the main objective and whose financial terms are intended to be concessional in character." [28] This includes official bilateral grants and grantlike flows, bilateral loans at concessional terms and receipts from multilateral institutions; it explicitly excludes military assistance, purely commercial flows and other nondevelopmental flows. This is a much narrower and more useful concept than is implied by the term *foreign aid* when it is used (as is commonly the case) to include all resource flows from DCs to LDCs regardless of terms, source or purpose. [29]

Aid Concentration Proportion of Official Development Assistance supplied by the principal donor, 1969–1971 average

The rationale of this indicator is similar to that for *export concentration* and *Investment;* it measures the extent to which LDCs rely on a single donor for the provision of development assistance.

Debt Service Adjusted annual 1–15 year scheduled debt service as a proportion of 1968–1971 export earnings

The intention of this indicator is to tap the burden of debt service facing LDCs. Attention to debt service rather than to total debt outstanding is useful in that it distinguishes among loans according to terms and duration, something which figures on total debt outstanding do not do. [30]

The data cover all public and publicly guaranteed loans. This includes "Official Development Assistance" loans (but not grants) as well as private export credits, bank loans and other commercial flows that receive some official guarantee in the borrowing (but not necessarily the lending) country; it excludes only purely private unguaranteed debt and some military credits. [31] All major sources are covered, including socialist nations and non-OECD countries.

On the basis of scattergram evidence this indicator was transformed by a natural logarithmic function. Perhaps the best way to view this transformation is to consider that this variable demonstrates a threshold effect, with increments at the upper end of the scale having less explanatory power than those at the lower end.

Reserves International reserves at the end of 1970 as a proportion of imports in the preceding year

The intention of this indicator is to measure the degree to which reserves holdings are available to LDCs; limited reserves are hypothesized to limit an LDC's "ability to ride out international trade fluctuations or interruptions of foreign capital" and to reduce "the room for manoeuvre open to the state in the external economic policy field." [32] The direction of this scale has, of course, been reversed.

Arms Transfers   Value of arms transfers from major arms suppliers,
1965–1974, as a proportion of 1970 GNP

This indicator attempts to tap the theoretically important external linkage represented by arms purchases from advanced countries. Several difficulties arose in constructing this indicator that were not present in constructing most of the others in this study. A first has to do with the fact that in comparison with, say, trade or economic assistance ties, arms purchases often fluctuate widely in amount from year to year. (The reason is obvious: weapons, particularly for small countries, usually represent very costly single items, or are purchased in large lots and then used for several years before further purchases are deemed necessary.) Consequently, it is necessary to employ averages over a number of years for this indicator, as has been done for several other variables. In this case, though, the data are such that three- or even five-year averages might cause serious distortions, particularly for small countries. Ten-year totals are thus employed, covering the period from 1965–1974. (The reader who wishes to examine the annual figures should consult the source cited in appendix IV.)

A second difficulty arises when considering concentration of arms suppliers. While figures broken down by major supplier are available, it was decided not to construct a summary index of concentration as was done for other variables. The reason is that this variable, much more than the others, assumes a Cold War dimension that makes a single summary concentration ratio problematic: surely arms purchases divided between the United States and Britain have different implications than do purchases divided between the United States and the Soviet Union, and the arms supply role of France and the People's Republic of China further complicates matters. This variable has been transformed by a natural logarithmic function.

Students Abroad   University students studying in fifty selected countries as
a proportion of total university students, 1970

The intention of this indicator is to measure educational linkages of LDCs with foreign countries. It is of special interest in that students abroad are particularly likely to be members of a hypothesized "comprador" elite and to be influential in determining policy for their countries.[33] The assumption is that if a high proportion of total university students is trained abroad, ties of external dependence in the cultural mode will be strong.

The index, while rarely used in quantitative tests of dependency theory, is straightforward. One comment should, however, be made: while the great majority of students attending universities abroad are resident in the United States, France, the Federal Republic of Germany, the United Kingdom and Canada, the index also covers LDC students resident in other LDCs such as Lebanon, Egypt, Argentina, India, Mexico, Singapore and the Ivory Coast. More will be said on the topic of regionally dominant LDCs in chapters 6 and 7.

A concentration ratio is not constructed for this indicator, although the figures are available, since for smaller countries the absolute numbers involved are rather small; it would be difficult to break them down further and still remain confident that the shift of a small number of students from one category to another would not make a major difference in the ratio.

As has been seen, the first section of this chapter has introduced some of the basic modes of interaction between DCs and LDCs; the second has proposed two dimensions along which they will be measured; and this section, the third, has described the actual indicators that will be used in this study. Our operational definition of external dependence has become clear: the higher an LDC measures on these indicators, the more *externally dependent* it is as the term will be used in this study. It is recognized that this operational definition is not comprehensive—a number of interesting interactions have for various reasons not been tapped—but it is submitted that it captures at least some of the most important interactions of interest to dependency theorists.

The rest of the chapter will focus on the dimensionality of the indicators introduced and will attempt to determine whether they can be shown empirically to be capable of being expressed in a smaller number of composite dimensions.

THE DIMENSIONALITY OF EXTERNAL DEPENDENCE: AN *R*-FACTOR ANALYSIS

Now that the principal independent variables of this study have been introduced, we can begin to explore interrelationships among them. Above all, we must consider whether from these thirteen indicators it is possible to derive a smaller number of distinct dimensions that explain a large proportion of the variance in the original indicators and at the same time have theoretical plausibility.

Before describing how this will be done, it is useful to place matters in a broader perspective by examining previous findings on the subject. Unfortunately, efforts along these lines have been few and limited in scope, perhaps because the range of indicators for which data have been collected has itself been limited. One effort was that of West, who retained from a "sizable number" of potential indicators only those which proved to be statistically significant on a Spearman rank-order test of consistency; but a test of this sort is of limited usefulness if we allow for the possibility that there coexist more or less distinct "modes" of external dependence, each with a somewhat different effect.[34]

Another effort was that of Kaufman et al., who collected data on four indicators of "trade" dependence and four of "capital" dependence for Latin American countries with the expectation that two distinct dimensions would be extracted. The results of the preliminary correlation analysis were encouraging: as put by the authors, "the correlation matrix . . . suggests that there is some clustering within each separate category" and "on the whole . . . correlations across categories were lower than those within categories."[35] In the factor analysis that followed, however, three, not two, factors emerged, and one indicator did not load highly on any of them. As a result the authors did not make use of factor scores based upon their analysis for further analysis.

But the real problem with this analysis seems to be the constitution of the variables themselves. A number of ratio variables, for example, differ not in the term of interest but only in the standardization term; what is really measured in these cases is the relationship between, say, population and GNP rather than a relationship among related indicators of external dependence. Similarly, the indicators are rather haphazard with regard to time, with two different points in time occasionally included for a single variable in the same analysis; this is not as serious a problem as the first, but it does result in certain statistical difficulties as well as the possibility that some foreign investments are counted twice. Given these problems, it is not surprising that the authors' findings in this area are inconclusive.[36]

Factor Analysis

Perhaps the most powerful statistical tool for exploring relationships among a large number of variables is R-factor analysis, a technique that allows the extraction from a set of variables of a smaller set of "factors" that are composites of related variables weighted according to their contribution. (The "R" distinguishes this form of factor analysis from the "Q" type which will be used later in this study; the latter differs in that it examines relationships among cases rather than among variables.) If a small number of composite variables explains a substantial proportion of the variance in the original variables, then we have a clear picture of a simpler structure inherent in the original variables. If, on the other hand, no such simpler structure exists, any factors that emerge will be weak and indiscriminate, less enlightening than the original variables.

In this section are the results of an R-factor analysis of the independent variables in this study, the indicators of the condition called "external dependence." The following variables will be included in the analysis:

Exports—Total exports / GNP.

Export concentration—Exports to the two principal export receiving nations / total exports.

Level of processing $-1 \times$ (Trade Composition Index).

Trade terms $-1 \times$ (Terms of trade).

Commodity concentration—Hirschman Commodity Concentration ratio.

Debt service ln (OECD debt service ratio + 1).

Investment concentration—Private direct investment stocks from firms in the principal investor country / total private direct investment stocks.

Aid—"Official development assistance" / GNP.

Aid concentration—"Official development assistance" from the principal donor / total "ODA."

As can be seen, this list does not include *students abroad, arms transfers* and *investment*. The reason for omitting these variables is that they tended to load positively on more than one factor and to demonstrate a not inconsistent, but still somewhat confusing pattern. Although this is an indication that the structure inherent in the thirteen indicators is not entirely clear-cut, it was decided that these variables were of such particular interest that to leave them submerged in a complex pattern, their variance apportioned among several factors, would be of little value; instead, they were retained in their original state for further analysis. It is emphasized that there is absolutely no methodological problem in doing this aside from a decrease in what would in any case be false parsimony: raw scores are perfectly capable of coexisting with composite factor scores in the multiple regressions that follow as long as the two are not so highly intercorrelated that collinearity becomes a problem. (They are not.)

A description of the *R*-factor analysis can now begin. First, the correlation matrix of all pairs of variables must be discussed.[37] The general finding is that most bivariate correlations are positive and the few that are negative are trivial, none greater than $-.15$ and only one greater than $-.10$. This finding is of considerable interest in that it shows that the condition of external dependence does not embody internal inconsistencies that would cast doubt upon its coherence even as a process that can operate through several distinct modes; instead, all bivariate correlations are positive (which implies interrelationship) or essentially zero (which allows for the coexistence of underlying modes that are distinct, but not incompatible).

When the variables were submitted to principal component factor analysis, four factors were extracted which accounted for 62.6 percent of their total variance. These factors were then rotated; instead of being forced to remain orthogonal, the factors were allowed to intercorrelate to some degree if this better depicted reality.[38] The results are reported in table 3.2.

Table 3.2 *R*-Factor Principal Component Factor Analysis of Modes of External Dependence (Factor Pattern/Factor Structure)

	Factor 1 (Trade)	Factor 2 (Finance)	Factor 3 (Concentration)	Factor 4 (Aid-Trade Terms)
Variables				
Level of processing	**.74/.76**	.09/.07	.10/.22	−.01/.04
Exports	**.75/.72**	−.04/−.06	−.13/−.03	−.19/−.16
Commodity concentration	**.83/.86**	−.03/−.05	.13/.29	.19/.25
Reserves	−.00/−.01	**.84/.84**	.13/.11	−.18/−.16
Debt service	.02/−.02	**.83/.83**	−.16/−.14	.17/.16
Export concentration	.09/.22	.05/.05	**.71/.74**	.15/.23
Investment concentration	.15/.28	−.08/−.08	**.69/.74**	.25/.33
Aid concentration	−.08/.02	−.02/−.02	**.72/.68**	−.27/−.20
Aid	−.09/−.03	.06/.06	.14/.19	**.64/.65**
Trade terms	.03/.06	−.06/−.06	−.11/−.03	**.76/.76**

Factor Correlations

	Factor 1	Factor 2	Factor 3	Factor 4
Factor 1	X			
Factor 2	−.02	X		
Factor 3	.16	.00	X	
Factor 4	.06	.00	.10	X

Percent Variance Explained

Factor 1	23.2%
Factor 2	14.2
Factor 3	13.6
Factor 4	11.6
	62.6%

What do the findings in this table indicate? In mathematical terms they suggest that almost two-thirds of the variance in the ten indicators is subsumed in four factors; that each of these is formed largely from the contributions of only two or three variables (those in boldface); that no variable loads substantially on more than one factor; and that factors 1 and 3 and factors 3 and 4 are very slightly positively correlated, while all other pairs of factors are virtually uncorrelated.

But, more importantly, what does this mean for the study of external dependence? It means, for one thing, that the broad condition of external dependence seems to be comprised of several distinct modes which do not necessarily presuppose one another but which do not preclude one another either. It means, further, that the factors which are extracted generally "make sense" in terms of the theoretical literature that they are intended to reflect. The first factor, for example, is comprised principally of contributions from *exports, level of processing* and *commodity concentration*—all variables measuring trade dependence. The second is formed primarily from the indicators *debt service* and *reserves;* it seems clear that the underlying theme being tapped here is financial dependence. The third factor, largely the product of contributions from *export concentration, investment concentration* and *aid concentration,* draws indicators from three separate modes, but it is immediately apparent that all three have something in common: they are all measures of partner concentration and thus indicate the degree to which a given LDC can be thought of as a "satellite" on the global "periphery." Only the fourth factor, comprised primarily from contributions from *aid* and *trade terms,* represents a less distinct pattern, although it is not entirely surprising that countries which have unfavorable terms of trade are also relatively dependent upon foreign aid—some of it perhaps in the form of assistance "tied" to purchases in the donor country.

These findings lead us to assign names to what have until now been called simply Factors 1, 2, 3 and 4: the first three are called *trade* dependence, *finance* dependence and partner *concentration* dependence, while the fourth is less satisfyingly called *aid-trade terms* dependence. These names represent composite dimensions which are functions of the weighted contributions of the ten indicators of external dependence, and scores can be assigned to individual cases along these dimensions for use in further analysis.

The structure that has emerged here is really quite distinct, given the vagaries of cross-national analysis. What has been found is that the condition of external dependence, at least insofar as it is represented by these indicators, operates through several relatively clear-cut modes and cannot accurately be depicted either as an undifferentiated unitary process or as simply the sum of many incompatible individual processes. This is a most significant finding, and it places the analysis to be done in the following chapters on a much firmer basis. It shows that when dependency theorists speak of "trade" or "finance" dependence, at least, they are indeed referring to something that has an empirical as well as a logical reality: three separate indicators of various elements of trade dependence tend to load together in the factor analytic model as do two indicators that clearly deal with financial dependence. Just as interesting is the fact that the composite indicators of "partner concentration," deriving from three very different modes of interaction, nonetheless load together on a single factor.

From the explicit attention to external dependence in this chapter flows one of the most important contributions that this study hopes to make: without first systematically operationalizing a concept and examining its dimensionality, it is very difficult adequately to test its effects. The next two chapters will be concerned with making use of factor scores derived from this analysis to explain variance among LDCs in internal political economy in an effort to determine whether LDCs actually do suffer, as a result of high levels of external dependence, the negative internal consequences that are hypothesized.

CHAPTER FOUR

The Domestic Consequences of External Dependence
I. A Survey of the Literature

THE FIRST SECTION OF THIS CHAP-
ter delves briefly into the intellectual antecedents of dependency approaches: it explores the contribution to dependency theory of two
earlier and related approaches to North-South relations, the traditions
of imperialism and structuralism, and highlights similarities and differences between these approaches and the dependency tradition. The
next sections deal directly with several major strands of the dependency literature. The second discusses the imagery of "center" and
"periphery" that is often employed by dependency theorists in con-
ceptualizing relations between developed and less developed countries; it first examines the hypothesized linkage role of a "bridgehead" elite in LDCs, and then discusses the process by which contact
between center and periphery is predicted to lead not to the diffusion
of values from center to periphery but instead to the intensification of
the subordinate position of dominated groups. The third section focuses more closely on the first of these themes: it examines dependency theorists' conception of the development of an "internationalized" bourgeoisie in dependent LDCs. The fourth section
develops a complementary theme: it examines the process whereby
nonelites in highly dependent LDCs are hypothesized to be marginalized and their subordinate status thus reinforced. A final section
deals with the hypothesis, controversial among dependency theorists,
that external dependence inevitably leads to stagnation and slow rates
of economic growth in underdeveloped countries.

The purpose of this chapter is to provide the theoretical background for the test, in chapter 5, of hypotheses relating modes of external dependence to inequitable patterns of income distribution, so-

cial marginality, political coercion and several other variables tapping elements of predicted internal "structural distortions" in underdeveloped countries.

INTELLECTUAL ANTECEDENTS OF DEPENDENCY THEORY: IMPERIALISM AND STRUCTURALISM

This book is not the place for a comprehensive discussion of the intellectual traditions upon which dependency theorists have drawn. Nonetheless, it is useful briefly to survey the contributions to dependency theory of at least two earlier and related approaches to North-South relations, the traditions of imperialism and of structuralism.

Imperialism

Part of the difficulty in assessing the tradition of *imperialism* is that the term has been used to denote approaches which, if not entirely inconsistent, are often at such different levels of analysis as to have little in common. Many of the ambiguities of dependency theory can be traced to an uncritical borrowing from various strands of the "theory of imperialism."

One approach is to use the term to refer, in the words of George Lichtheim, to "the relationship of a hegemonic state to peoples or nations under its control." [1] Imperialism in this sense can be applied to relationships at any time or place, ranging from the Roman to the British Empire, and is distinguished from relationships of pure physical coercion only by "an imperial creed held by the governing class and a corresponding sense of dependence on the part of its subjects." [2] Within this conception would be included what Karl Deutsch calls "folk" theories of imperialism—the notions that the impetus for external domination is ultimately "biological-instinctive," "demographic-Malthusian," "geographic-strategic" or "psychological-cultural"; also included, perhaps, would be Schumpeter's concept of imperialism as the result of "atavistic" impulses which are essentially dysfunctional and backward looking, but which often come to dominate even the most modern countries. [3]

A second and very different use of the term *imperialism* has arisen among scholars who, "while not denying the influence of forces which are mainly super-structural, . . . reject . . . the view that the course of history can be explained in terms of power drives, love of war, desire for glory and the influence of outstanding personalities." [4] Scholars within this tradition speak of imperialism in a much narrower sense, referring exclusively to the extension of Western dominance abroad since 1870, and for them the causes of this dominance have to do mostly with economic patterns within Western countries.

Among the seminal ideas in this mode are those of Hobson and Lenin.[5] In Hobson's view, the impetus for the rapid extension of European dominance to "backward" areas in the late nineteenth century was the evolution of Western capitalism into a system firmly dominated by a relatively small number of monopoly interests. The process of consolidation of previously competitive firms allowed production to become more efficient than ever before but at the same time did nothing to change the ability of employers to keep wages low, rendering workers less and less able to consume what was ever more efficiently being produced. The result was a lack of profitable investment opportunities that impelled investors to seek more remunerative uses for their capital in "backward" areas. The flag followed investment in this case, as monopolist interests encouraged political control that would solidify control of their foreign investments.

For Hobson imperialism was only one possible response to the problem of underconsumption that he saw as the dominant feature of late capitalism, and in many ways it was the least desirable for a country as a whole. A much more rational response, in his view, was simply to increase the consuming power of workers by distributing to them a larger share of their country's income. He is vague as to exactly how this might be done, but he makes it clear that he considers the irrational policy of imperialism capable of being changed without a fundamental alteration of the system of capitalism itself: he specifically mentions "Trade Unionism" and "Socialism" as the enemies of a policy of imperialism.[6]

For Lenin the condition of imperialism is not so easily reversed. In his view the distribution of wealth under capitalism is a given that can be altered only if the entire system is overthrown; as he puts it, "as long as capitalism remains what it is, surplus capital will never be utilized for the purpose of raising the standard of living of the masses in a given country, for this would mean a decline in profits for the capitalists."[7] Imperialism for Lenin, far from being a misguided policy, is a *stage* of capitalism that allows the bourgeoisie temporarily to postpone the working out of capitalism's contradictions (and its own demise) by profitably investing surplus capital abroad.

Lenin does not concentrate on the impact of imperialism on less developed areas of the world; his primary concern is with outlining the conditions for the rise of imperialism in the West. But he does make it clear that the effect of capital export on "backward" areas is ultimately to foster their development:

> The export of capital affects and accelerates the development of capitalism in those countries to which it is exported. While, therefore, the export of capital may tend to a certain extent to arrest development in the countries exporting capital, it can only do so by expanding and deepening the further development of capitalism throughout the world.[8]

Is the receipt of foreign capital in LDCs, then, a necessary evil in that it introduces the highly productive, if brutal, condition of capitalism into a precapitalist environment? Or can industrial development be accomplished in more internally oriented ways in which LDCs "copy . . . Western industrialism [but] avoid duplicating the superstructure of Western capitalist property relations"[9]—thus telescoping the historical dialectic of Marx? Lenin's thought on these matters (prodded by events) gradually evolved from a strict application of the Marxist historical dialectic to an approach which eventually came almost to redefine the bourgeoisie-proletariat dichotomy on a North-South basis, with the South the revolutionary proletariat to the North's bourgeoisie (which includes, of course, the corrupted, trade-unionized working classes in the North).[10]

The issue cuts both ways: either the export of capital from DCs to LDCs results in the development of capitalism in the latter (as the result of which they can be expected, for better or for worse, eventually to come to resemble the developed capitalist countries), or it accelerates a process of proletarianization of the Third World in which revolution becomes imminent. Neither of these outcomes seems really to resemble the enervating peripheralization that dependency theorists see as the result of LDC dependency, a condition in which the prospects for capitalist development and true revolution seem equally chimerical.[11]

In a sense, though, the Leninist approach is not so much contradictory to the LDCs' experience as less than fully relevant. The reason is that Lenin and his contemporaries were primarily concerned with the conditions that gave rise to imperialism and its role in the domestic political economy of advanced capitalist states. Imperialism was seen as a function of the internal development of advanced capitalism, in which "backward" countries participated mainly in the negative sense of serving as an outlet for surplus Western capital; in the words of one commentator, "the old masters['] . . . analyses, deduced more from first principle than empirical observation, appear to be ideas about European society projected outward rather than systematic theories about the imperial process as such."[12]

Much the same might be said of the very different approaches discussed at the beginning of this section: these approaches, too, concentrate on the sources of imperialism but say little of its effects. The theory of dependency arises from a very different historical experience, and, as will be seen later in this chapter, its emphases are very different.

Structuralism

A second precursor of dependency approaches is the tradition of *structuralism,* an approach which was first formulated in the early 1950s and is closely associated with such scholars as Gunnar Myrdal, H. W. Singer and, of course, Raul Prebisch and other economists of the United Nations Economic Commission for Latin America (ECLA or, in Spanish, CEPAL) and later the United Nations Conference on Trade and Development (UNCTAD).[13] This approach rests on the observation that technological progress tends to reduce the importance of primary products in overall production and that, moreover, as income increases, demand for food and other primary products generally fails to keep pace. Given these tendencies, the structuralists argue, it is inevitable that prices of the primary products on whose export less developed countries are heavily reliant will tend over the long run to deteriorate relative to prices of the manufactured goods they import, chiefly from developed countries. This long-term secular trend means that developed countries will in effect expropriate most of the reward for any increases in LDCs' primary product production, while underdeveloped countries will be plagued by chronic balance of payments difficulties and slow economic growth.[14]

What alternatives are available to LDCs in responding to so negative a situation? One strategy proposed by the structuralists is that they coordinate production and encourage trade among themselves by means of regional integration efforts, and, indeed, the 1960s and early 1970s have witnessed the formation of a wide range of LDC regional organizations.[15] Another is that developed countries be encouraged to become more open to manufactured imports from underdeveloped countries, especially through the enactment of generalized nonreciprocal tariff preferences on LDC manufactures. A third is the policy of import substitution, based on the direct encouragement of industrialization in LDCs through the construction of a protective tariff structure to shelter domestic "infant industries" from foreign competition, and the encouragement of foreign financing and direct investment in manufacturing enterprises.

The structuralists' central argument that the international market structure works to the disadvantage of LDCs has generally been retained by dependency theorists as *part* of their argument.[16] But in many respects dependency theorists go far beyond what they deem the essentially reformist character of the structuralist approach. They consider, for example, the inequities of global markets to be much more than a matter of the nature of the particular products exchanged; as put by Arghiri Emmanuel,

> it is not possible for low-wage countries to cancel [the] advantage enjoyed by the rich countries by themselves specializing in the branches favored by the unequal exchange of the moment. As soon as a branch is taken over by the low-wage countries, the rich ones drop it and turn to producing something else. . . . Branches that political economy has recently described as dynamic . . . are only "dynamic" because they belong to the high-wage countries, and would cease to be so the moment they cross over to the underdeveloped countries, as happened with the textile industry.[17]

Moreover, dependency theorists see North-South contacts as cumulative and mutually reinforcing and are very skeptical of the structuralists' hope that foreign investment in LDC manufacturing will reduce capital scarcity bottlenecks and foster meaningful industrialization. A final, and perhaps the most fundamental, difference is that structuralists and dependency theorists conceive very differently of the nature and purpose of development itself: while structuralists seem to share with liberal economists and sociological modernization theorists a goal of rapid industrialization and aggregate economic growth, dependency theorists have expressed disenchantment with the "distorted development" or "growth without development" that they see as the outcome of externally oriented development strategies, and they have stressed the need for more pervasive and equitable alternatives. In short while the structuralists have argued that the structure of international economic relations needs reform, dependency theorists posit the need for fundamental change in both the overall framework of North-South relations and the inequitable distribution of power and wealth within LDCs that they see as its product.[18]

CENTER-PERIPHERY IMAGERY

The time has now come to discuss several central themes of dependency theory itself. The first notion to be explored is the imagery, so frequently invoked by dependency theorists, of "center" and "periphery" in global relations.

One of the clearest theoretical discussions of the concepts "center" and "periphery" is by Johan Galtung.[19] Among the many ideas he proposes is the notion that the impact of rich upon poor nations can best be understood if the global political economy is viewed as the relationship between a "Center" (the developed countries) and a "Periphery" (the less developed countries), each of which is further subdivided into its own "center" (the governing elite) and "periphery" (groups without much power or wealth). Galtung suggests that there exists an overall disharmony of interest between nations of the world Center and Periphery (designated with a capital "C" and "P") and that there is also a disharmony of interest between center and periphery (designated by a lowercase "c" and "p") in any given nation. The pattern is not, however, neatly symmetrical, since in Galtung's estimation there is *more* disharmony of interest between center and periphery in nations of the Periphery than in those of the Center.

This sets the scene for the pattern of interaction that in Galtung's mind distinguishes relationships of dominance-dependence (or "imperialism") from other power relationships: the exercise of power not directly, through the offer of benefits or threat of sanctions by Center to Periphery nation, but instead indirectly, by means of a two-stage process in which the center of the Center nation structures the options of the periphery of the Periphery nation *by way of* a collaborating elite in the Periphery nation itself. As put by Galtung, "the basic idea is . . . that the center in the Center nation has a bridgehead in the peripheral nation, and a well-chosen one: the center of the Periphery nation."[20] The actual structure is best described in a diagram, which is offered in figure 4.1

The implications of this two-stage process are discussed by Karl Deutsch in a commentary on Galtung:

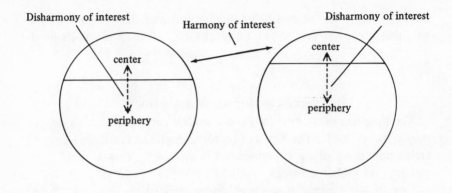

Center (DC)   Periphery (LDC)
Figure 4.1   Center-Periphery Relations
Adapted from Johan Galtung, "A Structural Theory of Imperialism," p. 84.

> The center of the center, of course, gets all the advantages. . . . The periphery of the center gets less than the center, but . . . it gets a rake-off. . . . In the periphery countries, the middle class will become somewhat reactionary. According to the Galtung theory, they are likely to be bought by the imperial system and to make up its bridgehead in their native countries. The middle classes of Buenos Aires, Rio de Janeiro, and Santiago de Chile, who completely accept the West European and North American standards of consumption . . . live about as well as, or better than middle class persons live in the advanced countries. But the poor of Brazil, Argentina and Chile are poor by the grim standards of the poor in Latin America.[21]

All of this is very simple and straightforward, but it does express a notion that is central to most theories of dependency, the idea that, while ties of external dependence act to the detriment of the population of an LDC as a whole, they do not operate directly, but instead work through and confer benefits upon a collaborating elite in the subordinate country. The treatment of this "comprador elite" in the literature will be dealt with in more detail in the next section.

But there is another element of the center-periphery imagery that Galtung does not directly bring out, although it is implicit in his analysis. This is the idea that nations on the periphery of the international system or groups on the periphery of a given national system are poor and backward not because they are isolated and insufficiently integrated into the international or their own national system (as the term *peripheral* might seem to imply) but rather because they *are* closely integrated, but in a manner unfavorable to their interests. This malintegration has the effect of rendering their objective standing progressively less and less favorable, putting them in a position worse than if they had never been in contact with the Center at all.

We need not belabor the point that this concept is radically different from conventional approaches to economic development and social modernization, which operate under the assumption that close contact among nations, regions or social groups at different levels of development will gradually result in the diffusion of advanced values and forms of organization from the better-endowed to the less-well-endowed entity. Political scientist Lucian Pye, for example, speaks of "modernization," a composite process which

> might also be called Westernization, or simply advancement and progress; it might, however, be more accurately termed the diffusion of a world culture . . . based upon a secular rather than a sacred view of human relations, a rational outlook, an acceptance of the substance and spirit of the scientific approach, a vigorous application of an expanding technology, an industrialized organization of production, and a generally humanistic and popularistic set of values for political life.[22]

Similarly, sociologists see contact between advanced and less developed nations, and between advanced and backward regions within the same nation, as resulting in "the transfer of technology, modern rational organizational forms, labor habits complementary to industrial production and 'modern' attitudes to the self, the family and society, which facilitate economic development."[23] Economists most often direct their attention toward international capital flows, which are viewed as important engines of growth, both directly and through linked effects on related sectors; and to the principle of comparative advantage in international trade, which is seen as allowing each partner in international trade to concentrate his resources in that sector in which they can be most efficiently utilized. The examples could go on *ad infinitum*. But in every case diffusion is the key, operating almost as if, in the words of Tibor Mende, "an invisible magician had been carrying around a spark from each stimulated sector to awaken the dormant possibilities of the remaining ones."[24]

The dependency perspective could not be more different. From this point of view, contact between poor and rich operates within a structure that is inevitably biased toward the dominant interests within it. The tendency is toward the progressive integration of isolated elements, that is clear, but their integration is not such that the subordinate partners will ever come to resemble the dominant; instead the dominated will come to be progressively malintegrated in a manner that solidifies their position as subordinates.

An example of this principle in practice is offered by Julio Cotler, who describes the penetration of the dominant world cultural and economic system from the coast into the sierra in Peru. He quotes Frank in concluding that the " 'marginal' or 'floating' population is in process of becoming, or in some cases is fully integrated into the society in a way which prejudices its welfare and opportunities to develop." [25]

Similarly, Eric Wolf describes how the Mexican Revolution propelled the norms of the dominant world economic system, capitalism, into the country's most remote and traditional regions, with the effect of marginalizing much of the rural population: as land became a commodity to be bought and sold, the peasant's traditional communal rights were undermined and his position became less and less secure. [26] Finally, Rodolfo Stavenhagen argues in more general terms that at the heart of Latin American underdevelopment is not the persistence of feudal modes of organization in backward regions because of isolation from more advanced forms, but rather the development of a malformed and stunted capitalism as the result of contact with just such forms:

> The spread of manufactured industrial goods into the backward zones often displaces flourishing local industries or manufacturers, and therefore destroys the productive base for a significant part of the population, provoking what is known as rural proletarianization, rural exodus and economic stagnation in these areas. [27]

In every case the process described is similar: peripheral elements are progressively integrated into an international structure on terms that are not to their advantage. In the next two sections more will be said about both the "internationalized" elites that serve as the transmitters of influence from center to periphery and the nonelites in LDCs which are at the receiving end.

CENTER OF THE PERIPHERY: NATIONAL BOURGEOISIE OR INTERNATIONALIZED ELITE?

One of the most basic of orthodoxies among traditional Marxists is that history proceeds according to certain immutable stages. Each stage represents an advance from a previous condition and each is led by a particular class whose function it is to hasten the demise of the previous order and to spearhead the establishment of the new.

In the late eighteenth and early nineteenth centuries, according to Marx, the progressive class was the bourgeoisie and the inevitable stage of history that it ushered in was capitalism. But by the middle and end of the nineteenth century capitalism was, in the industrial countries, becoming outmoded and laden with contradictions, and was expected to spawn within itself a new leading class, the proletariat. This class was destined imminently to lead a revolution that would destroy the existing order and bring about a new order, this time the final organization of society, communism.[28]

But this is not what happened. Instead of becoming progressively immiserated and ripe for revolution, the proletariat in the industrial nations gradually won political and economic concessions without a single and decisive upheaval, and the scene of potential revolutionary activity seemed to many scholars to shift from the industrial nations to countries that, far from being in the late stages of capitalism, were in many respects precapitalist. In such countries the misery and marginality of much of the population made revolution seem much more imminent than in the developed capitalist countries.

At the heart of much Marxist-oriented dependency theory is an attempt to reconcile this apparently changed set of circumstances with a theory whose central feature is an immutable dialectic in which no more advanced stage of history can be achieved until all previous struggles have been played out, in which socialism cannot be built until capitalism has provided "the economic and technological infrastructure that will enable society to allow for the free development of every member according to his capacities."[29]

One view on this issue is taken by theorists whose position derives from a clear and straightforward interpretation of the inevitable historical dialectic. For them today's less developed countries are indisputably precapitalist, and what they need for the present is, quite simply, a good dose of capitalism, whose ability to destroy feudal structures and to organize the accumulation of the material preconditions of socialism is unquestionable, nowhere more forcefully expounded than in the works of Marx. The leadership of this capitalist revolution would not, of course, derive from the tired capitalist interests in the developed countries (mired as they are in the decadent monopoly stage of capitalism, imperialism) but would instead be a youthful and vibrant capitalism reminiscent of early nineteenth century Europe, led by a nationalistic but thoroughly capitalist group called the "national bourgeoisie."

A good example of this line of thought is expressed by Raul A. Fernandez and Jose F. Ocampo, in the context of Latin America:

> The basis of Latin American backwardness cannot be attributed to the capitalist character of its economies and their integration within the world capitalist system, but rather to the *lack* of capitalist development and the persistence of feudal forms of agriculture.[30]

One of the central themes of most dependency theorists is that the expectations of Marxist scholars like Fernandez and Ocampo for the emergence of a progressive and nationalistic bourgeoisie that will achieve a true capitalist revolution, are misplaced. They assert, quite simply, that times have changed since Marx wrote and that the possibility of a bourgeois revolution in the underdeveloped world is not viable within the present international environment, a world order that impinges directly on the autonomy of less developed countries.

Paul A. Baran, writing in 1957, provides one of the earlier discussions of the potential of the national bourgeoisie in newly independent countries when he speaks of the rapid degeneration of avowedly nationalistic independence movements into decidedly collaborationist elites, which not long after independence begin to

> make common cause with the feudal elements representing the main obstacle to [their] own development, with the imperialist rulers just dislodged by the national liberation, and with the comprador groups threatened by the political retreat of their foreign principals.[31]

Baran, though, still holds some hope for a move "in the direction of industrial capitalism" led by the exceptional national bourgeoisie that is "determined to overcome the opposition of feudal and comprador interests."[32]

Such a possibility has seemed much more remote to more recent dependency theorists. Fernando Henrique Cardoso, for example, describes how the potential national bourgoisie in Brazil, despite some proclivities for independence, has been driven by fear of the "popular classes" to join forces with "internationalized" elites:

> The alliance among the military, the bourgeoisie and the middle classes is the contrivance of a development model and a political regime in which their interests are balanced as against more serious enemies.

> This balance could be achieved, quite obviously, because the internal
> contradictions are not as antagonistic as the threat of a development pol-
> icy generally favorable to the popular classes.[33]

Although Cardoso views the emergence of this hybrid class as a re-
markable, indeed, "revolutionary" development, he doubts that this
group could ever achieve the fundamental alteration of the existing
social order that is part of a true capitalist revolution:

> I do not believe that the Brazilian bourgeoisie, a child of dependent
> capitalism, can stage a revolution in the strong meaning of the term. Its
> "revolution" is limited to integrating itself into the scheme of interna-
> tional capitalism, to associating itself with international capitalism as a
> dependent and minor partner.[34]

Reginald H. Green describes a similar process in the context of
sub-Saharan Africa; he speaks of an African political leadership
which

> is not a class in either the bourgeois or the socialist sense. In a majority
> of cases it forms either an expensive facade for a nation remaining
> basically stagnant and deprived, or a *de facto* intermediary for, ally of,
> and expense upon, continued foreign economic penetration and domina-
> tion.[35]

And Harold Brookfield, in assessing the Latin American dependency literature, describes a stunted and retarded "comprador"
bourgeoisie which does not challenge, but rather reinforces, existing
authority patterns: "The middle class, so far from being progressive,
enterprising and expanding, is tied to foreign consumption patterns;
policies designed to strengthen the middle class reinforce the ruling
class, and do not lead to any 'diffusion' of development."[36]

All of these arguments are rather general in tone. What empirical
evidence is there that an internationalized bourgeoisie of the sort described really exists in LDCs, or that it is linked to the interests of developed countries within the sorts of structures described? Some evidence is provided in case studies of elites in LDCs whose external
ties are unusually extensive. Richard Sklar, for example, cites as
"the central issue of Zambian political development" the question
whether "technocratic elitism, sheltered by the influence of multinational corporations, will transform the populist party into a willing instrument for capitalist development."[37] In answering the question,

he speaks of the development of a "managerial bourgeoisie" and suggests that "in Zambia, as elsewhere, the bourgeoisie takes care to contain radicalism and maintain its position as the predominant class."[38] Indeed, Sklar finds that in Zambia even apparently highly nationalistic elements of the ruling elite are reconciled with international interests: he asks whether the "corporate international elite" can be reconciled with such "staunchly parochial patriotism," and concludes that "in fact, parochial nationalism on the part of the ruling class in a newly developing country may be entirely consistent with the broad interests of the corporate international bourgeoisie." He continues by suggesting that "insofar as parochial nationalism blocks the formation of wider political unities among neighboring underdeveloped countries, it fortifies international capitalism by reducing the potential viability of anticapitalist alternatives."[39]

Examination of a very different situation in a very different country leads Petras and Cook to a similar conclusion; they conclude from a survey comparing attitudes toward foreign investment of Argentine executives of foreign-based multinational corporations with those of executives of Argentine-owned firms that

> the assumption of conflict between national and foreign [-employed] industrialists that might lead the former to play a nationalist developmentalist role is incorrect. Foreign and national socioeconomic elites have been intertwined with each other through financial, technical-economic, political and/or ideological links.[40]

Other case studies in this mode could be cited; among the most frequently referred to are studies of Kenya by Leys and of Chile by Moran.[41] But the purpose of this study is not to add directly to the understanding of the ways in which DC actors' interests interact with those of elites in individual LDCs, but instead to complement these studies with analysis of a very different sort: the emphasis will be not so much on LDC elites themselves as on the implications of their ascendancy for nonelites. A few of these implications will be discussed in the next section.

PERIPHERY OF THE PERIPHERY: MALINTEGRATION AND MARGINALIZATION

Although the previous section has focused on internationalized elites in LDCs as the principal agents in transmitting foreign influence to the national scene, it has probably become evident that the consequences of the ensconcement of a "comprador elite" are in no way favorable to the interests of the "popular classes" (to use Cardoso's term) in LDCs. In fact the outcome most commonly hypothesized by dependency theorists is that external influence, far from resulting in the diffusion of modernization or even in the appending of a modern enclave onto an unaffected precapitalist base, draws the masses into an integrated structure that results in an absolute decline in their "level of living." As put by Cardoso: "Associated-dependent development . . . entails costs; . . . this path of development is based on a regressive profile of income distribution . . . and contributes to social marginality and the underutilization and exploitation of manpower resources." [42]

Exactly how does this process of marginalization and impoverishment occur? One of the most comprehensive discussions is provided in an article by Osvaldo Sunkel entitled "Transnational Capitalism and National Disintegration in Latin America." [43] Sunkel's basic argument is that social marginality is related to external dependence (especially investment dependence) in Latin America because reliance on foreign investment represents an investment strategy that, while profitable for the investing firms and their domestic agents and less direct beneficiaries, is profoundly inappropriate to the needs of the majority of the population:

> If the modern sector, apart from expanding relatively faster than the primitive sector, further replaces to some extent its output, technological modernization would result, on the one hand, in the *creation* and on the other in the *destruction* of employment opportunities. If demand remains constant during this process of technological substitution, an increase in investment in the modern sector would create idle capacity and unemployment, since the number of persons employed per unit of capital in the modern sector is less than in primitive activities. In this way it is conceivable that an *increase in the rate of investment* could lead to an *increase in the rate of un- and underemployment,* and, therefore, of marginality. In fact, I would suggest that this is not just an extreme hypothetical situation, but is perhaps the best working hypothesis to explain the growing problem of unemployment, underemployment, and marginality in Latin America. [44]

But, while a process has been posited that demonstrates the employment of an inappropriate development strategy that may or may not be the inevitable outgrowth of unplanned capitalist growth, it has not yet been demonstrated that such an outcome is the result of specifically *international* contact. This element enters to some degree when Sunkel describes in more detail the groups that have chosen this path of development:

> The international capitalist system contains an internationalized nucleus of activities, regions and social groups of varying degrees of importance in each country. These sectors share a common culture and "way of life," which expresses itself through the same books, texts, films, television programmes, similar fashions, similar groups of organization of family and social life, similar style of decoration of homes, similar orientations to housing, building, furniture and urban design.[45]

But, still, while a sort of colonialism by emulation has been vividly invoked, Sunkel has yet to describe the actual mechanisms linking external forces to internal marginality. This he begins to do when he identifies "transnational conglomerates" as the key institutional link between external forces and internal marginalization, suggesting that these "tend . . . to disrupt the rest of the economy and society, segregating and marginalizing significant sectors of the population."[46]

We would expect, then, that the more fully private direct investment dominates the economic life of an LDC, other things being equal, the stronger the position of internationalized elites, and the greater the marginalization of the rest of the population. But Sunkel himself does not provide any direct empirical evidence for the validation of this hypothesis, and in fact seems to assume that this outcome is self-evident: he suggests that "it *becomes apparent* that there *must be* a close correlation . . . between the extension of the developed countries into the underdeveloped countries, and the developed, modern and advanced activities, social groups and regions of these countries" (emphasis added).[47]

Since these are the very groups whose ascendancy is associated with marginalization of the lower classes according to the process described above, testing the proposed correlation becomes essential; one attempt at such a test is the present study. A previous analysis of these issues was done by Jose Serra for the single case of Brazil. In it the author contends that Brazil's "economic miracle," which has been closely identified with an open policy toward foreign investment since the 1964 coup, has been based upon steadily worsening patterns of social distribution.[48] The author cites statistics on literacy, income distribution, primary education and public health, finding that many aggregate levels have actually declined despite the enormous growth in aggregate national product in recent years. He evaluates the government's social welfare and social insurance programs and finds them "almost totally useless to the workers" and indicates that the government's taxation policy, largely based on indirect taxes, has, instead of reducing income inequality, served only to reinforce it.[49]

In another study in this vein Thomas Weisskopf examines both external ties and internal conditions in a number of LDCs and concludes that development strategies heavily reliant on external linkages have resulted in widespread marginality; in a typical conclusion he suggests that

> the power and influence of the urban middle classes operate to bias the educational expenditures of the state in favor of urban and higher education at the expense of rural and lower education. Yet there is evidence that returns to primary education are much greater than to higher education in most poor countries.[50]

Not only are subordinate groups in highly dependent LDCs hypothesized to receive a relatively small share of the income of these countries and to experience a relatively poor quality of life as the result of a process of progressive marginalization, they are also hypothesized to be the object of a relatively high level of physical coercion on the part of political authorities. As put by the authors of one summary of the literature in this area:

> Basically, [dependency] theory argues that external dependence of poor nations on rich nations produces distortions in the economic structures of poor societies. These distortions create a large potential for conflict. Under pressure from external and domestic actors, the dependent state attempts to stabilize the situation by the use of coercion to control conflict. Thus, the interaction of external dependence with latent conflict leads to escalation of levels of violence used by both the state and opposition.[51]

While it would be easy to cite additional theoretical propositions on this subject of malintegration and marginality, or more examples of attempts to test them, the main points are clear. What is needed now is an attempt to operationalize at least some of these concepts in order that their relationship to the various modes of external dependence in LDCs may be evaluated for the seventy nation sample. Such an effort will be the task of the next chapter. But, first, a more controversial dependency hypothesis must be discussed.

DEPENDENCY, GROWTH AND DEVELOPMENT

Every dependency theorist would accept that the consequences of external dependence are, on balance, negative. But on one particular consequence there is less agreement. This is the issue of whether extensive and asymmetrical foreign ties inevitably lead to economic stagnation in LDCs or whether, instead, some form of economic growth can and does occur within a framework of external dependence.

One view is that of Andre Gunder Frank, who in a frequently cited passage very unambiguously poses several hypotheses averring that external dependence and economic growth are negatively linked:

> The first hypothesis [is] that in contrast to the development of the world metropolis which is no one's satellite, the development of the national and other subordinate metropoles is limited by their satellite status. . . . A second hypothesis is that the satellites experience their greatest economic development and especially their most classically capitalist industrial development if and when ties to their metropole are weakest. . . . A third major hypothesis derived from the metropolis-satellite structure is that regions which are the most underdeveloped and feudal-seeming today are the ones which had the closest ties to the metropolis in the past.[52]

Frank does not systematically test these hypotheses, but he does cite evidence in their support: he suggests, on the one hand, that the greatest economic growth in Latin America has occurred during the First and Second World Wars and the Depression of the 1930s, periods in which Latin American external ties were weakest, and also that his research indicates that economic growth has been most rapid in regions and countries that have been least closely integrated into the world capitalist system; he notes, on the other hand, that economic growth has been slowest in precisely those regions (such as Northeast Brazil and the sugar-exporting areas of the West Indies) that have had the earliest and most intensive contact with external interests.[53]

These hypotheses express a major theme in the dependency literature, proposed in various contexts by, among other writers, Osvaldo Sunkel, Susanne Bodenheimer, Thomas Weisskopf, Walter Rodney,

Kwame Nkrumah, James O'Connor, Samir Amin and Theotonio dos Santos.[54] The mechanisms cited by these authors linking external dependence and economic stagnation are many and varied. Among them are excessive profit repatriation on investment holdings; value lost from declining terms of trade; capital outflows owing to excessive debt service; the failure of "spin off" effects of industrial production to occur within a raw-materials-for-industrial-goods trade relationship; inappropriately large expenditures for arms by a worried or emulative LDC elite; the "boom or bust" nature of external capitalist influences that renders the planning essential for sustained growth impossible; and distortion of the internal economic integration necessary for economic growth through the imposition of outwardly oriented forms of economic organization.

But the hypotheses themselves remain (a rarity in the genre) clear, unambiguous and eminently testable—the higher the level of external dependence, the lower the rate of economic growth—and, perhaps for this reason, they have constituted the basis for a good many of the cross-national "tests of dependency theory" that have been attempted to date. As has been shown in chapter 2, data on growth rates of gross domestic product and similar measures of economic growth have been used as a dependent variable (i.e., a variable whose variance is explained by the modes of external dependence) in studies by Chase-Dunn, Kaufman et al., Alschuler, McGowan and Smith and a number of others. The results of these studies have been mixed; a good review of this rapidly expanding branch of the literature, as well as an attempt at further specification, is provided in a 1977 article by Richard Rubinson.[55]

But critics have been quick to point out what appear to be striking exceptions to any general confirmation of Frank's hypotheses: it is difficult to state that external dependence leads directly to economic stagnation without in some way accounting for such apparent dramatic exceptions as Brazil, the Republic of Korea or the Ivory Coast, all of which have followed aggressively outwardly oriented development strategies and yet have experienced very rapid rates of economic growth. One study in this mode that has been particularly noted in the dependency literature (perhaps because it derives from a socialist perspective) is a 1973 article by Bill Warren in the *New Left Review* entitled "Imperialism and Capitalist Industrialization."[56] In this article the author concludes from an examination of data on growth rate of gross domestic product, the proportion of GDP in manufacturing and similar measures that "'stagnation' in the Third World is largely a myth. There has been a very substantial growth of capitalist social relations of production throughout the Third World where they were previously non-existent or in a very primitive state."[57] Warren suggests that a frank acknowledgment of these facts will allow scholars of the left to concentrate their attention on "internal contradictions of the Third World itself" and to avoid "supporting bourgeois regimes which, as in Peru and Egypt, exploit and oppress workers and peasants while employing anti-capitalist rhetoric."[58]

These conclusions have not gone without response from within the general dependency perspective. Perhaps the most common rejoinder is that sheer economic "growth," as measured by GDP growth rates and similar measures, does not necessarily imply "development," a broader concept that includes overall improvement in the condition of life of the population of a country rather than mere aggregate accumulation.[59] Arghiri Emmanuel, for example, suggests that it is "unwarranted" to assume that "industrialization . . . and development are the same thing"; if this were the case, he says, we would have to conclude (at least on the basis of figures on the proportion of output and labor in the manufacturing sector) that Argentina is already as developed as the United States and Hong Kong more so.[60] McMichael, Petras and Rhodes make a similar point for another indicator when they express their doubt about the assumption that for Third World and developed countries, "similar historical experiences are subsumed under the statistical concept 'Gross Domestic Product.' "[61]

Fernando Henrique Cardoso goes a step further when he discusses Brazil, one of the most dramatic apparent exceptions to the dependence-results-in-stagnation hypothesis. Cardoso maintains that Brazil and some other LDCs have embarked upon what is quite simply a new form of development that he terms "associated-dependent development," which is based on heavy foreign investment in the manufacturing sector with emphasis on supplying the internal rather than export markets. He holds that this form of development is not only different from the development historically experienced by now-developed countries but also from the mining and agricultural trade-oriented foreign investment common to less developed LDCs. In Cardoso's view this form of development "is *not* without dynamism . . . [but is] based upon a new international division of labor [in which] part of the industrial system of the hegemonic countries is now being transferred under the control of international corporations, to countries that have been able to reach a relatively advanced level of industrial development.'' [62] The problem is that, while economic *growth* may result from this relationship, "this path of development also entails costs," among them inequitable patterns of income distribution, poor levels of living for the masses and the other characteristics of marginalization (non*development*) discussed in the last section. [63]

The disagreement, then, is clear. On the one hand, there is a long list of scholars and some cross-nationally derived evidence that external dependence does lead to economic stagnation (as well as marginalization) in LDCs. On the other hand, there are many scholars who, while they agree that high levels of external dependence lead to economic marginality and worsening conditions for much of the population of LDCs, maintain that economic growth per se can and does occur within such a framework.

CONCLUSION

Chapter 3 directly analyzed several of the ties most frequently cited as characteristic of the condition of "external dependence." From that analysis there emerged a series of indicators that tap the degree and partner concentration of these ties and allow us to determine not only whether a given LDC is more externally dependent than another but also how much more dependent it is and on what dimensions.

But analysis of the interaction of LDCs with their international environment is only the first step in addressing the hypotheses of dependency theorists. For the literature suggests not only that dependent LDCs interact with the world political economy in a certain manner and to a certain degree but that this interaction is in a decisive way *to their detriment,* or at least to the detriment of the bulk of their populations. The central issue is not so much that a dependency relationship infringes upon the autonomy of subordinate LDCs, but that it infringes upon it in a manner whereby some value is achieved or retained by the dominant country (or at least the dominant groups within that country) and surrendered or foregone by the subordinate country (or at least the subordinate groups within it).

A good deal of the literature of imperialism, especially the early literature, focuses on the first part of this exploitative relationship:

68 DOMESTIC CONSEQUENCES

there has been extensive debate over the degree to which the working as well as the ruling class in developed countries is incorporated into a system of imperialism; the extent to which imperialism serves as an outlet for inevitable surplus production in advanced capitalist countries; the amount of gain accruing to developed countries from direct investment "decapitalization" of LDCs or the maintenance of an assured supply of raw materials at prices artificially low relative to those they receive for their manufactures; and on many other aspects of the effects of DC-LDC relationships on the *developed* partner.

The emphasis of this study, in contrast to these approaches but in accordance with the emphasis of most current dependency theorists, is not on the developed partner in a DC-LDC relationship, but on the other member of the exploitative relationship described above, the less developed partner.[64] Some of the consequences that have been proposed by dependency theorists as suffered as a result of relations marked by a high degree of external dependence have been detailed in this chapter. To summarize, almost all dependency theorists agree that extensive and highly concentrated LDC ties with DCs in the areas of trade, aid, investment, debt, higher education and arms transfers tend to result in the ascendancy within LDCs of co-opted elites whose interests are more in harmony with those of elites in the world "Center" than with those of peripheral groups in their own countries. These elites can be expected to prevent meaningful distributive or social welfare policies that might threaten their dominance at home, to devote considerable attention to expanding the coercive apparatus of their countries and, in general, to follow a development strategy that meets their own needs but is inappropriate to the needs of nonelites in their countries. The ultimate result of a distorted development pattern of this sort is that nonelites are drawn into a set of structural relationships in which their relative position can only deteriorate.

In addition some but not all dependency theorists argue that high levels of external dependence are directly associated with economic stagnation in LDCs; some views on this more controversial hypothesis were also discussed.

CHAPTER FIVE

The Domestic Consequences of External Dependence II. The Basic Regression Model

THIS CHAPTER WILL TEST SOME OF the broad hypotheses that have been proposed in chapter 4 for the cross-national sample of seventy less developed countries on which this study is based. To this end several important dimensions of economic and social marginality and of economic growth will be operationalized by means of a series of indicators of income distribution, the progressiveness of national taxation systems, the extent of military and internal security efforts and rates of unemployment and of economic growth. These indicators will first be related to one another by means of R-factor analysis in order to determine whether most of their variance can effectively be expressed in a smaller number of composite dimensions. If clear composite dimensions do emerge, they will be entered as dependent variables in a series of multiple regression equations in which as large a proportion of their variance as possible will be explained using the seven modes of external dependence developed in chapter 3 and two necessary control variables, gross national product per capita and natural resource endowment.

What broad outcomes are possible in an anlysis of this sort? Several might be identified. First, it is possible that all findings will be strong and in the direction that dependency theory would have us expect; if this is the case, we could say that the theory has withstood one, fairly difficult, cross-national test. Second, it is possible that all or most of the modes of external dependence will not be in any way related to political and economic characteristics of LDCs; if this is true, we would have to conclude that such factors are of little use in predicting militarism, inequality or economic stagnation, and that future researchers might do well to look to more traditional cultural, social and economic factors in explaining the division of power and wealth in LDCs. Finally, it is possible that any relationships found will be strong, but in the opposite direction from that predicted by dependency theorists, and will more closely resemble the economic and social diffusion model described in chapter 4.

But a test of the sort proposed need not be an all-or-nothing proposition. As has been indicated, relating a number of modes of external dependence to a number of dependent variables results in a large number of individual propositions, each of which may or may not be empirically validated. Moreover, the model will include control variables and will be constructed for a number of separate subgroups of the original seventy nations. All of this suggests that the number of individual relationships to be examined is quite large, and it is hoped that this profusion of hypotheses will result in a more subtle and detailed test of a very rich body of theory than has previously been attempted. The ultimate result may well be not an outright acceptance or rejection of dependency theory as such, but rather the emergence of more refined and sophisticated sets of propositions that have withstood cross-national testing and are ready for further exploration.

DEPENDENT VARIABLES: INDICATORS AND DIMENSIONS

In this section the dependent variables that will be used in the regression exercise, that is, some of the particular internal characteristics of LDCs that dependency theory would lead us to expect to be related to the level of external dependence, will be briefly introduced. The sources of all of these indicators and more detailed information about them are provided in appendix IV.

Educational Enrollment   Gross educational enrollment ratio for
the first and second levels of schooling, c.1970

The intention of this indicator is to measure the demonstrated effectiveness of government efforts in one representative area of social policy. It measures the number of students attending primary and secondary schools in relation to the size of the school-aged population. While the measure of foreign educational ties used as an indicator of external dependence (*students abroad*—university students studying abroad / total university students) was compiled for students at the university level, at which stage children of a "comprador elite" might be expected to be generously represented, this measure concentrates upon primary and secondary education, which would be difficult for a small elite to monopolize. In addition and in contrast to many other commonly used indicators of social policy (such as measures of the pervasiveness of public health programs), this indicator is identified with social mobility and eventual change in a society's distribution of social and economic resources. As was seen in chapter 4, low levels on this indicator have been explicitly invoked by several dependency theorists as representative of the negative effects of external dependence.

Social Insurance Programs   Extent of social insurance coverage, early 1971

This indicator is intended to suggest the degree to which the public in a country is protected from loss of earnings on account of injury, sickness, maternity or old age and after the death of the principal earner; is provided with medical care in the event of such occurrences; and is subsidized if family earnings fall below a certain minimum level. The indicator is based on data assembled by the United States Department of Health, Education, and Welfare and is similar to that used in a comparative cross-national study of social insurance efforts by Phillips Cutright.[1]

The indicator ranges from 0 to 5, depending upon the number of five major categories of social insurance (as defined by the source) in which coverage is provided.[2] The categories are

Work injury programs   Family assistance programs
Sickness and maternity programs   Unemployment programs
Old age, invalidity and death programs

If a program existed in a given category in early 1971, one point was tallied; a few exceptions were made in cases in which programs existed but were very limited in scope or applied only to very restricted groups.

Social Welfare   Social welfare index

This indicator was formed by collecting data on four basic welfare characteristics—infant mortality, life expectancy, literacy and caloric consumption—linearly transforming these data to fit four parallel scales ranging from 0 to 100 and averaging country scores on the four scales. This rather primitive but effective method of scaling these variables was patterned on previous work by Douglas Hibbs and Robert Jackman.[3]

The purpose of this indicator is to measure as closely as possible the general social welfare of the "masses" in a given LDC. Although figures are based on aggregates for entire countries, it is submitted that they can still be relatively effective in indicating general social welfare since there is an upper limit beyond which the values on which these indicators are based cannot easily be accumulated. As put by Douglas Hibbs, "it is difficult to imagine infant live births . . . and caloric consumption being monopolized by a small group. After all, a privileged elite can only eat so much, produce so many children."[4] We might also note that, as a consequence of including GNP per capita and natural resource endowment as control variables, the proportion of variance in *social welfare* attributable to these "givens" can readily be isolated from that associated with the modes of external dependence; this is true of all of the dependent variables in the study, but it is particularly relevant for this indicator.

Education Budget   Public educational expenditures as a proportion of
total public expenditures, c.1970

The intention of this indicator is not to measure the present condition of
public education (as was the case with *educational enrollment*) but rather to
tap the government commitment to public education programs. The indicator
is based on budget shares, since it is in actuating a budget that program
priorities are most readily evident: an increase in funding for one program,
other things being equal, entails a decrease in funding for others. Figures for
this indicator include both current and capital expenditures at all levels of
government and reflect reported government expenditures rather than commitments. It is hoped that this indicator will supplement *educational enrollment* by including some notion of the possibility of future advances in education (as particularly reflected in the capital budget) as well as of the
quality as opposed to the pervasiveness of efforts in public education.

Direct Taxes   Direct taxes as a proportion of total
government revenue, 1970

This indicator is intended to measure the progressivity of a country's tax
structure. The topic is an important one, since a country's tax mechanisms
represent the government policy with perhaps the most direct potential for
altering (or maintaining) an existing pattern of income distribution and are
thus important indicators of efforts to encourage or discourage a wider distribution of income.

The main lines of justification of this particular indicator of tax progressivity are provided by one of a large number of scholars who have used it,
Robert Jackman (quoting Musgrave):

> Essentially, this variable involves a distinction between direct and indi-
> rect taxes, wherein direct taxes are those "assessed on *objects* rather
> than individuals and therefore not adaptable to the individual's special
> position and his taxable capacity." In other words, direct taxes are
> usually assessed by the criterion of ability to pay, while indirect taxes
> are not, . . . [and the former] are likely to be considerably more pro-
> gressive.[5]

Top 20 Income Share, Bottom 40 Income Share   Shares in household
income, as near as possible to 1970

Income distribution is one of the central variables in this analysis and, indeed, taps directly one of the central dimensions of all social science. Unfortunately, however, data on this dimension are perhaps the least readily available and least reliable of those for any major socioeconomic variable.[6] As
recently as 1972, for example, Taylor and Hudson, in compiling the second
edition of the *World Handbook of Political and Social Indicators,* were
forced to rely on figures for income distribution across eight broad economic
sectors rather than across households, and even for this very imperfect
measure they were able to assemble data for only fifty-two countries worldwide.[7]

Only in the last few years has the situation improved, mostly through the efforts of Irma Adelman and Cynthia Taft Morris, Felix Paukert, and Hollis Chenery, Shail Jain and other World Bank associates, in collating the many and diverse individual studies in this area into a more or less compatible set of data on income shares to the level of household.[8] The most recent figures from Paukert, Chenery et al. and Chenery and Syrquin have been integrated to make up the indicators used in this study; even so data are unavailable for 25 of the 70 cases (most of them in Black Africa), making this one of the few variables for which data are missing for more than one or two cases.[9]

These data have been reported separately for upper and lower income groups instead of being presented in the form of a single summary Gini or Schutz index, because it is quite possible that certain external linkages will be more strongly related to the income share of the elite (the top 20 percent of the population) than to that of the masses (the bottom 40 percent), while for other linkages the opposite will be true. It should be noted that although income distribution figures were selected to represent a year as near as possible to 1970, they vary more than any other variable in the actual year covered and should be viewed with this in mind.

Unemployment Unemployment rate, 1970

One of the most direct indicators of marginality in any country is its rate of unemployment. Unfortunately accurate and comparable data on unemployment rates, like those on income distribution, are difficult to come by. The data used here are from World Bank statistics and provide data for only 43 of the 70 members of the sample. They derive principally from International Labour Organisation figures, but the IBRD has supplemented ILO data (which are often of limited comparability in their raw form) with data from labor force surveys, retirement insurance statistics, labor union benefit statistics, work registration program enrollments and national and IBRD country estimates.

Military Expenditures Total military expenditures as a
proportion of gross national product, 1970

The intention of this indicator is to measure the extent to which the leaders of a country devote their nation's resources to military spending. The figures generally coincide with the expenditures of the defense ministry of the country, although where possible the figures have been adjusted to exclude military assistance grants and civilian-type expenditures by the military and to include military-type expenditures by civilian agencies. The figures are standardized to GNP.

Military Manpower Manpower in military service
per 1,000 population

This indicator measures the relative extent to which a country devotes manpower resources to military service. The figures cover only active personnel. Paramilitary forces are included "where these resemble regular units in their organization, equipment, training or mission."[10] Since this indicator is based on manpower, it is standardized to population. It has been transformed by a natural logarithmic function.

Internal Security Forces   Internal security forces
per 1,000 population

This indicator is intended to contribute to the measurement of the extent of government effort directed toward the suppression of internal opposition. The measure itself is straightforward. It is standardized to population.

GDP Growth Rate   Average annual growth rate of total real gross domestic product at market prices, 1970–1974

Chapter 4 discussed the hypothesis, controversial among dependency theorists, that a high level of external dependence necessarily results in economic stagnation in LDCs. This indicator focuses on the rate of growth of gross domestic product from 1970 to 1974, the period immediately following the point in time (c.1970) for which the indicators of external dependence are measured.[11]

Unlike the Chase-Dunn and Alschuler studies, but like the Kaufman et al. study and in line with the general parlance of the economic growth literature, this study measures increases in absolute GDP and not GDP per capita. This is done because when the growth rate of GDP per capita is focused upon it will often occur that country X, in which overall economic growth was very rapid but population growth almost as rapid, will be rated as having demonstrated less economic dynamism than country Y, with a slower overall increase in economic output but much slower population growth. This is hardly what most people have in mind when they speak of relative economic growth; indeed, it means that countries with rapid rates of population growth will be judged economically stagnant almost irrespective of how rapidly their economy is growing in absolute terms. Thus, although the growth rate of GDP per capita is in some ways a more realistic measure than the one used here, it was decided that the measure used provided a more meaningful test of the hypotheses in question.[12]

It is recognized that the period for which GDP growth is measured was, to say the least, a highly unstable one, owing especially but not exclusively to the 1973 oil price rises. Part of the influence of this factor is mitigated by the fact that this study does not include major oil producers; for the purposes of this regression it has been seen fit also to exclude Indonesia, Nigeria, Ecuador and Tunisia, countries which were in 1970 moderate-scale oil producers with relatively large populations and thus were included in the general analysis. It is hoped that the inclusion of a natural resource endowment index as a control variable will, at least in part, mitigate the influence of oil resources for the moderate-scale oil producers (such as Mexico or Brazil) that remain.[13]

As has been seen, twelve individual indicators have been introduced, a rather large number, perhaps, readily to analyze and digest. Matters would be greatly simplified if we could, using R-factor analysis, extract from these individual indicators a smaller number of composite dimensions that embody most of their variance. While there is no compelling substantive reason for doing this, it turns out that we can, at little cost in specificity and precision, render the findings that must be reported much less voluminous.

As is seen in table 5.1 and *R*-factor analysis was performed on eight of the indicators introduced. The indicators of income distribution and unemployment, since they contain a large amount of missing data, were not included and will be entered independently into the forthcoming regressions. The indicator *GDP growth rate* was also excluded because it represents a hypothesis more controversial than the others, making its integration with the other variables undesirable.

Using the Kaiser criterion, three factors were selected and rotated. The first factor is derived primarily from contributions of *educational enrollment, social welfare, social insurance programs* and *direct taxes,* the variables dealing with demonstrated social welfare and government efforts in this area. The composite indicator will be called "welfare." The second factor is defined by the three indicators *military expenditures, military manpower* and *internal security forces;* since each of these clearly deals with the coercive resources available to LDC governments, the composite indicator defined by

Table 5.1 *R*-Factor Analysis of Dependent Variables
(Factor Pattern/Factor Structure)

	Factor 1 (Welfare)	Factor 2 (Coercive Potential)	Factor 3 (Education Budget)
Variables			
Educational enrollment	**.77/.81**	.34/.40	.24/.23
Social insurance programs	**.81/.79**	−.13/−.04	−.03/.00
Social welfare	**.85/.87**	.19/.28	−.06/−.05
Direct taxes	**.79/.76**	−.25/−.17	.02/.06
Military expenditures	−.10/−.02	**.82/.82**	−.19/−.26
Internal security forces	−.09/.01	**.85/.82**	.25/.19
Military manpower	.38/.45	**.72/.78**	−.26/−.31
Education budget	.06/.08	−.04/−.10	**.94/.95**

Factor Correlations

	Factor 1	Factor 2	Factor 3
Factor 1	X		
Factor 2	.10	X	
Factor 3	.03	−.07	X

Percent Variance Explained
Factor 1   38.2%
Factor 2   24.7
Factor 3   13.3
             76.2%

this factor is called "coercive potential." A third, much weaker, factor is formed essentially from the contribution of only one variable, *education budget;* it is simply called "education budget," although it must be remembered that it differs slightly from the original variable of this name.

As can be seen, the loadings on these factors are in general very cleanly differentiated, and it appears that we can with confidence use the composite dimensions derived here as dependent variables in the multiple regressions that follow.

ISSUES OF CONTROL

The variables introduced in this section are focused upon not so much for their intrinsic interest as for another value: if they were not introduced, the possibility would remain that many of the findings of the regression analyses to come would be spurious, since they would be derived from the joint action of these variables on both the independent and dependent variables in the regression model. The need for *post facto* statistical control arises from the fact that cross-national research is nonexperimental and must operate within a given set of countries that often vary so widely as to make comparison without taking some of these differences into account hazardous. Although the number of potentially confounding variables is virtually infinite, it is most important explicitly to control for those that previous theory or research have indicated might be expected to have a major impact on both the independent and the dependent variables in a particular study.[14]

Among the most important of these in studies of less developed countries are gross national product per capita and natural resource endowment. Chenery and Syrquin, for example, in a study of development patterns in 101 countries from 1950 to 1970, found that GNP per capita explained a large proportion of the variance in twenty-seven structural characteristics of the countries of their study, while Grant Reuber, in a study of private direct investment in 113 LDCs, found that GNP per capita was an important factor in explaining the extent of investment ties between developed countries and LDCs: a spurious effect based on GNP per capita thus seems possible, at least for investment dependence.[15] Similarly, in a summary of the literature in this area, Carlos F. Diaz-Alejandro concludes that "if one knows the per capita income, the population and the resource endowment . . . for a given LDC, one can make a very good guess about the structure of production and foreign trade in that country.''[16]

In line with these authors this study will directly control for the level of GNP per capita and general natural resource endowment by including indicators of these dimensions at every step of the regression analysis as independent variables in competition with the modes of external dependence; the partialling process that governs the construction of multiple regression coefficients will have the result that, in effect, only countries at similar levels of these variables will be compared, and any impact their inclusion may have on the dependent variables will be isolated.[17] Absolute population and another variable, absolute GNP, will be less fully controlled by physically dividing the sample into two subsamples based on these variables, for which regressions will then be done separately. This technique will also be used for two other variables, region and former colonial metropolis, which might be thought of not so much as variables whose effect needs to be controlled as contextual factors outside the general model, the impact of which is worth examining. The latter findings will be reported only in summary form.

All of these variables are discussed next.

GNP per capita   Gross national product, 1970, in market prices in current
United States dollars, based upon average 1965–1970 exchange rates,
divided by mid-1970 population estimate

Gross national product is perhaps the most widely used indicator in cross-national research of all kinds. Its use has come under two basic criticisms. First, it is argued that this variable measures only aggregate accumulation with no regard for the distribution or pervasiveness of the economic activity indicated. This objection is directly addressed in this study by the introduction of a number of distributive and social welfare indicators that give at least some indication of the penetration of the benefits of economic activity throughout the population. A second objection is that GNP per capita is a concept that exists mainly on paper, based as it is on extensive estimates, especially of activity in the nonmonetized sector in LDCs. Criticism from this point of view suggests that aggregate development might better be measured by a more concrete indicator such as energy consumption per capita. The national product indicator was nevertheless used in this study, because its use will enhance comparability of this study with others, most of which also use it. The reader is referred to a review of the recent technical literature in this area by Chenery and Syrquin, on the basis of which the authors conclude that ''while systematic bias in national income converted at official exchange rates is a well-established phenomenon, there is not at present any preferred alternative.''[18]

On the basis of scattergram evidence this indicator has been transformed by a natural logarithmic function. This means that a given increment in GNP per capita is weighted somewhat more strongly if it separates countries at low levels of GNP per capita than if it separates those at higher levels.

Natural Resource Endowment   Index of natural resource endowment, c.1970

This is another of the few indicators in this study that are measured at the ordinal level. It was compiled by assigning LDCs to categories based upon the relative extent of their endowment of oil, natural gas, iron ore, phosphates, manganese, diamonds, bauxite and similar ores, copper, nickel, tin, zinc and lead; the basic data source is a United States Geological Survey Professional Paper entitled *Summary of Petroleum and Selected Mineral Statistics for 120 Countries and Offshore Areas.*[19] The figures are generally based on production, although reserves figures were also examined where available. The four-category ordinal variable created is admittedly rough, but it is probably as discriminatory as we might realistically expect in an indicator based on such a large number of very different commodities, the relative importance of which is very difficult to judge and is constantly changing.

1. Very limited mineral or petroleum resources
2. Limited amounts of one or two mineral or petroleum resources
3. Moderate to large amounts of a single resource or moderate to small amounts of more than one
4. Large amounts of a single resource or moderate to large amounts of more than one

All designations were based on relative production in comparison to world production figures.

Absolute Population, Absolute GNP   Absolute population and gross national product estimates, 1970

In order to examine the possibility that large and moderate-sized LDCs demonstrate contradictory patterns that make whole-sample analysis misleading, parallel regression analyses have been constructed based on subsamples of the general sample dichotomized according to absolute population and GNP. The demarcation point for population is ten million, which distinguishes 26 large-population LDCs from the rest of the sample. The cutting point for absolute GNP is also rather arbitrary: it is set at $5,000 million, which isolates high-level countries somewhat more closely, resulting in 18 high-level countries and 52 at lower levels.

Region   Geographical region

The geographical region of each country in the sample is also coded; the designations are as follows:

1. Sub-Saharan Africa
2. Latin American and Caribbean
3. Mideast, Asia, Southern Europe

(For the present the final three regions have been combined; more detailed attention will be given to geographical region in chapters 6 and 7.)

Former Colonial Metropolis

Former colonial metropolis is categorized as follows:

1. Former British colonies
2. Former French colonies
3. Former Spanish or Portuguese colonies
4. Former Belgian, Dutch, Italian, Japanese or American colonies
5. "Never a colony"

Countries that have been subject to more than one colonial power in recent times were assigned to the category of their metropolis in 1939. Countries that were colonies at some point before 1939 but not since were coded 5, except for Latin American former Spanish and Portuguese colonies, which were coded 3.

THE BASIC REGRESSION MODEL

Now that the principal dependent and control variables have been introduced, it is possible to present the multiple regressions by which they are related to the independent variables (modes of external dependence) that were introduced in chapter 3.

All of the basic regression statistics are presented except the b coefficients, which have little intuitive meaning in themselves since, for the most part, the regression relates standardized factor scores to one another.[20] Beta-weight coefficients are reported and an indication is made in parentheses if the b coefficients on which they are based are statistically significant at the .01, .05 or .10 level. In the interest of economy of presentation, beta weights are not reported if their corresponding b coefficients are not significant at at least the .10 level; every equation, however, includes all independent and control variables. If beta-weight coefficients predict a relationship in the direction hypothesized by dependency theory they are designated "expected" and if they predict a relationship in the opposite direction they are designated "unexpected."[21]

For reference a full list of the independent, dependent and control variables used in the basic regression model is presented in table 5.2.

Now, to the actual equations. The first equation deals with the relationship between the nine competing independent variables and the dependent variable *welfare*.

Table 5.2 Reference List of Variables in Multiple Regressions

I. *Independent Variables* (x_i)
  Modes of External Dependence (see chapter 3 for discussion)

Trade	Composite trade dependence indicator
Finance	Composite finance dependence indicator
Concentration	Composite aid, trade and investment concentration indicator
Aid-trade terms	Composite aid-trade terms dependence indicator
Investment	Private direct foreign investment indicator
Arms transfers	Arms transfers indicator
Students abroad	Foreign higher education indicator
Control Variables	
GNP per capita	Gross national product per capita
Natural resource endowment	Natural resources endowment index

II. *Dependent Variables* (y)

Social welfare	Social welfare composite indicator
Unemployment	Unemployment rate
Top 20 income share, bottom 40 income share	Household income shares of the top 20 and bottom 40 percent of the population
Education budget	Education budget composite indicator
Coercive potential	Coercive potential composite indicator
GDP growth rate	Growth rate of absolute GDP, 1970–1974

Welfare as Dependent Variable ($R^2 = .71, N = 70$)

Students abroad	−.17	(.05)	Expected
Trade	−.16	(.05)	Expected
Arms transfers	−.14	(.05)	Expected
Concentration	−.11	(.10)	Expected
GNP per capita	+.68	(.01)	Control
Natural resource endowment	+.15	(.05)	Control

What do these statistics indicate? For one thing, we see that .71 of the variance in *welfare* is explained by the model. Of the individual predictors six are found to demonstrate a significant relationship with *welfare*. The strongest of these is with the control variable *GNP per capita*, which is just as might be expected: it is reasonable that countries at higher levels of economic development demonstrate higher levels of social welfare.

But inspection reveals that even after the control variables are taken into account, four of the indicators of external dependence— *students abroad, trade, arms transfers* and *concentration*—significantly predict *welfare* in the direction that dependency theory would lead us to expect. What this means, in effect, is that among countries at similar levels of GNP per capita and with similar endowments of natural resources, those with higher levels of educational, trade and arms transfers dependence and with a higher concentration of trade, aid and investment partners tend to have lower levels of general social welfare. Dependency theorists would suggest that several patterns are at work: that in countries in which a large proportion of university students have studied abroad the "internationalization" of the domestic elite has been consolidated; that higher levels of trade dependence have reinforced the position of dependent LDCs as disadvantaged partners in a vertical trade structure and thus fostered malintegration of their economies; that high levels of arms imports have been maintained at the expense of other goods and services that might more directly benefit the masses in LDCs; and that relatively concentrated aid, trade and investment ties have reinforced the subordinate position of LDCs by solidifying their status as "satellites" in a global "feudal interaction structure." Other explanations are possible, but the general dependency hypotheses do seem to be borne out.

Unemployment as Dependent Variable ($R^2 = .48, N = 43$)

Trade	+.35	(.05)	Expected
Finance	+.34	(.01)	Expected
Investment	+.29	(.10)	Expected
Arms transfers	+.25	(.10)	Expected
Students abroad	+.25	(.10)	Expected

The next dependent variable is *unemployment.* The hypothesis that high levels of external dependence lead to high levels of unemployment in LDCs has been proposed by many dependency theorists. Cardoso, for example, suggests that "associated-dependent development" leads to the "underutilization of manpower resources" in LDCs.[22] Similarly, Sunkel proposes that the hypothesis that an increase in the rate of foreign investment leads to an increase in the rate of unemployment and underemployment is "perhaps the best working hypothesis to explain the problem of underemployment and marginality in Latin America."[23] And Thomas Weisskopf suggests that

> forces are at work [in dependent LDCs] to bias the choice of technique
> used to produce any given good or service in favor of physical capital
> and skilled labor and against unskilled labor. The tendency to adopt

techniques that have been developed under conditions in rich countries, where capital is more plentiful and labor more scarce, results in just such a bias.[24]

The findings presented here provide persuasive evidence supporting these hypotheses: five of the seven modes of external dependence are positively and significantly related to the rate of unemployment in LDCs and none is negatively related. We thus find quite clear confirmation of the marginalization hypothesis for one very specific area of social marginality, the pervasiveness of unemployment.

Education Budget as Dependent Variable $(R^2 = .22, N = 70)$

Investment	+.34	(.05)	Unexpected
Concentration	+.23	(.10)	Unexpected

The next dependent variable, *education budget,* is predicted by the general model much less well than either of the first two: R^2 is only .22. Moreover, the individual independent variables that are significantly related to this variable show a relationship in the opposite direction from that predicted by dependency theory: the higher the level of *investment or concentration* the higher the level of *education budget.*

How might these findings be explained? A possibility, relevant to the stronger relationship, is that DC-based multinational corporations, whatever their overall impact on LDCs, do pay taxes which help to support educational and other social programs. This finding casts doubt on the most extreme dependency prediction that private direct investment has a uniformly negative effect on social welfare in LDCs, although it does not necessarily mean that negative effects do not occur that balance this positive effect.

Top 20 Income Share as Dependent Variable $(R^2 = .29, N = 45)$

Investment	+.52	(.01)	Expected
Students Abroad	−.30	(.05)	Unexpected

As can be seen, two independent variables make a statistically significant contribution to explaining variance in *top 20 income share.* The weaker of these relationships concerns the independent variable, *students abroad;* it suggests that, contrary to dependency predictions, strong foreign educational ties are negatively related to inequitable patterns of income distribution. Apparently, foreign study does have a distributive effect, either directly or through the dissemination of progressive foreign ideas.[25]

The stronger of these relationships does, however, confirm dependency predictions: it shows a pattern in which private direct foreign investment stocks are positively related, with a beta weight of +.52, to the income share of the top fifth of the population. This is as dependency theorists would predict—private direct investment, they would say, furthers a form of "development" that enriches a small, collaborative elite at the expense of the bulk of the population. If they were interpreting this finding, dependency theorists would probably cite it, in conjunction with the findings for the dependent variables *welfare* and *unemployment,* as indicative of a process in which marginalization and maldevelopment in LDCs are closely associated with extensive foreign-owned private investment holdings.

But other explanations are possible. One might respond to this finding by suggesting that it represents only a temporary shift toward less equitably distributed income, resulting from a very real increase in the income of the "modern" sector directly affected by foreign investment, superimposed on an as-yet-unaffected mass base. Since in a transitional society increases in productivity and income rarely diffuse gradually through an entire population, but instead tend to occur unevenly as one person or group at a time crosses the boundary from the traditional to the modern economy, a temporary trend toward inequality might be expected.

One way of addressing this divergence of interpretation is to consider distribution figures for a smaller group of high-income persons. Along these lines data have been assembled for the income share of the top 5 percent of the population in LDCs, allaying the argument that data from the top 20 percent might actually incorporate the income share of an emerging middle class. Unfortunately, these data are available for only twenty-nine cases, which is not enough for reliable estimates for the full multiple regression model. But when a multiple regression is done using only *investment* and the two controls *GNP per capita* and *natural resource endowment* in an effort to explain variance in *top 5 income share,* the positive relationship between *investment* and *top 20 income share* is confirmed—the beta weight is an even stronger +.56, significant at the .01 level.

Still, the discussion has not gone beyond high-income groups. What of low-income groups, the other side of the maldevelopment picture? Part of the answer was given in the preceding analysis of *welfare* and *unemployment*—as has already been indicated, these variables were chosen to reflect the level of social welfare of the masses in a given country. But it is also of interest to examine directly figures for the household income distribution of the bottom two-fifths of the population of LDCs.

Bottom 40 Income Share as Dependent Variable $(R^2 = .43, N = 45)$

Investment	−.50	(.01)	Expected
Concentration	−.21	(.10)	Expected
Arms transfers	−.24	(.10)	Expected
Aid-trade terms	+.24	(.10)	Unexpected

Here we find statistically significant relationships for four independent variables, three in the expected direction. The strongest by far is for *investment,* confirming the notion that private direct foreign investment stocks are negatively related to income shares for the bottom 40 percent of the population of LDCs as well as positively related to income shares of the top 20 and 5 percent.

Two other relationships are in the predicted direction, although weaker. The first of these is with *arms transfers;* the obvious explanation is that heavy expenditures on foreign-produced arms often occur at the expense of alternative uses for scarce resources that might benefit lower income groups and, indeed, are often financed in part by these groups. The relationship of *concentration* is also as predicted.

As can be seen, one independent variable (*aid-trade terms*) is related to *bottom 40 income share* in an unexpected direction. This finding suggests that economic assistance (to the extent that it contributes to *aid-trade terms*) is not as negative a factor as some of its critics have suggested.

Coercive Potential as Dependent Variable $(R^2 = .66, N = 70)$

Students Abroad	+.28	(.01)	Expected
Concentration	+.20	(.05)	Expected
Arms Transfers	+.71	(.01)	Expected
Trade	−.17	(.05)	Unexpected
GNP Per Capita	+.39	(.01)	Control

Here the proportion of the variance in the dependent variable explained by the competing independent variables is a strong .66. Once the effect of the controls is taken into account, we find that three modes of external dependence are related to *coercive potential* in the variance in *coercive potential* that was not already accounted for by the nine other independent and control variables. Thus at least one additional test confirms the validity of the multiple regression in explaining *coercive potential*.[28]

The final dependent variable is *GDP growth rate*. Since the predicted relationship for this variable is more controversial among dependency theorists than for the others analyzed in this chapter, discussion of its relationship to the modes of external dependence will be deferred until later in the chapter.

Absolute GNP and Population, Region, and Former Colonial Metropolis

Although the analysis just conducted has included two of the most important control variables, there are good reasons to consider (although in a somewhat less systematic manner) the effects of several other outside variables on the general regression model. For this purpose separate series of regression have been constructed for parallel subsets of the general sample subdivided according to the categorical variables *absolute GNP, absolute population, region* and *former colonial metropolis* (the final variable for only former French and British colonies). Since the principal reason for constructing parallel regressions is to determine whether the effects of these variables invalidate the general model, and since these findings are rather voluminous, all that will be presented here are summary figures; the main purpose is not to detail particular findings but simply to determine whether these regressions are more or less consistent with those for the analysis of the whole sample. (Former colonial metropolis and geographical region will, of course, be more fully dealt with in chapters 6 and 7.)

The findings can be summarized as follows: 30 separate multiple regressions were constructed (in many instances there were too few cases for *top 20 income share, bottom 40 income share* and *unemployment* for them to be further subdivided). In these regressions 69 significant ($p \leqslant .10$) relationships were established between modes of external dependence and various dependent variables; of these 53 were in the direction predicted by dependency theorists and 16 in the opposite direction. Furthermore, it was found that for each of the four series of parallel regressions, relationships in the expected direction outnumbered those in an unexpected direction: 15 to 4 for the regressions based on *absolute GNP*, 16 to 6 for those based on *absolute*

expected direction and one, the weakest, in an unexpected dire
By far the strongest explanatory power (beta weight = +.71)
tributed to the indicator *arms transfers*. We might conclude fror
that LDCs with a large coercive potential tend to bolster that pot
with purchases of foreign-produced arms—or, conversely, tha
arms merchants, aggressively seeking expanded export markets.
to play a large role in directing scarce LDC resources to weap
the expense of more productive uses. (Recall that *arms transf*
also negatively related to *welfare* and *bottom 40 income shar*
positively related to *unemployment*.)

But what about the most obvious unincluded potentially inte
ing variable, the presence or threat of foreign war? Does this no
ern both the level of arms transfers *and* the level of coercive
tial? If this factor were taken into account might not
demonstrated relationships disappear? I would argue that matte
not quite this simple, since it is possible that the presence or thr
war is itself a function of the extent to which the parties are arr
just as a tavern quarrel is likely to turn violent when weapo
readily available.

Still, the possibility of a spurious relationship is worth exam
While it is most difficult to measure quantitatively the magnit
threat of war, some notion of the relative extent of external c
might be achieved by considering the indicator "external int
tions" from the *World Handbook of Political and Social Indic*
This indicator reports the number of times a given country ha
fered "an attempt by an actor, whether another nation-state or a
group operating from outside the country, to engage in military
ity within [it] with the intent of influencing [its] authority
ture."[26] Data on this indicator were totalled for the years 1963
for each country to establish whether that country had in l
recent history of intervention from abroad. The raw number of
nal interventions was then transformed by a $\log_{10}(x+1)$ funct
order that countries with a very large number of external int
tions would not unduly influence the indicator. (We can think
transformed variable as representing the symbolic intensity of
nal intervention.)[27]

The indicator thus produced was entered into the multiple r
sion equation as an additional control variable. It was found t
beta weight changed by more than ± .01 as a result of its inc
and that external intervention itself accounted for only .00185

population, 10 to 3 for those based on *region* and 12 to 3 for those based on *former colonial metropolis.* Finally, all but one of the individual dependent variables in the parallel regressions was related to modes of external dependence in an expected direction considerably more frequently than in an unexpected direction: 16 to 2 for *welfare,* 14 to 2 for *coercive potential,* 4 to 2 for *top 20 income share,* 6 to 3 for *bottom 40 income share* and 5 to 0 for *unemployment;* the exception, as for the whole-sample regressions, was *education budget,* for which the ratio of expected to unexpected relationships was only 8 to 7.

Although these findings are presented only in summary form, it is clear that they are more or less consistent with those of the whole-sample regressions, and offer some confidence that the multiple regressions described above have not been seriously affected by the four underlying characteristics *absolute GNP, absolute population, region* and *former colonial metropolis.*

EXTERNAL DEPENDENCE, GROWTH AND STAGNATION

As was suggested in chapter 4, dependency theorists disagree whether high levels of external dependence tend inevitably to result in economic stagnation in LDCs, or whether they may result in a process Cardoso terms "associated-dependent development," whose chief characteristics are rapid economic growth accompanied, however, by poor distribution and high levels of marginality. Cross-national research in this area has been inconclusive: Chase-Dunn and Alschuler, for example, found some evidence of a positive relationship between external dependence and economic stagnation, while Kaufman et al. and McGowan and Smith did not.[29] Because hypotheses in this area are more controversial among dependency theorists than are other dependency hypotheses considered in this study, efforts in this area are reported separately in this section.

How might this issue best be dealt with? Two basic approaches have been taken. First, a careful effort has been made in previous sections to relate external dependence to a broader range of phenomena than can be encompassed by data on the average annual growth rate of gross domestic product and similar measures. Careful attention has been given to figures on income distribution, basic welfare, tax progressivity, social insurance expenditures and other aspects of a broad concept of "development" as opposed to a narrow concept of "growth." It is hoped that this has resulted in an understanding of whether "growth without development" has indeed occurred in ostensibly externally dependent LDCs whose economies are rapidly expanding—the Brazils and South Koreas of the Third World.

But it would be a mistake to leave the matter at this, facilely dismissing a major strand of the literature and the five or six previous cross-national tests of dependency theory that rely on GDP growth rates by suggesting that they are missing the point that dependence can result in "growth without development." Rapid economic growth in itself is not everything, and evidence that it is or is not related to external dependence certainly does not prove or disprove dependency theory as a whole, but it is hard to deny that economic growth rates are important and eminently worthy of study in their own right.

For this reason, GDP average annual growth rate from 1970 to 1974 has been introduced as a dependent variable and related to the modes of external dependence in the same manner as were the marginality, distribution, social policy and political coercion indicators in the previous section of this chapter. The first multiple regression is for the full sample. The findings are as follows:

GDP Growth Rate as Dependent Variable $(R^2 = .35, N = 65)$

Investment	+.39	(.05)	"Dynamism" hypothesis confirmed
Arms transfers	+.32	(.01)	"Dynamism" hypothesis confirmed
Students abroad	−.24	(.05)	"Stagnation" hypothesis confirmed

What does this regression indicate? It suggests, in summary, that the relationship of the modes of external dependence to economic dynamism is an inconsistent one: private direct foreign investment is positively associated with *GDP growth rate,* as is *arms transfers,* while *students abroad* is negatively related. Here we have some evidence confirming the Cardoso hypothesis: as was indicated, Cardoso's "associated-dependent development" is closely identified with foreign investment which is itself associated (as was noted earlier) with income inequality. But the picture is still rather indistinct, with two other relationships not directly confirming either the Frank or the Cardoso hypothesis, and the R^2 rather low.

How might these findings be further specified? One possibility is to dichotomize LDCs according to level of development. It is possible that in countries at low levels of GNP per capita the stagnation resulting from a typically vertical trade relationship is dominant, while in LDCs at a higher level of development, with a potential market of some substance to satisfy, external dependence results in significant (if poorly distributed) economic growth. Cardoso, for example, speaks of associated-dependent development as representative of countries that "have already been able to reach a relatively advanced level of industrial development"; Emmanuel agrees, likening private direct investment, particularly in manufacturing, to liquid in communicating vessels, which "is not attracted by a low level . . . but is, on the contrary, sucked up by a siphon effect, towards active markets and high levels of consumption."[30]

The following figures represent parallel regressions in which countries are divided according to GNP per capita level so that thirty-seven countries are in a "low" category and the other twenty-eight are in a "high" grouping. (The control variable, *GNP per capita,* is retained in the regressions, even though its variance is reduced, in order to account for the still considerable variance in this variable that remains after dichotomization.)

GDP Growth Rate as Dependent Variable
(Sample divided according to *GNP per capita level*)
Low *GNP per capita* level ($R^2 = .26, N = 37$).
No significant predictors
High *GNP per capita* level ($R^2 = .46, N = 28$).

Trade	$-.54$	(.05)	"Stagnation" hypothesis confirmed
Concentration	$-.59$	(.05)	"Stagnation" hypothesis confirmed
Students abroad	$-.62$	(.05)	"Stagnation" hypothesis confirmed
Investment	$+1.26$	(.01)	"Dynamism" hypothesis confirmed
Arms transfers	$+.51$	(.05)	"Dynamism" hypothesis confirmed
GNP per capita	$-.48$	(.05)	Control

As can be seen, for low per capita income countries no independent variable is significantly related to GDP growth rates. It is clear that for poorer LDCs the relationship between various modes of external dependence and the rate of economic growth is limited, that for these countries the rate of short-term growth, at least, does not seem to be closely related in either direction to levels of external dependence.

But for high GNP per capita countries a relationship does finally emerge, providing evidence that "associated-dependent development" is a distinct phenomenon confined to certain (but not all) high-income LDCs: we see that *GDP growth rate* is positively related to *investment* (beta-weight = +1.26), which is as Cardoso and others have predicted, while the relationship of *trade, concentration* and *students abroad* to growth is negative (beta weights = −.54, −.59 and −.62, respectively), confirming the hypotheses of Frank and others.[31] These findings suggest that patterns of economic dynamism through contact are doubly limited—they apply only to high-income countries which are also host to a relatively large stock of private direct foreign investment—but that they do, nevertheless, exist.

It would be unwise to read too much into these findings. For one thing economic growth over only a four-year period indicates a short-term trend, one that, moreover, covers a period of unusual instability in the world economy and a general slowdown of economic growth. Future explorations in this area might extend the analysis over a longer period of time and introduce additional controls.

Nevertheless, this is a most interesting finding since it appears to reconcile apparently conflicting dependency hypotheses: the "associated-dependent development" model seems applicable to high-income LDCs which are host to large stocks of foreign direct investment, while the "stagnation" model seems more representative of high-income LDCs with high levels of trade and concentration dependence. Neither approach, however, seems unambiguously to explain variance in economic growth rates for low-income LDCs. To my knowledge no previous study of growth-stagnation dependency hypotheses has constructed parallel analyses according to level of economic development, and this may be one reason for the inconclusive findings that have been derived.

GETTING DOWN TO INDIVIDUAL CASES: RESIDUALS AND OUTLIERS ANALYSIS

Regression residuals represent, most simply, the extent to which values of individual cases on a dependent variable stray from the predictions of the multiple regression model. Their careful examination is always well-advised, since if residuals are not more or less randomly distributed it is likely that the regression equation on which they are based has violated necessary assumptions, and the use of multiple regression for a particular set of data is called into question. An analysis of residuals in these terms is described in appendix III.

But while in many analyses the "cases" analyzed are anonymous and can be examined only in terms of general trends, in a cross-national analysis quite the opposite is true: the units of analysis are readily identifiable countries about which one has a great deal of prior information. Individual regression residuals thus have meaning in themselves and we are likely to learn something by directly examining countries that do not fit the regression-based generalizations very well. In this section residuals will be listed if they place a particular country more than ±1.5 standard deviation units from the regression line, certainly a conservative limit.

The y-predict values in regression represent values on the dependent variable that summarize the information offered by the regression coefficients about its relationship to the independent variables. We might think of them as symbolizing the generalizations the regression allows us to make, while the residuals indicate the degree to which individual cases deviate from these generalizations.

In examining y-predict values, it is important to identify any that are exceptionally high or low in relation to the others. The reason is that such values are usually the result of outliers, extreme values that can dominate a regression equation, artificially raising R^2 and distorting relationships. The form in which the variables in this study have been expressed and the occasional use of logarithmic transformations have ensured that no really extreme values have been included, but in the interest of comprehensiveness all y-predict values greater than ±2.00 standard deviation units from the mean are reported.

The results of residuals and outliers analysis are reported for the whole-sample model. For ease of comprehension residuals and y-predict values are always reported in pairs, even if only one or the other exceeds the established limits. Table 5.3 lists the principal findings.

We begin with the dependent variable *welfare*. Here we find no large residuals (as would be expected in an equation with an R^2 of .71) and only one moderately high y-predict value, that of Spain, probably the most developed country in the entire sample.

The next variable is *top 20 income share*. Here we find three residuals greater than ±1.50 standard deviation units from the regression line, all positive: Kenya, Sierra Leone and El Salvador. Explanations for these deviances are possible: the first country is one of the most aggressively capitalist-oriented in sub-Saharan Africa, while the second and third are strongly dominated by culturally distinct elites.

For *bottom 40 income share* only Greece has a relatively large residual. It is perhaps not unreasonable to suggest that this derives, at

Table 5.3 Residuals and y-Predict Values for the Whole-Sample Regressions

Country	Residual	y-Predict
Welfare as dependent variable		
Spain	+.51	+2.19
Top 20 Income Share as dependent variable		
Kenya	+1.53	+.06
Sierra Leone	+1.67	−.20
El Salvador	+1.65	+.69
Bottom 40 Income Share as dependent variable		
Greece	+1.69	+.22
Education Budget as dependent variable		
Congo	+2.44	+.60
Benin	+1.86	+.16
Colombia	+1.68	+.77
Uruguay	+1.62	−.26
Philippines	+1.66	+.18
Coercive Potential as dependent variable		
Congo	+1.89	+.95
Jordan	+1.78	+3.72
Burma	+1.64	−.75
Syria	−.10	+2.41
Unemployment as dependent variable		
Nicaragua	+1.69	−.06
Sierra Leone	−1.52	+.21
Liberia	+.23	+2.23
Somalia	+1.59	+.88
GDP Growth Rate as dependent variable		
Dominican Republic	+1.71	+.31
Gambia	+1.66	−.90
Uganda	−1.54	−.61
Niger	−1.65	−.92
Senegal	−1.84	+.39
Chile	−1.51	+.36
Uruguay	−1.96	+.23

least in part, from the unusual facility of Greeks in earning income abroad and then returning home to spend it, or sending funds home to support relatives.

The variable, *education budget,* as would be expected in a predictive equation with an R^2 of only .22, shows several more residuals than the previous regressions: five, all positive. We might begin to think of reasons why at least some of these countries have higher educational budgets than the general model would predict: for the Philippines and Colombia this is perhaps the result of years of experience with very particularistic democratic political systems that may have tended to distribute a larger-than-predicted share of benefits as a result of elite competition for mass support; for Uruguay the deviance may be the result of a cultural tradition of emphasis on formal education deriving from its largely European settler population.

Next, there is the dependent variable *coercive potential*. The most atypical case here is Jordan, which has a large positive y-predict value and a positive residual beyond that. The reasons are obvious: Jordan has long been beset by serious threats, both external and internal. Since this is the only really deviant case in the entire series of regressions, the basic regression for *coercive potential* was redone without it. The results were the same in terms of significant predictors and direction of prediction, although the actual beta weights were slightly different and the R^2 was reduced from .66 to .60. We can conclude that the semioutlier Jordan does not seem to have seriously distorted findings in the general regression model.

Another moderately high y-predict value (but not, this time, residual) is that of Syria, a major Soviet arms purchaser which, of course, feels a serious external threat to its security. Finally, Burma has a relatively large positive residual, although its y-predict is negative; this may be the result of a heavy preoccupation with security coupled with a relatively limited reliance on foreign arms supply on the part of the extremely xenophobic Burmese military regime.

The next dependent variable is *unemployment,* for which three residuals and one y-predict value are reported. The reason for this is unclear, and some of the deviation may simply be measurement error; as has been indicated, measurement of unemployment is one of the less certain areas of statistical research.

The final dependent variable is *GDP growth rate*. Here there are no extreme y-predict values, but seven residuals are more than 1.50 standard deviation units from the regression prediction. Some reasons for the deviance of these cases might be surmised: Gambia and the Dominican Republic have positive residuals, the former, at least, perhaps because of the stimulative effect of a stable political system. Niger and Senegal have negative residuals, no doubt because of the drought in the Sahel during this period. Uganda also has a negative residual, perhaps because of the political and economic instability in

that country following the 1971 coup. The same might be said for
Chile, which underwent during this period not only intense political
instability but also an abrupt reversal of the very essentials of economic policy.

We might go further in exploring residuals, but the analysis will
cease here. Much more comprehensive attention will be paid to
regional and subregional groupings in chapters 6 and 7.

SUMMARY

In the series of multiple regressions linking modes of external
dependence to internal characteristics of LDCs it was found, first,
that *trade, students abroad, arms transfers* and *concentration* dependence were significantly related in the predicted direction to the composite indicator of social welfare and policy in LDCs (*welfare*) even
after the effect of GNP per capita and natural resource endowment
were taken into account; this means that, other things being equal,
populations in externally dependent LDCs do as hypothesized tend to
experience a lower level of social welfare than those in less dependent LDCs. It was found, second, that the level of unemployment in
LDCs was significantly related in the predicted direction to four indicators of external dependence, *trade, finance, arms transfers* and
students abroad, confirming dependency hypotheses for a very specific indicator of social marginality. It was found, third, that investment dependence was, as predicted, related to the income share of
the top 20 percent of the population in LDCs, and that this relationship persisted when a regression was computed linking investment dependence to the income share of the top 5 percent of LDC
households; the relationship between *students abroad* and *top 20 income share* was, however, in the opposite direction from that predicted, and suggests that foreign study does have a moderately distributive effect. It was found, fourth, that the income share of the
bottom 40 percent of households in LDCs was negatively related, as
predicted, to *investment, concentration* and *arms transfers,* although
a final relationship, with *aid-trade terms,* was positive. Fifth, it was
found that the relative emphasis, in terms of manpower and expenditures, devoted by LDCs to their coercive apparatus was positively
related to three modes of external dependence and negatively related
to only one; the strongest relationship by far was that with *arms*

transfers, and this relationship did not change substantially even when the indicator "external interventions" was entered into the equation. Finally, it was found that the various modes of external dependence together explained only .22 of the variance in *educational budget* and that both of the significant relationships that did occur were in an unpredicted direction.

In addition these findings were generally confirmed for subsets of the general sample based on absolute GNP and population, region and former colonial metropolis: 53 of 69 significant relationships were as predicted by dependency theory.

As can be seen, dependency predictions were in most cases confirmed by the multiple regression analysis conducted in this chapter. For the whole-sample model there were found fifteen significant relationships linking modes of external dependence to internal characteristics in the predicted direction and only five in the opposite direction, two of these for the dependent variable *education budget*. Moreover, every mode of external dependence except one was significantly related to dependent variables more frequently in expected than in unexpected directions; the only exception was *aid-trade terms*.

The two anomalous findings must be briefly mentioned. One question is why so little of the variance in *education budget* was explained by the seven modes of external dependence and why the few significant relationships that did occur were at variance with those of the other dependent variables. It is possible that *education budget* (based, it will be recalled, on educational expenditures / total government expenditures) is not as good an indicator of distributive social policy as are some of the other indicators of the study; one problem may be that this variable represents expenditures at all levels of public education (figures for capital expenditures are widely available only on this basis), including for higher education, the benefits of which may tend to be monopolized by a small elite. Future studies might pursue this matter further, perhaps by means of a more intensive analysis of budgetary appropriations for a smaller sample of LDCs than used here.

A second anomaly has to do with the independent variable *aid-trade terms:* it was found to be significantly related to a dependent variable only once, and this in an unpredicted direction. It is of note that the unexpected relationship was with *bottom 40 income share;* as has been mentioned, this suggests that high levels of economic assistance may not be as unambiguously negative a factor as radical critics like Hart, Goulet and Hudson or Hayter have proposed.[32]

Hypotheses linking the dependent variable *GDP growth rate* to levels of external dependence are controversial even among dependency theorists, and they were discussed in a separate section. For neither the whole sample nor the parallel subsets of the whole sample based on geographic region, former colonial metropolis, absolute GNP or absolute population, did the modes of external dependence have much power in explaining variance among LDCs in rate of economic growth. But when the sample was divided by level of GNP per capita a very interesting finding, confined to high-income LDCs, did occur: it was found that relatively rapid economic growth was related to levels of private direct foreign investment stocks, while relative stagnation was related to levels of trade and concentration dependence.

The final section of this chapter briefly examined regression residuals and extreme y-predict values for the whole-sample regressions. It is hoped that this analysis has helped bring the study nearer to the level of individual cases, an effort that will be further pursued in the next two chapters.

The tests of hypotheses conducted in this chapter, and thus the findings, were intentionally very complex, and cannot adequately be summed up in a few words: they are as stated, and conclusions should not, strictly speaking, go beyond the particular coefficients that have been derived. Nevertheless, it does seem clear that the modes of external dependence identified in chapter 3 do together explain a substantial proportion (although by no means all) of the variance among LDCs in income distribution, marginality, general social welfare and coercive potential, and that the direction of prediction is generally as dependency theory hypothesizes.

CHAPTER SIX

A Regional Perspective on
External Dependence
I. A Q-Factor Analysis

IT IS NOW TIME TO CONSIDER RE-
lationships not among variables but among countries for these variables; the basic question to be asked is whether there exist distinct
clusters of LDCs that share a common pattern of external dependence
or the lack thereof. This is an area of inquiry rarely pursued either in
the quantitative literature on dependence, which has almost always
examined relationships among variables rather than among cases, or
in the nonquantitative literature, which is often either very broad in
scope or very narrowly oriented toward a single case. It is hoped
that the intermediate-level analysis that follows will effectively
address a definite gap in the literature.

But, while analyses of dependency from a subregional perspective
have been few, there is at least one strand of the literature that is of
some relevance in this area. The central theme of this approach is a
variation on the familiar center-periphery dichotomy, applied not to
DC-LDC relations but rather to inter-LDC relationships. The argument is that there exist among LDCs middle-level regional powers
which link fully developed countries on one side and the least developed countries on the other. Along these lines Immanuel Wallerstein
proposes that the world be divided into not two but three tiers: core,
periphery and "semiperiphery."[1] Samir Amin employs similar terms
to describe the position of migrant laborers from the West African
"hinterland" of Upper Volta in the foreign-oriented coastal plantations of the "semiperipheral" Ivory Coast.[2] And, finally, Stephen
Hymer stresses the role of middle-level powers in discussing the geographical implications of the organizational structure of multinational
corporations, which

> tend to produce a hierarchical division of labor between geographical
> regions corresponding to the vertical division of labor within the firm
> [that is likely to] centralize high-level decisionmaking occupations in a
> few key cities in the advanced countries, surrounded by a number of
> regional sub-capitals, and confine the rest of the world to lower levels
> of activity.[3]

A comprehensive examination of relations between semiperipheries
and their own peripheries would probably require a series of intensive
case studies, and would no doubt necessitate primary research into
data, such as those concerning labor migrations, which are poorly
documented even for advanced countries. Still, it seems reasonable to
suggest that if the application of center-semiperiphery-periphery imagery to inter-LDC relations is valid, LDCs on the periphery will
cluster separately from those on the semiperiphery when examined in
terms of the overall pattern of their external relations. The identification of distinct clusters of LDCs sharing a similar orientation should,
then, provide at least the foundation for a more intensive and more
direct exploration of an area of dependency theory that is often neglected in cross-national tests of dependency hypotheses.[4]

Even beyond any light it may shed on the existence and role of
semiperipheries, the identification of clusters of LDCs with similar
external linkages is of considerable interest in that it provides a perspective that is complementary to that of most previous studies in the
field, a perspective that allows us to go beyond the unspoken assumption of most cross-national analyses that individual countries are
merely interchangeable ''cases'' whose regional context may safely
be ignored. Analysis of clusters of LDCs with common traits will
allow us to explore whether external dependence operates through
certain channels in certain sorts of countries in certain areas of the
world, and by so doing it will provide a fuller picture of what all
would agree is a very complex and many-layered phenomenon not
only in terms of the number of variables encompassed but also in the
nature of the networks of influence through which they operate.

Although several statistical techniques exist for exploring interrelationships among individual countries in a cross-national analysis,
perhaps the most effective for variables of the sort considered in this
study is Q-factor analysis.[5] While this form of factor analysis is
infrequently used in political science or sociological research, it is a
straightforward variation on the more familiar R-factor analysis that

was employed earlier in this study: scores are standardized and then the country-variable matrix is transposed, with cases becoming, in effect, "variables" and variables "cases." A standard factor analysis program can then be employed for this transposed matrix; the only difference is that the factors which are extracted are weighted composites of countries with similar traits rather than vice versa. In the context of this study the thirteen original indicators of external dependence become "cases" in the Q-factor analysis while the seventy LDCs become "variables," interrelationships among which are analyzed. The original variables (i.e., the indicators of external dependence) are lost in this process, but they can be recovered by means of a multiple regression model that uses them to explain variance in LDC loadings on extracted factors.[6]

Initially, a Q-factor analysis was done for all seventy countries simultaneously for the thirteen indicators of external dependence, but this seventy-variable model proved rather unwieldy and difficult to interpret. A much clearer picture emerged when the full sample was divided according to geographical region. The results of regional analyses are reported separately for each region. In general, loadings greater than ±.55 are considered to indicate membership in a cluster, although this criterion is occasionally slightly relaxed in the interest of clarity of interpretation.

BLACK AFRICA

Samir Amin has suggested that Black Africa's links to the dominant world political economy be viewed as operating through three separate modes, each the result of a particular historical heritage and each applicable to a particular area in Africa.[7] The first "macroregion" proposed is "Africa of the Colonial Economy," which includes former French West Africa as well as Togo, Ghana, Nigeria, Sierra Leone, the Gambia and Liberia.[8] According to Amin, the legacy of the slave trade that dominated this region in the eighteenth and nineteenth centuries and the colonial plantation system that followed is a trade-based economy relying on foreign-owned or foreign-oriented monopoly interests at the highest level of the economy and nonindigenous merchant classes at the middle levels. At the lowest levels are the peasant farmers and laborers who were brought into the system during the colonial period by the imposition of monetary taxes that "forced them to produce what the monopolists offered to buy" or, in the most extreme cases, by means of forced labor *corvees*.[9]

Amin suggests that this subregion can be further divided into "semiperiphery" and "hinterland" components:

> At the regional level, the colonial trade necessarily gave rise to a polarization of dependent peripheral development. The necessary corollary of the "wealth" of the coast was the impoverishment of the hinterland. . . . The culmination of the colonial trade system was balkanization, in which the "recipient" micro-regions had no "interest" in "sharing" the crumbs of the colonial cake with their labour reserves.[10]

Based on Amin's characterization, we can assume that the "semi-periphery" of "Africa of the Colonial Economy" encompasses at least the coastal and riverine regions of Senegal, Ghana, Togo, the Ivory Coast, Nigeria and perhaps Benin, the Gambia, Liberia and Mauritania, while the "hinterland" includes Chad, Mali, Niger and Upper Volta; Amin considers the Sudan a third category with its own special characteristics.

A second major region is termed by Amin "Africa of the Concession-Owning Companies," a group which includes the Congo, the Central African Empire and Zaire. In this region low population density, a hostile climate and a relative lack of indigenous hierarchy made the "colonial economy" model impossible and the region was opened up to "any adventurers who would agree to 'get something out of it' without [colonial] resources."[11]

A third major region is "Africa of the Labour Reserves," which includes Kenya, Tanzania, Uganda, Zambia, Rwanda, Malawi and the other nations of Southern Africa. In this region the exploitation of mineral resources and the existence of large-scale settler communities entailed "[the need] to have a large proletariat immediately available."[12] The result was a system in which " 'enclosure acts' were applied to entire peoples,"[13] and colonists "dispossessed the African rural communities and drove them back deliberately into small regions," forcing the traditional society "to be a supplier of permanent migrants on a vast scale, thus providing a cheap proletariat."[14]

Amin places Ethiopia, Somalia, Madagascar and Mauritius in a final catchall category which "do[es] not form part of these macro-regions, although here and there one finds aspects of one or the other of the three systems."[15]

Table 6.1 reports the results of a Q-factor analysis of the twenty-nine sub-Saharan African countries included in this study. As can be

Table 6.1 A Q-Factor Analysis of Twenty-nine Black African Countries for Thirteen Indicators of External Dependence (Factor Pattern/Factor Structure)

	Factor 1	Factor 2	Factor 3	Factor 4	Factor 5
Countries					
Cameroun	.09/.23	.15/.31	**.63/.58**	.08/.09	**.66/.63**
CAE	−.22/−.26	**.83/.86**	−.22/−.27	.19/.14	.21/.39
Chad	−.01/−.09	**.87/.88**	−.22/−.17	−.05/−.09	.11/.31
Congo	**−.72/−.76**	.49/.49	−.06/−.10	.20/.12	−.15/−.12
Benin	**−.55/−.61**	**.62/.66**	.01/−.02	−.23/−.31	.01/.08
Ethiopia	.12/.14	−.31/−.33	.51/.53	−.40/−.37	−.28/−.39
Gambia	**.67/.67**	**.60/.61**	.07/.17	.08/.11	.24/.42
Ghana	.04/.17	−.05/−.01	**.67/.68**	.51/.52	.06/−.02
Ivory Coast	.43/.55	−.31/−.22	.09/.06	.39/.45	**.60/.57**
Kenya	−.16/−.11	−.04/−.01	**.75/.74**	−.26/−.26	−.16/−.27
Liberia	−.23/−.14	−.02/−.03	.07/.05	**.85/.83**	.01/.02
Madagascar	−.05/.02	−.11/.05	−.21/−.31	.09/.09	**.86/.86**
Malawi	−.13/−.06	.23/.40	.20/.12	−.12/−.13	**.71/.72**
Mali	**−.83/−.81**	.03/.07	.04/−.05	.26/.18	.01/−.07
Mauritania	.47/.51	.21/.12	.05/.15	**.77/.80**	−.23/−.14
Mauritius	**.86/.83**	.31/.25	−.15/−.02	.05/.11	.02/.18
Niger	−.08/−.06	**.57/.72**	.23/.19	−.33/−.35	**.57/.65**
Nigeria	.35/.46	−.03/.03	**.77/.79**	−.01/.04	.16/.11
Rwanda	−.05/−.02	**.68/.71**	.40/.44	.23/.21	.05/.15
Senegal	−.11/−.09	−.04/.10	−.40/−.50	−.07/−.08	**.78/.80**
Sierra Leone	.49/.53	.21/.24	.20/.25	.16/.20	.25/.32
Somalia	−.01/−.08	.11/.14	.15/.15	**−.86/−.87**	−.04/−.04
Sudan	−.32/−.28	.09/.02	.50/.53	.41/.39	−.54/−.60
Tanzania	−.46/−.39	−.05/−.00	**.77/.72**	−.12/−.15	−.14/−.28
Togo	.21/.22	.42/.49	**.58/.62**	−.53/−.51	.14/.18
Uganda	.28/.39	−.08/−.09	**.81/.86**	.24/.28	−.15/−.22
Upper Volta	.23/.13	**.91/.85**	−.01/.10	−.18/−.20	−.27/−.06
Zaire	**.89/.89**	−.21/−.29	.02/.13	−.06/.03	−.14/−.10
Zambia	**.78/.80**	−.07/−.18	.17/.30	.21/.28	−.32/−.27

Factor Correlations

	Factor 1	Factor 2	Factor 3	Factor 4	Factor 5
Factor 1	X				
Factor 2	−.06	X			
Factor 3	.12	.06	X		
Factor 4	.09	−.04	.01	X	
Factor 5	.09	.20	−.11	.01	X

Percent Variance Explained

Factor 1	23.0%
Factor 2	20.4
Factor 3	16.8
Factor 4	12.1
Factor 5	8.3
	80.6%

seen, five factors account for 80.6 percent of the variance of these countries on the indicators of external dependence. High loadings on these factors represent no more than clusters of countries similar to one another in mode and extent of external linkages.

Do the clusters of countries that emerge fit the patterns predicted by Amin? Do they fit another readily evident pattern? Or do they adhere to no apparent pattern at all? These questions can only be answered by examining the factors one by one.

Factor 2 is discussed first.[16] For convenience, countries loading on this factor at better than ±.55 are listed along with their pattern and structure loadings:

Upper Volta	.91/.85
Chad	.87/.88
Central African Empire	.83/.86
Rwanda	.68/.71
Niger	.57/.72
Gambia	.60/.61
Benin	.62/.66

How does this grouping fit the classification proposed by Amin? At first glance, it would seem, not well: all three of the principal categories are represented in this single cluster. But a closer look reveals that the two countries not members of Amin's first group, "Africa of the Colonial Economy"—the Central African Empire and Rwanda—are hardly typical of the categories to which Amin assigns them ("Africa of the Concession-Owning Companies" and "Africa of the Labour Reserves," respectively). In the Central African Empire, for example, accumulated private direct investment represented 20 percent of current GNP in 1971, moderately high but not nearly as high as the percentage of Zaire (33 percent) or the Congo (37 percent), the other members of its proposed subgrouping. Similarly, Rwanda, while heavily populated, has hardly been as subject to mineral exploitation or colonial settlement as Zambia, Kenya or the other southern African countries.[17]

Aside from these exceptions all of the countries in this cluster are members of Amin's "Africa of the Colonial Economy" group. Moreover, all but the Gambia and Benin are landlocked and thus share the geographical features of the "hinterland" group within that category.

But these countries have even more in common. For one thing except for the Gambia (which is bordered on three sides by former French colony Senegal) all countries in this group are former French or (in the case of Rwanda) former Belgian colonies, and thus share a francophone political and cultural tradition. For another these countries are among the poorest in Africa, with an average per capita GNP in 1970 of $91 compared to an average of $174 for the other countries of Black Africa.

In examining the regression equations relating this factor to the thirteen original indicators of external dependence, we find, further, that countries' loadings on this factor are positively related to foreign-trade concentration, levels of economic assistance from abroad and the proportion of university students enrolled in foreign universities, but negatively related to debt service and arms transfers indicators of external dependence.[18]

What is the overall picture that emerges of this group? The group represents, in summary, a coherent cluster of countries that are very poor, are generally former French colonies, are generally in the interior of the continent, are relatively dependent upon foreign aid but are not deeply in debt, engage in a relatively concentrated set of trade linkages, generally with France, and maintain strong francophone educational ties both with France and with such regional cultural powers as Senegal and the Ivory Coast. While this grouping does not exactly coincide with the "hinterland" of "Africa of the Colonial Economy" as proposed by Amin, it surely points in that direction and might be thought of as a refinement of Amin's category in light of further empirical evidence.

Factor 5 is next. The principal loadings are as follows:

Cameroun	.66/.63
Ivory Coast	.60/.57
Madagascar	.86/.86
Malawi	.71/.72
Niger	.57/.65
Senegal	.78/.80

As can be seen, four of these six countries are members of Amin's "Africa of the Colonial Economy" group, the exceptions being Malawi and Madagascar. Beyond this these countries have two major characteristics in common: all but one are former French colonies and maintain close ties with the former mother country; and all are host to important export-oriented tropical product enterprises, gener-

ally specializing in products that are grown on plantations or otherwise require large-scale, often foreign-generated, capital investments.
Table 6.2 makes this concentration clear.

**Table 6.2 Shares in Total Exports of Two Principal Export Commodities,
1970, Six African Countries**

Countries	Share	Product
Cameroun	24.3%	Cocoa beans
	21.9	Cotton lint
Ivory Coast	32.2	Coffee beans
	8.0	Lumber
Madagascar	27.2	Coffee beans
	9.0	Vanilla
Malawi	41.1	Tobacco
	27.1	Tea
Niger	56.2	Groundnuts
	10.2	Live animals
Senegal	30.7	Groundnut oil
	10.9	Groundnut cake

SOURCE: United Nations, Economic Commission for Africa, *Survey of Economic Conditions in
Africa, 1971,* part 1, table A62.

The characteristics just mentioned are reflected in the finding of the
supplementary multiple regression analysis that the exports of these
countries tend to be concentrated by receiving country (France, in
every case but that of Malawi) although they are somewhat less concentrated by commodity than is typical. It is also found that these
countries tend to receive a large amount of economic assistance relative to their size, again reflecting close ties to the former mother
country, although arms transfers are less concentrated by source than
is the norm for African countries.

What can we conclude about this cluster? Its most striking characteristic is its resemblance to the group of francophone members of the
"semiperiphery" of Amin's "Africa of the Colonial Economy":
both Amin's category and this cluster include countries that are
strongly tied to the former mother country and are deeply involved in
the production of plantation-type tropical products for export. The
main difference is that these countries are more diverse geographi-
cally than are those of the group proposed by Amin and, of course,
that they include only the francophone members of the group.

Factor 4. The following countries load strongly on this factor:

Liberia	.85/.83
Mauritania	.77/.80
Somalia	−.86/−.87

The two countries with positive loadings have a good deal in common. Both are small West African countries rich in mineral resources, and each is host to a relatively few enclave-based foreign companies exploiting a relatively narrow range of natural resources: iron ore, for example, comprises 89.5 percent of Mauritania's exports, while in Liberia it accounts for 70.3 percent, with rubber comprising another 16.9 percent. Somalia's negative loading simply means that it is very *different* from the first two countries along the same dimension; the fact that it loads alone is in line with Amin's placing it in his catchall category of countries that fit none of his groups.

The countries loading positively on this factor nicely complement those loading positively on factor 5, the previous factor discussed, and together factors 4 and 5 might be thought of as subcategories within a somewhat revised formulation of the "semiperiphery" of Amin's "Africa of the Colonial Economy": both clusters are oriented toward the production of primary products for export, but the countries defined by the former tend to specialize in agricultural exports and by the latter in exports of nonscarce mineral ores. The "hinterland" of this two-part "semiperiphery" consists, of course, of the countries defined in factor 2.

Factor 3. The following list contains all loadings better than ±.55 on this factor:

Cameroun	.63/.58
Ghana	.67/.68
Kenya	.75/.74
Nigeria	.77/.79
Tanzania	.77/.72
Togo	.58/.62
Uganda	.81/.86

This time the cluster does not correspond very well to any of Amin's categories: in fact it cuts directly across two of the subgroupings. But it is rather striking that, with the exception of Togo and Cameroun (both League of Nations Mandates, the latter in part administered by Britain), all of these countries are former British dependencies. Another interesting characteristic of these countries is their large size: their average population is 15.3 million (or 8.5 million excluding Nigeria) compared to 5.5 million for the rest of Black Africa (or 3.8 million excluding Ethiopia and Zaire).

When we examine the multiple regression equations relating this factor to the original variables, we find that these countries tend to receive a relatively large amount of economic assistance in relation to GNP (as perhaps befits their importance) but that this assistance tends to be less concentrated than average (which suggests the ability of former British colonies to diversify aid sources more effectively than former French colonies). With regard to trade it is found that the position of these countries in a vertical trade structure (i.e., the level of Galtung's Trade Composition Index) is relatively less favorable than average, but also that this trade is less concentrated by partner than is the norm.

In summary the third factor seems to define a group (not proposed by Amin) of large, former British colonies which are relatively high in the extent of aid and trade ties but which tend to measure lower in the concentration of external ties among DC partners than do their principally francophone counterparts identified with the first two factors discussed.

Factor 1. Principal loadings on this factor are as follows:

Gambia	.67/.67
Mauritius	.86/.83
Zaire	.89/.89
Zambia	.78/.80
Congo	$-.72/-.76$
Mali	$-.83/-.81$
Benin	$-.55/-.61$

The composition of this cluster is somewhat puzzling: it cuts across all of Amin's categories and includes three former British and one former Belgian colony loading positively and three former French colonies loading negatively. What do these countries have in common that causes them to cluster? One underlying dimension seems to be raw material exploitation: Zaire and Zambia, two very different countries that have in common an economy highly oriented to copper exports, exhibit similar loadings as do Mauritius, highly specialized in export-oriented sugar production, and the Gambia, strongly dependent upon the export of groundnut products. The Congo, Benin and Mali, on the other hand, which have negative loadings, are not particularly export oriented: exports represent 13, 13 and 5 percent of the GNP of these countries, respectively, compared to a 23 percent average for all Black African countries in the study and a 43 percent average for the four countries loading positively on this factor.[19]

The multiple regression equation relating this factor to the original indicators of external dependence reveals that the exports of these countries are indeed unusually concentrated by both partner and commodity. In addition it is found that positively loading countries tend to be faced with a particularly heavy debt burden, but tend not to receive a large amount of economic assistance and not to send a large proportion of their university students abroad to study.

Finally, we come to the countries that do not load highly on any of these factors, or whose loadings are divided among a number of factors. Ethiopia, one of the nations which Amin does not place in any of his categories, is one of the two sub-Saharan African countries that escaped nineteenth century European colonialism; it is not at all surprising that this country fits no common pattern. A second, the Sudan, is a country that Amin places in "Africa of the Colonial Economy," but in a subgroup of its own; again, we would expect this country to be isolated. The third country is Sierra Leone; the reasons for its isolation are not clear.

At this point a brief summary is in order. What has been attempted in this section is to examine similarities among African countries in the extent and nature of their linkages to more powerful and wealthy countries. A classification scheme proposed by Samir Amin was used as the baseline from which the analysis proceeded. It was found that five distinct clusters of countries accounted for most of the variance of African nations in the mode and concentration of ties of external dependence: one group exhibited many of the characteristics of the "hinterland" subcategory of Amin's "Africa of the Colonial Economy"; two other groups were represented principally by large tropical product exporters and small West African exporters of nonscarce minerals, respectively, and had many of the characteristics of the "semiperipheral" members of the same group; a fourth group consisted of relatively large countries that were generally former British colonies and generally maintained less concentrated external relations than did countries of the first groups; and a final group was defined by a fairly mixed group of trade-oriented countries.

Table 6.3 summarizes these findings. (A few minor simplifications of the actual findings were made in compiling this table.) As can be

**Table 6.3 African Subregions Defined in Terms of the Extent and
Concentration of Ties of External Dependence**

I. *"Africa of the Colonial Economy"*
  A. "Semiperiphery"
    1. Plantation products
      Cameroun
      Ivory Coast
      Madagascar
      Malawi
      Senegal
    2. Nonscarce minerals
      Liberia
      Mauritania
  B. "Hinterland"
      Chad
      Central African Empire
      Rwanda
      Niger
      Gambia
      Benin
      Upper Volta

II. *Large Former British Colonies*
  Ghana
  Kenya
  Nigeria
  Tanzania
  Uganda
  Togo (?)

III. *High Trade–Private Direct
Investment Orientation*
  Zaire (pos.)   ⎫ "Africa of the con-
  Zambia (pos.)   ⎬ cession-owning com-
  Mauritius (pos.)⎭ panies"—revised?
  Mali (neg.)   ⎫ to I.B. above?
  Congo (neg.)   ⎬

seen, the first of Amin's categories, "Africa of the Colonial Economy," is well-represented, although principally by its francophone members, and his "semiperiphery-hinterland" distinction seems to be more or less borne out by these findings. His second category, "Africa of the Concession-Owning Companies," seems, however, not to be represented at all, although some of its characteristics are shared by the countries in group III; we might consider redefining this category in terms of these countries. His third category, "Africa of the Labour Reserves," seems also not to be borne out, although it does bear some similarity to the countries in group II above. We can conclude that Amin's historically based categories do have some relevance to defining African subregions within an overall structure of external dependence but that former colonial metropolis and overall product composition are important factors in modifying his classifications.

LATIN AMERICA AND THE CARIBBEAN

Table 6.4 represents the findings of a Q-factor analysis of the twenty countries of South and Central America examined in this

Table 6.4 A Q-Factor Analysis of the Twenty Latin American Countries for Thirteen Indicators of External Dependence (Factor Pattern/Factor Structure)

	Factor 1	Factor 2	Factor 3	Factor 4	Factor 5	Factor 6
Countries						
Argentina	−.11/.04	.00/.13	−.10/−.12	**.99/.97**	.02/−.10	−.14/−.02
Bolivia	.19/.35	**.81/.80**	−.06/−.13	−.21/−.02	−.25/−.24	−.04/.04
Brazil	.16/.29	−.20/−.07	.13/.05	**.67/.74**	−.37/−.49	.24/.28
Chile	.14/.15	**.44/.59**	−.11/−.14	**.40/.46**	−.52/−.43	.35/.45
Colombia	.22/.45	**.54/.60**	−.19/−.31	.12/.33	**.57/.64**	.11/.20
Costa Rica	**.81/.84**	−.16/−.01	.13/.10	.26/.35	−.10/−.31	−.07/−.09
Dominican R.	**.82/.86**	.10/.18	.00/−.03	−.19/−.05	−.21/−.36	−.19/−.21
Ecuador	.11/.28	**.51/.60**	.22/.17	**.61/.69**	.01/−.06	−.05/.06
El Salvador	**.29/.48**	.14/.17	.20/.07	−.07/.13	**.83/.87**	.21/.20
Guatemala	**.82/.85**	−.13/.06	−.32/−.36	.17/.30	−.10/−.34	.11/.13
Guyana	−.23/−.23	−.14/−.23	**.93/.92**	.07/.01	−.18/−.04	.02/−.06
Haiti	**.53/.45**	**−.73/−.66**	−.12/−.08	.03/−.02	−.09/−.25	−.30/−.38
Honduras	**.90/.94**	.03/.15	−.08/−.11	−.06/.09	−.17/−.37	−.11/−.12
Jamaica	.45/.38	.19/.19	**.76/.79**	−.07/−.08	.35/.35	−.17/−.24
Mexico	.20/.25	.24/.19	−.09/−.01	.08/.03	.15/.10	**−.92/−.88**
Nicaragua	**.39/.58**	−.04/.05	−.03/−.14	.19/.36	**.74/.86**	.14/.16
Panama	**.69/.67**	.21/.34	.11/.08	−.02/.10	.21/.07	.19/.19
Paraguay	−.13/.13	.18/.15	−.15/−.25	.15/.28	**.93/.94**	−.12/−.05
Peru	−.04/.14	**.81/.82**	−.08/−.13	.22/.33	.05/.05	−.16/−.03
Uruguay	.20/.22	.25/.40	−.36/−.44	.02/.18	.09/.00	**.76/.82**

Factor Correlations

	Factor 1	Factor 2	Factor 3	Factor 4	Factor 5	Factor 6
Factor 2	.16	X				
Factor 3	−.03	−.06	X			
Factor 4	.14	.15	−.04	X		
Factor 5	−.22	.03	.11	−.14		
Factor 6	−.02	.12	−.09	.11	−.01	X

Percent Variance Explained

Factor 1	32.4%
Factor 2	16.3
Factor 3	13.0
Factor 4	9.9
Factor 5	8.5
Factor 6	7.3
	87.4%

study. The strongest loadings are in boldface. The six factors extracted are focused upon.

Factor 1. The following figures represent the strongest pattern and structure loadings on this factor:

Costa Rica	.81/.84
Dominican Republic	.82/.86
Guatemala	.82/.85
Honduras	.90/.94
Panama	.69/.67
El Salvador	.29/.48
Haiti	.53/.45
Nicaragua	.39/.58

What do these countries have in common? The answer is obvious and striking: all are small Central American or Caribbean countries that maintain close ties with the United States. In examining multiple regression equations relating the thirteen indicators of external dependence to loadings on this factor, it is possible to specify further the pattern of external dependence operative here: we find that these countries are inclined to receive economic assistance from a single donor (in every case the United States), to be host to private direct investment from a single investor country (again in every case the United States), and to experience relatively unfavorable terms of trade. These findings suggest that in these countries external dependence, while not necessarily greater in relative extent than in other areas of Latin America, does tend to be more concentrated by partner.

Factor 2 is almost as clear-cut as factor 1. The principal loadings are:

Bolivia	.81/.80
Chile	.44/.59
Colombia	.54/.60
Ecuador	.51/.60
Peru	.81/.82
Haiti	−.73/−.66

It is fairly easy to see a common thread running through this cluster as well: all of the positive loadings represent countries that are wholly or partly Andean, and nearly all of these countries are important exporters of mineral or petroleum resources. When we examine the multiple regressions underlying these findings, we see that the exports of these countries do indeed, as we might expect, tend to be heavily concentrated by commodity (although, contrary to what might be expected, they are about average in trade verticality and terms of trade). In addition we find fairly heavy expenditures for arms purchases, as well as foreign assistance relatively unconcentrated by donor. Haiti, of course, with its negative loading, is distinguished by being very *different* from these countries along a common dimension.

Factor 3 features the following strong loadings:

Guyana .93/.92
Jamaica .76/.79

The common characteristics of these countries are again obvious: both are former British colonies that have only recently become independent; both are heavy exporters of bauxite; and both have maintained close ties with the United Kingdom and Canada as well as the United States. These characteristics are reflected in the relationship between this factor and the variables from which it was formed: these countries tend to exhibit a good deal less partner concentration than is usual, at least in the areas of private direct investment and economic assistance, and both have an export structure that is highly concentrated by commodity, relative to the other countries of Latin America.

Factor 4 has the following strong loadings:

Argentina .99/.97
Chile .40/.46
Brazil .67/.74
Ecuador .61/.69

Certainly, it is not unexpected that the first three of these countries cluster together: these are the ABC countries, historically the most powerful and important in Latin America.[20] All have a large and highly developed modern sector and all are relatively autonomous, at least in comparison with the "Central American," "Andean," and "former British colonies" groups already discussed. Why Ecuador loads on this factor is a mystery, since it clearly seems to fit better with the "Andean" factor on which it also loads.

The underlying regressions indicate that these countries are, as we would expect, relatively autonomous in terms of the partner concentration of external linkages, at least with regard to direct foreign investment and export outlets; in the extent and trade verticality of these linkages, however, the countries are about average for Latin America.

Factor 5 has the following principal loadings:

Colombia	.57/.64
El Salvador	.83/.87
Nicaragua	.74/.86
Paraguay	.93/.94
Chile	$-.52/-.43$

Precisely what the first four of these countries have in common is not immediately evident, although they do seem to echo in some ways the first factor discussed, "Central America." Multiple regression analysis shows that loadings on this factor are positively related to a high ratio of external trade to GNP and a high concentration of aid donors and trade partners, the principal partner being in every case the United States; these relationships are similar to those for the "Central America" factor.

Factor 6 features the following principal loadings:

| Mexico | $-.92/-.88$ |
| Uruguay | .76/.82 |

This final factor tells us little more than that Mexico and Uruguay do not belong to any of the previous groups and that, moreover, they are very different from one another on a common dimension.

Table 6.5 presents a proposed scheme of subregions within Latin America defined on the basis of the mode and extent of external link-

**Table 6.5 Latin American Subregions Defined in Terms of Extent
and Concentration of Ties of External Dependence**

I. *Central American and Caribbean Countries* Costa Rica Dominican Republic Guatemala Honduras Panama El Salvador Haiti Nicaragua	III. *ABC Countries* Argentina Brazil Chile IV. *Former British Colonies* Guyana Jamaica V. *Countries Belonging to No Group* Mexico Uruguay Paraguay (loads on factor 5)
II. *Andean Countries* Bolivia Chile Colombia Ecuador Peru	

ages. (The scheme adheres closely to the findings of the Q-factor analysis, but again, as can be seen, a few consolidations and simplifications have been made.) This empirically grounded typology clearly confirms the rough generalization of Kaufman, Geller and Chernotsky, on the basis of their own research, that "dependency seems to operate quite differently within . . . two subregions" which they define as "Middle America" and "South America," but the Q-factor methodology allows the derivation of a more detailed classification scheme than these authors' dichotomy.[21] It is hoped that these findings, like those for Black Africa, will provide an impetus for further systematic study of the neglected area of regional analysis, for which, in the words of Kaufman, Geller and Chernotsky, "the general literature of dependency offers few guidelines or clues."[22]

ASIA

The next region to be examined is Asia. Table 6.6 presents the factor pattern / factor structure matrix of a Q-factor analysis of the Asian members of the general sample, as well as a few other necessary statistics. Supplementary regression analyses could not be performed because of the limited number of Asian cases, but a bivariate correlation matrix relating the original variables to factor pattern loadings was examined.

The first factor is dominated by the following loadings:

Afghanistan	.66/.73
India	.95/.94
Pakistan	.90/.91
Republic of Korea	.79/.78

It is not difficult to see what the first three of these countries have in common: all are large, very poor and relatively lacking in natural resources. Examination of bilateral correlations between the indicators of external dependence and loadings on this factor indicates further that these countries do not exhibit highly vertical trade patterns (primarily because India and Pakistan, at least, export a fair amount of manufactures and are poorly endowed with mineral or agricultural resources which might lead to primary product exports), nor are their exports highly concentrated by commodity, nor do they receive a large amount of private direct investment relative to the magnitude of their GNP. On the other hand, all are faced with a relatively large debt service burden.

**Table 6.6 A *Q*-Factor Analysis of Eleven Asian Countries for Thirteen
Indicators of External Dependence (Factor Pattern/Factor Structure)**

	Factor 1	Factor 2	Factor 3	Factor 4	Factor 5
Countries					
Afghanistan	**.66/.73**	.50/.52	−.18/−.37	−.12/−.03	.18/.18
Burma	.05/.21	**.60/.65**	−.40/−.52	**.49/.54**	−.08/−.12
India	**.95/.94**	−.04/.03	−.02/−.22	.12/.21	−.14/−.06
Indonesia	−.07/−.05	−.50/−.57	−.07/−.06	−.07/−.06	**.49/.56**
South Korea	**.79/.78**	−.04/−.06	.10/−.09	−.13/−.07	.39/.44
Malaysia	−.27/−.40	.22/.12	**.85/.84**	.31/.18	.11/−.11
Pakistan	**.90/.91**	−.02/.06	−.05/−.26	.22/.30	−.18/−.11
Philippines	.03/.13	.05/−.06	−.08/−.21	.16/.19	**.89/.90**
Singapore	.18/−.03	−.08/−.10	**.85/.87**	−.17/−.27	−.24/−.31
Sri Lanka	.18/.23	−.23/−.25	.10/−.05	**.91/.91**	.16/.21
Thailand	−.05/−.06	**.90/.88**	.16/.14	−.31/−.34	.04/−.11

Factor Correlations

	Factor 1	Factor 2	Factor 3	Factor 4	Factor 5
Factor 1	X				
Factor 2	.06	X			
Factor 3	−.21	−.08	X		
Factor 4	.08	−.00	−.13	X	
Factor 5	.07	−.14	−.11	.02	X

Percent Variance Explained

Factor 1	32.3%
Factor 2	18.8
Factor 3	14.1
Factor 4	11.3
Factor 5	9.6
	86.1%

It is not completely unexpected that the Republic of Korea also fits
this pattern, although not as strongly as India or Pakistan: it too
engages in relatively favorable trade relations in terms of the level of
processing continuum, it too is relatively poor in natural resources
and it too exports a wide range of commodities. This is not to say
that the integration of South Korea into the world economy is not
very different from that of India or Pakistan but only that there are
also certain similarities. (Certain of the problems that this grouping of
very different countries poses were resolved in the general multiple
regression analysis of chapter 5 when the effect of gross national
product per capita and natural resource endowment were included as
independent variables along with the indicators of external dependence, their effects thus controlled.)

A second factor has the following principal loadings:

Burma .60/.65
Thailand .90/.88

These countries are notable in that they are both located on the mainland of Southeast Asia, but beyond this it is difficult to see obvious similarities between intensely introverted Burma and externally oriented Thailand. The bivariate correlation matrix shows that these countries tend to have an unfavorable reserves position and unfavorable terms of trade ratios.

A third factor links Malaysia and Singapore:

Singapore .85/.87
Malaysia .85/.84

The relationship between the countries of this cluster is immediately evident: these countries have always had close relations and prior to 1965 were united politically.

The fourth factor has the following strong loadings:

Sri Lanka .91/.91
Burma .49/.54

The upshot of this factor, on which Sri Lanka loads very strongly and Burma moderately, seems to be that Sri Lanka constitutes a group of its own which shares some similarities with Burma. The strongest external linkage defining this factor is export commodity concentration: Sri Lanka devoted 56 percent of its total exports in 1970 to tea and most of the rest to rubber, while Burma devoted 49 percent of a smaller export base to rice and most of the rest to hardwood.[23]

The final factor has the following principal loadings:

Philippines .89/.90
Indonesia .49/.56

These countries have several characteristics in common: they are the only archipelago nations in the region, both have strong ties to both the United States and Japan, and both are relatively populous. The bivariate correlation matrix shows that the export partner concentration of this subgroup tends to be relatively high for the region.

The reader has probably noted that the structure emerging from the Q-factor analysis of Asian countries is less distinct than that for other regions that have been considered. One reason for this is that Asia seems to constitute a much less distinct region than does, say, Africa or Latin America. Another factor may be that the colonial legacy in Asia, interrupted for many countries during the second World War and superimposed upon countries which often had long histories as large and complex nations with their own traditions of external relations, may simply not have penetrated as deeply as in other regions of the world. The countries that we would expect to load similarly—India and Pakistan, Singapore and Malaysia—have indeed tended to load highly on the same factor, but there does seem to be in Asia a number of countries that are *sui generis*—Sri Lanka, Burma and South Korea, for example—and the pattern of loadings of these countries has been indistinct and occasionally puzzling. While this outcome is theoretically inelegant, it is perhaps only an accurate reflection of the fact that for Asia there simply does not seem to exist a clear-cut subregional dimension to the structure of external dependence.[24]

THE MIDEAST AND SOUTHERN EUROPE

Since only six Mideastern nations are included in this study, the clustering pattern is much easier to elucidate than for the regions that have been previously discussed. Table 6.7 presents the loadings on the two factors that were rotated.

What differentiates these two subgroupings? The most obvious dis-

Table 6.7 A *Q*-Factor Analysis of Six Middle Eastern Countries for Thirteen Indicators of External Dependence (Factor Pattern/Factor Structure)

	Factor 1	Factor 2
Countries		
Egypt	**.75/.75**	−.37/−.38
Jordan	−.12/−.11	**−.82/−.82**
Lebanon	−.00/.00	**−.87/−.87**
Morocco	**.81/.81**	.36/.36
Syria	**.73/.74**	**−.58/−.59**
Tunisia	**.65/.64**	.27/.27
Factor Correlation	−.01	
Percent Variance Explained		
Factor 1	38.4%	
Factor 2	33.2	
	71.6%	

external dependence, Turkey can be considered a distinct subregion of the more general region of Southern Europe.

Do coherent regional subgroupings of LDCs exist, which demonstrate common patterns of external dependence or the lack thereof? Such subgroups are indeed in evidence, particularly for the African and Latin American regions, based primarily upon geographical proximity, colonial heritage and common patterns of export product composition. It is hoped that this exercise will stimulate further attention to the neglected area of subregional analysis, without which our conception of a hypothesized system of dominance-dependence will remain unsatisfyingly one dimensional.[25]

tinction is geographical: the principal loadings on factor 1 all re
sent countries on the African continent (with the exception of S)
which has long had close ties with Egypt and which loads moder;
highly on both factors), and loadings on the other factor are all re
sentative of Western Asia countries. The supplementary multiple
gressions could not be constructed for this region because of
small number of cases, nor were the bivariate correlations sufficie
discriminatory to be of much use, so it is difficult to go beyond
simple observation on the basis of the Q-factor analysis for tl
countries.

Table 6.8 presents findings of the Q-factor analysis of Soutl
European countries. The pattern here is very evident. Despite sti
ideological differences between NATO members, Greece and '
key, and leader of the "nonaligned" world, Yugoslavia, the foi
countries load strongly on a single factor along with Spain, w
Turkey loads strongly on a factor of its own. The bivariate correla
matrix shows almost opposite correlations between these loadings
a whole series of indicators of external dependence: Turkey is 1
tively high on the Trade Composition Index, has a relatively p
terms of trade ratio, has a pattern of exports relatively concentr
by commodity and destination, receives a large amount of exte
economic assistance and military transfers and is highly burdenec
debt service; Spain, Greece and Yugoslavia, on the other hand,
relatively low on each of these indicators. All of this implies that
purposes of categorizing countries according to degree and mod

**Table 6.8 A Q-Factor Analysis of Four Southern European Countries f(
Thirteen Indicators of External Dependence (Factor Pattern/Factor Struct**

	Factor 1	Factor 2
Countries		
Greece	**.80/.85**	.30/.44
Spain	**.86/.80**	−.32/−.15
Turkey	.05/.22	**.94/.95**
Yugoslavia	**.84/.88**	.20/.35
Factor Correlation	+.18	
Percent Variance Explained		
Factor 1	57.8%	
Factor 2	23.9	
	81.7%	

CHAPTER SEVEN

A Regional Perspective on External Dependence
II. Linking LDCs to Their Principal Partners

DISCUSSION UP TO THIS POINT HAS remained incomplete in that no systematic attempt has been made to identify the actual partners with which LDCs interact and to analyze their external ties on this basis. The purpose of this chapter is to address just this topic, by analyzing a series of data matrices linking individual LDCs to the nations with which they principally interact for several of the most important modes of external dependence.

The contribution to the dependency literature that is most relevant to this discussion is the core-periphery concept that has already been examined at some length. The emphasis here is, however, not on the hypothesized linkage between elites in core nations and their counterparts in peripheral countries, but rather on a more general formulation that posits a *feudal interaction structure* linking closely interacting "core" nations, each with its own group of LDC "satellites." The key characteristics of this proposed structure are close interaction on relatively equal terms among a group of "core" industrial nations; intense but highly asymmetrical interaction between individual nations of the core and groups of much less powerful and wealthy LDC "satellites"; and limited interaction both among individual LDCs and between developed countries and LDCs outside their sphere of influence.[1] Figure 7.1 shows graphically the main characteristics of a structure of this sort.

Two major consequences are hypothesized to flow from LDC participation in a feudal interaction structure. First, an effective perception of common interests among LDCs becomes unlikely to the extent

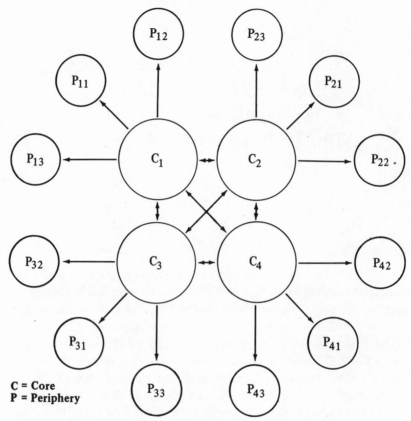

Figure 7.1 A Feudal Interaction Structure
Adapted from Johan Galtung, "A Structural Theory of Imperialism," p. 89.

that they are involved in extensive and exclusive relationships with DC partners, ties that may be in many details incompatible with the interests of LDCs linked to different partners or less closely integrated into the system; the long reluctance of African states associated with the European Community (EC) to support generalized trade preferences to LDCs because these would erode their own preferential access to EC markets is only one example. Many scholars, both within and outside the dependency tradition, argue that the lack of effective collective action by LDCs is one of the most serious hindrances to the improvement of their objective standing.[2]

Second, as has been noted, an individual LDC closely linked to a single dominant partner is almost inherently less likely to have the bargaining power and freedom of action of one whose external ties are dispersed among several partners.[3]

To what degree does there exist a feudal interaction structure linking groups of Third World nations to particular DC partners, and what are the main characteristics of this interaction? To answer these questions a series of data matrices has been assembled relating all seventy LDCs of the sample to potential DC partners for most of the indicators of external dependence dealt with in this study, including trade, aid, investment, educational and military ties.[4] The resulting dyads have then been reduced to more manageable form by means of tables that group individual LDCs with their most important DC partner or partners according to certain common criteria. From these tables we should get a good idea of the extent to which a feudal interaction structure exists for a given mode of external dependence, of the degree to which particular LDCs fit into such a structure and of the developed countries to which various groups of LDCs are most closely linked.[5]

TRADE TIES

The first North-South linkages considered are those of international trade. From the source cited in appendix IV, a large matrix was drawn relating the seventy LDCs examined in the study to eighteen of the world's most important trading countries.[6] The value of imports that each LDC received in 1970 from each partner was then recorded for each country-partner dyad.[7] The resulting matrix was large and contained many zero and near-zero cells, so it is not reproduced in full; instead, tables based upon it are presented which indicate LDCs' principal and secondary trade partners and also give some indication of the relative extent of trade ties.

An LDC is grouped with a trade partner if more than 20 percent of its total imports are received from this single source. (In the few instances in which more than one partner accounts for more than 20 percent of imports, a country is listed with the partner that provides the largest value.) If secondary partner(s) account for at least 10 percent of the imports of a given LDC, they are listed in parentheses in order of the proportion accounted for. If no partner accounts for as much as 20 percent of its imports, a country is listed in the category "diversified trade" along with all partners accounting for at least 10 percent of its total imports. Finally, all LDCs for which external trade is both absolutely and relatively limited in extent—that is, accounts for less than 15 percent of GNP and is valued at less than $200 million—are denoted with an asterisk(*).[8]

The following listing represents LDCs whose principal trade partner is the United States:

Colombia	Chile (also W. Germany)
Costa Rica	Jamaica (also U.K.)
Dominican Republic	Peru (also W. Germany)
Ecuador	*Paraguay (also Argentina)
Honduras	Argentina (also W. Germany, Neth.)
Mexico	
Nicaragua	Bolivia (also Japan, W. Germany)
Panama	Liberia (also W. Germany, Neth.)
*Haiti	Pakistan (also U.K., Japan, W. Germany)
Brazil (also W. Germany)	
El Salvador (also Japan)	India (also U.S.S.R., U.K., W. Germany, Canada)
Guatemala (also Japan)	

The pattern here is fairly clear. The grouping contains twenty-one countries, all but three from the Western hemisphere. A first "inner circle" is comprised of nine nations, all from the Caribbean, Central America or northern South America; for none of these countries does a source other than the United States supply as much as 10 percent of total imports. A second ring includes seven more LDCs, again all from the Western hemisphere, that receive at least 20 percent of their imports from the United States but also have a secondary source that accounts for at least 10 percent of imports. A third ring of countries, those with two important secondary sources of imports, consists of two South American countries and the African state of Liberia; the former two might be thought of as states within the United States trade orbit but near its edges, while Liberia is a country with historically strong trade ties with the United States which are under some pressure from West Germany and the Netherlands, European countries which did not recently have their own African colonies and thus have no strong, exclusive African ties of their own. A final outer ring consists of India and Pakistan, which maintain strong trade ties with the United States, but which also have moderately strong ties with three or four other important sources.

The next important trade partner is France. The following countries received at least 20 percent of their imports from France:

Mauritania	*Benin
Central African Empire	*Niger
Ivory Coast	*Upper Volta
Madagascar	Morocco (also U.S.A.)
Senegal	Tunisia (also U.S.A.)
Cameroun	Togo (also U.K.)
*Chad	*Mali (also U.S.S.R.)
*Congo	

The common characteristics of these countries are obvious: all are former French colonies, all are located on the African continent, all were in the colonial period closely linked to France through an intensive system of trade preferences and subsidies. In fact this grouping *exactly* coincides with the list of all of France's former African colonies that are included in this study.[9]

The pattern of "orbits" maintained by LDC "satellites" whose trade is conducted principally with France is drawn much tighter than that around the United States: an inner circle consists of eleven former French colonies while a second ring includes two North African and two sub-Saharan African states. Not a single LDC within France's orbit receives as much as 10 percent of its imports from two or more secondary partners.

The next categories include countries for which Belgium-Luxembourg[10] and Italy are the principal trade partners:

Belgium-Luxembourg	*Italy*
Zaire (also U.S.A.)	Somalia
*Rwanda (also Japan)	

The principal partners are again the former colonial metropolises.

Since all of the LDCs listed with France, Belgium-Luxembourg and Italy were associates of a six-member European Community (EC) in 1970, the date for which data are presented, interesting questions arise that deserve a brief digression: What effect did the identical trade preferences that each of these countries had in the markets of all six EC members have on the trade relationships between associated states and their former metropolises? Did tariff-free access to the markets of five major industrial nations in addition to the former colonial metropolis broaden ties? From examining the listings just presented, it would appear that the effect of this access has been limited: while the United States, the United Kingdom and the Soviet Union are moderately important secondary sources for several of the countries, not one EC member besides the former metropolis has managed to supply as much as 10 percent of the total imports of any associate.[11]

But more detailed data suggest that the primacy of France, Belgium and Italy in the trade of their former colonies, considerable even by colonial standards (especially for the former French colonies), has been to some extent eroded by other EC members; table 7.1 shows the trend. While, however, association with the European Community has resulted in some diversification of trade ties, the great preponderance of these ties is still with the former metropolis. The association experience, then, represents, depending upon the observer's point of view, either a gradual but genuine diversification of historically highly concentrated ties or an only slightly ineffective fossilization of these ties.

Table 7.1 Imports of the Former French, Belgian and Italian Colonies Included in This Study from the Six Members of the European Economic Community, 1961 and 1973 (or nearest available date), in Current Millions of Dollars

EEC	1961	1973	Percent Increase
France	$827.7	$1,698.0	105%
West Germany	75.1	373.9	398
Netherlands	31.4	151.6	383
Italy	43.1	209.5	386
Belgium Luxembourg	110.2	239.5	117

SOURCE: Computed from United Nations, *Yearbook of International Trade Statistics,* 1963 and 1975.
NOTE: The Associated African and Malagasy States covered are Benin, Chad, Central African Empire, Congo, Madagascar, Rwanda, Somalia, Togo, Zaire, Cameroun, Ivory Coast, Mali, Mauritania, Niger, and Upper Volta. Morocco and Tunisia, associated under a different agreement, are also included.

The next group consists of countries whose principal import source is the United Kingdom:

Malawi	Guyana (also Japan)
Mauritius	Zambia (also U.S.A.)
Sierra Leone	Kenya (also Japan)
Gambia (also Japan)	Ghana (also U.S.A., W. Germany)
Uganda (also Japan)	Nigeria (also U.S.A., W. Germany)

In the case of Britain, unlike that of the United States and, especially, France, the "inner circle" of LDCs with no important secondary import source is small: it contains only three small former African colonies. The second ring of influence (countries with only a single secondary source providing at least 10 percent of imports) includes five other former African colonies, with Japan the most common secondary source. Finally, a third ring consists of Ghana and Nigeria, large West African countries for which both the United States and West Germany are secondary import sources.

What do the countries linked to the United Kingdom by trade ties have in common? For one thing each member of this group is a former British colony and was historically the beneficiary of Commonwealth Preferences in the British market. For another all of the countries in this group are located in Africa or (in one case) South America: no Asian former British colony is included.

But, despite these common characteristics, it seems evident that this group is not at all as closely knit or as strongly dominated by Britain as are the former French colonies by France or the Latin American countries by the United States. There are several likely reasons for this: one is Britain's long advocacy of free trade policies, which rendered the trade preferences offered to her colonies less effective than were similar preferences in the more highly protected French market; another is the recent difficulty of British exports effectively to compete in foreign markets worldwide, including, apparently, even those of her former colonies.[12]

The next group consists of the LDCs for which Japan is the principal import source:

Indonesia (also U.S.A.)   Thailand (also U.S.A.)
Republic of Korea (also U.S.A.)   *Burma (also India)
Phillippines (also U.S.A.)

As can be seen, all of these are relatively large East or Southeast Asian countries. It is interesting that none of these countries is without a secondary partner from which it received at least 10 percent of its imports: all have exactly one secondary partner, and in every case but one it is the United States.

There is a sixth category of LDC whose principal trade partner is the Soviet Union. This category contains only one member:

*Afghanistan (also Japan)

Primacy in the market of only one LDC does not, however, necessarily indicate an unimportant role for the Soviet Union in the external trade of all LDCs; certainly for such socialist nations as Cuba, Vietnam, North Korea or Mongolia its role is very considerable. But

relations among socialist nations is a subject that, for reasons that
have been noted in chapter 1, is not directly considered in this study.
For the seventy LDCs covered here, we would have to conclude that
the position of the Soviet Union and other socialist states in the pattern of trade linkages is very limited. As will be seen in later sections, this is not the case for all external ties.

Among the final group of countries none receive as much as 20
percent of their imports from a single source. These countries are
listed along with all partners which supply at least 10 percent of imports in order of the proportion supplied:

Sudan	U.K., U.S.S.R., India, W. Germany, Japan
Tanzania	U.K., U.S.A., W. Germany, P. R. China
Uruguay	Brazil, Argentina, U.S.A., U.K.
Jordan	U.K., U.S.A., W. Germany, Japan, Italy
Lebanon	U.S.A., France, W. Germany, Japan, Italy
Egypt	U.S.S.R., France, W. Germany, Japan, Italy
Syria	U.S.S.R., W. Germany, Italy
Malaysia	Japan, U.K.
Singapore	Malaysia, Japan, U.K.
Sri Lanka	U.K., P. R. China, India
Greece	W. Germany, Japan, Italy, U.K., France, U.S.A.
Spain	U.S.A., France, U.K., W. Germany, Italy
Turkey	U.S.A., W. Germany, U.K.
Yugoslavia	W. Germany, Italy, U.S.S.R., U.S.A.
*Ethiopia	Italy, W. Germany

What can we say about this grouping? For one thing, we find that
countries whose trade is relatively diversified are most common in
Southern Europe (where they include all 4 countries included in this
study) and in the Mideast (where 4 of 6 countries have diversified
trade patterns), but are less common in Asia (3 of 11 countries) and
scarce in Africa and Latin America (3 of 29 and 1 of 20 countries, respectively). Second, we find in this group a large number of countries
whose formal association with developed countries in the nineteenth
and twentieth centuries has been limited: Ethiopia, for example, was
never a European colony, Tanganyika was a League of Nations Mandate instead of a Crown colony, the Sudan was subject to an Anglo-
Egyptian Protectorate rather than full colonial authority, Jordan and
Egypt were formally independent by the 1920s, the 4 Southern European countries were not recently colonies, and even Malaysia and
Singapore experienced a lapse of British control during World War
II. Third, we find that several countries in this group—Tanzania, the
Sudan and Syria, for example—are among the few countries for

which the Soviet Union or the People's Republic of China are important import sources: apparently, trade relations with noncapitalist states are at least one means by which an LDC's trade partners are diversified.

In summary, a feudal interaction structure does seem to define the external relations of LDCs in the area of trade. The strongest and most exclusive relationship is between France and her former African colonies. Trade ties with the United States are strongest in Central America and the Caribbean, with progressively less exclusive relationships spreading in waves to South America and, finally, to South Asia. A third and looser grouping forms around the United Kingdom, consisting mainly of her former African colonies. Japan has a moderately exclusive group of trade satellites of her own, in East and Southeast Asia, but is also important as a secondary partner to countries in every area of the world. The latter characteristic also applies to the Federal Republic of Germany, but this country is primary partner to no LDCs. Finally, Belgium-Luxembourg, Italy and the Soviet Union each have one or two countries for which they are the principal trade partner, but are only occasionally important secondary partners to countries outside this principal sphere of influence.

On the fringes of this network from the point of view of the *extent* of trade ties are thirteen small, poor, often landlocked countries (those marked with an asterisk) which conduct a limited volume of trade overall. Deeply involved in the trade network, but beyond the dominant influence of a single DC partner, are fifteen other LDCs whose trade is relatively dispersed among a variety of import sources.

PRIVATE DIRECT INVESTMENT TIES

The methods used in this section are similar to those used in the examination of trade ties. Only the criteria for inclusion in various groupings are different, governed as they are by the particular characteristics of private direct investment ties. In this case an LDC is listed with a partner if more than half of the private direct investment stocks in that country are controlled by firms based in a single partner; otherwise, sources are listed as "diversified." Substantial secondary sources of investment are listed in parentheses; the criterion for inclusion of a secondary source is that the partner controls investments valued at more than $10 million. (No more than three secondary investors are, however, listed.) LDCs which are host to foreign-owned private direct investment stocks valued at less than 5 percent of current GNP are marked with an asterisk (*).[13]

Countries whose principal investment source is the United States
are listed first:

Costa Rica

Guatemala

Haiti

Honduras

Panama

*Urguay

*Jordan

*Syria

*Republic of Korea

Afghanistan (also W. Germany)

Dominican Republic (also Canada)

El Salvador (also Canada)

Ecuador (also U.K.)

Paraguay (also U.K.)

Nicaragua (also Canada)

*Egypt (also Italy)

Bolivia (also U.K., Canada)

Jamaica (also Canada, U.K.)

Lebanon (also France, U.K.)

Indonesia (also France, U.K.,
Japan)

Colombia (also U.K., Netherlands,
W. Germany)

Mexico (also U.K., Switzerland,
Japan)

Argentina (also Italy, U.K., Switzerland)

Chile (also Japan, W. Germany,
U.K.)

Peru (also Japan, Canada, U.K.)

Philippines (also U.K., Japan,
Netherlands)

Liberia (also W. Germany, Sweden, Italy)

As can be seen, this group includes all but two of the Western
Hemisphere countries included in this study, four of the six Middle
Eastern nations and Afghanistan (although the relative magnitude of
private direct investment stocks is not high for the latter countries), as
well as Liberia, the Republic of Korea and Indonesia, countries with
which the United States has historically maintained close ties. While
similar in many respects to the group of countries linked to the
United States by trade ties, this grouping is considerably larger and
more diverse. Another interesting feature is the prominent secondary
role played by the United Kingdom and Canada, both of which have
had a long history of investment in Latin America, particularly in
utilities.

A second group consists of LDCs receiving over half of their
private direct investment from French firms:

Central African Empire

Congo

Chad

Benin

Ivory Coast

Madagascar

Mauritania

Niger

Senegal

Togo

Upper Volta

*Cameroun

*Mali

Two characteristics of this grouping are of particular interest. One
is that it exactly coincides with the former French colonies of sub-

Saharan Africa that are included in this study. Another is that for *none* of these countries is there a single substantial investment source other than France. The clear conclusion is that, as was the case for trade ties, France's investment "satellites" are a much more exclusive preserve than those of any other major DC partner.

Next, the British group. The LDCs for which British firms control over half of the outstanding foreign investment stocks are the following:

Sri Lanka	Kenya (also U.S.A.)
Sierra Leone	Zambia (also U.S.A.)
Malawi	Pakistan (also Japan, U.S.A.)
Gambia	Malaysia (also U.S.A., Japan, France)
*Sudan	Nigeria (also U.S.A., France, W. Germany)
*Burma	India (also U.S.A., W. Germany, Netherlands)
Ghana (also U.S.A.)	

This grouping, which consists entirely of former British colonies, is identical to the group for which the United Kingdom is the principal trade partner, except for the addition of four large Asian countries. The indication is that Britain's investment linkages are stronger than its trade linkages, although this grouping, too, is far from an exclusive preserve for British firms.[14]

Next, the countries where ownership of foreign investment stocks is dominated by Belgian and Italian firms:

Belgian Partners	*Italian Partners*
Zaire	Somalia
Rwanda	

Again, each country is linked to its former colony or colonies.

Finally, we come to a group of LDCs where none have received as much as half of their total private direct foreign investment from a single source:

Brazil	U.S.A., Canada, W. Germany
Guyana	Canada, U.K., U.S.A.
Morocco	France, U.S.A., Italy
Tunisia	France, Italy, U.S.A.
Singapore	U.K., U.S.A., Netherlands
Thailand	U.S.A., U.K., Japan
Greece	U.S.A., France, Italy
Spain	U.S.A., France, Italy
Turkey	U.S.A., U.K., Netherlands
*Ethiopia	France, U.S.A., Denmark
*Tanzania	U.K., Italy
*Uganda	U.K., Canada

As was the case with trade ties, only a small number of these countries are from the Western Hemisphere: included are only Brazil, very hospitable to foreign investment and attractive to firms of many nations, and Guyana, a small country with imperial ties to Britain and Canada as well as more recent ties to the United States. Other countries with relatively diversified investment sources are Morocco and Tunisia, where the exclusive influence of French firms is tempered by Italian and United States holdings, and Thailand and Singapore, where both the United States and Britain have important interests. Finally, there are included three countries of Southern Europe, whose trade ties are also diversified, and three East African countries, the absolute amount of investment in which, however, is small.

In summary private direct investment ties present the following picture. First, there is a very large group of countries, the bulk of whose foreign investment stocks is owned by United States firms; this group includes all but two of the Western Hemisphere countries included in this study, but also includes a number of countries elsewhere, especially in Asia. Next, there is a grouping, exactly coinciding with the former French colonies included in the study, in which French interests dominate private direct investment; as was the case for trade ties, these linkages are more nearly exclusive than those for any other DC partner. Third, there is a British group, consisting of former British African and Asian colonies; an important secondary investor for almost half of these countries is the United States, indicating that American firms have made inroads into Britain's investment relations with her former colonies that have not been made in LDCs linked to France. Britain is, however, more important as a secondary investor than it is as a secondary trade partner in countries outside its primary sphere of influence. Fourth, there are the former Belgian and Italian colonies, each of which is linked to its former metropolis. And, finally, there is a group of twelve LDCs which are host to foreign direct investment from a relatively diversified group of DC partners.

More generally, we might note that in the field of private direct investment the position of the United States is more pervasive than in the trade network: not only are United States firms the principal investors in a large number of LDCs but these firms are also secondary investors in a large and diverse group of countries. West Germany and Japan, on the other hand, have a less prominent position in the investment matrix than in the matrix of trade ties. Some possible reasons for these findings come immediately to mind. For one United States corporations were pioneers in the multinational movement and have been among the foremost proponents of this mode of international business; because of this American firms were the first to enter many promising areas for investment in LDCs. For another American corporations have rarely experienced serious government or union pressure against foreign investments and in favor of a strategy of export promotion; Japan and West Germany, on the other hand, have devoted considerable resources to export promotion and have often heavily subsidized domestic export industries and maintained large and influential trade missions abroad.

DEVELOPMENT ASSISTANCE TIES

Now that two modes of external dependence have been elaborated in some detail it is becoming unnecessary (and tedious) to expand fully upon DC-LDC relations for each new mode of external dependence. Therefore, for the remaining modes the data will be presented in the form of summary tables, and the analysis will be much less detailed, except where there emerge significant differences from the general pattern of the first two modes.

Table 7.2 represents ties of Official Development Assistance (ODA) from OECD-DAC countries, categorized by principal donor. How do these data relate to those reported for trade and investment ties? Several comments are in order. First, the dominant position of the United States in Latin America is reconfirmed, but in addition to strong ties in this region the United States maintains dominant aid linkages with a number of large Asian countries; there was some evidence of ties in this region for previously discussed linkages, but for this mode of external dependence the pattern is much more distinct. Second, France is again seen to have the most cohesive group of satellites of any DC partner; bilateral aid to her former African colonies is high in both relative amount and donor concentration, and France allots only limited aid to other regions. Third, the position of the United Kingdom in the aid matrix is both less extensive and less exclusive than in any of the previous networks. And, finally, the "diversified" group contains many more African and a few more Latin American countries than was the case for other ties. In summary the picture that is presented is of a network dominated by the United States, France and, to a lesser degree, Britain, but with a

Table 7.2 Official Development Assistance from OECD-DAC Countries, Categorized by Principal Donor

United States Partners

Jordan	Liberia
Panama	Uruguay*
Haiti	Turkey (also France)
Guatemala	Thailand (also Japan)
El Salvador	Ecuador (also W. Germany)
Costa Rica	Brazil (also W. Germany)
Bolivia	Paraguay (also W. Germany)
Colombia	Indonesia (also Japan)
Dominican Republic	India (also U.K.)
Honduras	Republic of Korea (also Japan)
Nicaragua	Pakistan (also W. Germany)

United Kingdom Partners

Zambia	Singapore (also Japan)
Kenya	Uganda (also U.S.A.)
Malawi	Gambia (also U.S.A.)
Malaysia (also Japan)	Mauritius (also U.S.A.)

French Partners

Chad	Ivory Coast
Mauritania	Madagascar
Central African Empire	Mali
Congo	Niger
Benin	Senegal
Cameroun	Upper Volta

Belgian Partners
Rwanda
Zaire (also U.S.A.)

West German Partners
Argentina*

large group of countries whose sources of aid are diversified among several donors. A feudal interaction structure is again in evidence, but it seems somewhat less pervasive than for ties of trade and foreign investment.

MILITARY TIES: ARMS TRANSFERS

The next external linkage to be examined is that of arms transfers. Since the distribution of arms transfers among LDCs is so much more skewed than that of other ties—with a few countries receiving enormous amounts and many very little—a clearer picture is presented when the table is divided into four categories according to the value of arms received. Absolute amounts are used as the criterion since

Japanese Partners

Philippines (also U.S.A.)   Burma (also W. Germany)

Diversified Partners

Ghana	U.S.A., U.K., Canada
Nigeria	U.S.A., U.K., W. Germany
Somalia	Italy
Tanzania	Sweden, U.S.A.
Togo	France, W. Germany
Morocco	U.S.A., France, W. Germany
Tunisia	U.S.A., France, W. Germany
Chile	U.S.A., W. Germany, France
Guyana	U.S.A., U.K., Canada
Sri Lanka	U.S.A., U.K., Canada
Afghanistan	W. Germany
Peru	U.S.A., W. Germany, France
Jamaica	U.K., U.S.A., Canada
Syria	U.N.
Sierra Leone	U.S.A., U.K., W. Germany
Ethiopia	U.S.A., Sweden, Italy
Mexico*	France, U.S.A.
Sudan*	U.N.
Egypt*	U.N.
Lebanon*	U.S.A., W. Germany

SOURCE: see appendix IV.

NOTE: Criteria employed in this table are the following: countries receiving less than a third of their total OECD-DAC aid from a single donor or receiving at least 10 percent of total ODA from three or more donors are classified as having diversified aid sources. All other countries are classified with their principal donors, with donors contributing more than 10 percent of total ODA listed in parentheses.

*ODA constitutes less than 1 percent of GNP. (As has been noted, Greece, Yugoslavia, and Spain receive so little aid that, to avoid misleading findings, they are excluded from this and other analyses.)

they more directly reflect the actual flow of arms, but a table categorized by relative amounts was also constructed and demonstrated only minor differences from the one presented in table 7.3.

The pattern here is somewhat different from those found for other external linkages. The most striking difference is the degree to which arms transfers are dominated by the United States and the Soviet Union. The principal exception is France, which is again linked, almost to the exclusion of other suppliers, with its former African colonies (although the absolute amounts of arms supplied are modest). A second difference is the fact that for this external linkage the range of secondary suppliers is much more limited than for the previous modes: Japan and West Germany, for example, are not much in evi-

Table 7.3 Arms Transfers from Major Arms Exporters to LDCs, 1965–1974

Recipients of the Largest Amounts of Arms (Arms receipts ≥ $1 billion)

United States	Soviet Union
Republic of Korea	Egypt
Greece	Syria
Turkey	India

Intermediate Recipients ($1 billion > arms receipts ≥ $100 million)

United States	Soviet Union	France
Ethiopia	Sudan	Lebanon
Jordan	Afghanistan	
Philippines	Yugoslavia	
Spain		
Thailand		

Diversified Suppliers

Nigeria	U.K., U.S.S.R.
Zaire	U.S.A., France, Belgium
Morocco	U.S.A., Czechoslovakia
Argentina	U.S.A., France, W. Germany
Brazil	U.S.A., France
Chile	U.K., U.S.A.
Colombia	U.S.A., France
Peru	W. Germany, Canada, France, U.K., U.S.A.
Indonesia	Netherlands
Malaysia	U.K.
Pakistan	P. R. China
Singapore	U.K., U.S.A.

dence in the arms supply picture, while the role of Britain is limited. The exception is again France, which emerges as an important secondary supplier even in regions (such as Latin America) where its aid, trade and investment linkages are weak.

In looking at the overall pattern of linkages, we find that very large amounts of arms are received from the world's two superpowers by a small number of very closely tied cients; at the highest level of absolute arms transfers, supplies are very highly concentrated by source. At intermediate levels of arms transfers, countries with diversified suppliers are much more in evidence; although a number of countries at this level are closely identified with either the United States or the Soviet Union, many more have received arms from several competing sources, in some cases from opposite sides of the bipolar rivalry that dominates the first category. Finally, the recipients of relatively small amounts of arms from abroad tend to be

Recipients of Limited Arms (Arms receipts < $100 million)
United States

Liberia	Guatemala	Nicaragua
Tunisia	Haiti	Panama
Burma	Honduras	Paraguay
Bolivia	Jamaica	Uruguay
Dominican R.	Mexico	

Soviet Union	*P. R. China*	*W. Germany*
Mali	Tanzania	Niger
Somalia		

France	*United Kingdom*	*Italy*
Cameroun	Ghana	Zambia
Cent. African Emp.	Kenya	
Chad		
Congo	*Diversified Suppliers*	
Benin	Uganda	U.S.S.R., Czech.
Ivory Coast	Sri Lanka	U.K., P. R. China
Madagascar	Ecuador	U.S.A., U.K., France
Mauritania	El Salvador	"Others" (not specified in source)
Rwanda		
Senegal		
Togo		
Upper Volta		

No Arms Transfers Recorded

Gambia	Sierra Leone
Malawi	Costa Rica
Mauritius	Guyana

SOURCE: see appendix IV.
NOTES: The criteria employed for this table are the following. A country is listed with its principal supplier if it received more than half of its arms imports from that supplier over the period indicated. In the "diversified" category all arms sources are reported that supplied more than $20 million in arms for the "intermediate recipients" group, and more than $5 million for the "limited" group.

closely identified with a single principal source, in most instances the United States or France; there are only four countries with diversified suppliers at this level of arms transfers.

In summary in examining the arms transfers picture, we again find something resembling a feudal interaction structure, although this time the lines are more closely drawn on a bipolar basis with only France playing a major secondary role. While other countries are occasionally important arms suppliers, their role is much more limited than for other modes of external dependence.

Table 7.4 University Students Studying Abroad, 1970

Less Than 2% of Total University Students Enrolled Abroad

Argentina	Indonesia
Egypt	Republic of Korea
Brazil	Pakistan
Mexico	Philippines
Burma	Spain
India	Yugoslavia

2% or More of Total University Students Enrolled Abroad

France

Senegal	Chad
Ivory Coast	Congo
Madagascar	Benin
Morocco	Mali
Cameroun	Tunisia
Cent. African Emp.	

United States

Chile	El Salvador
Colombia	Liberia
Costa Rica	Nigeria
Dominican R.	Sierra Leone
Ecuador	Guyana
Guatemala	Honduras
Nicaragua	Jamaica
Ethiopia	Panama
Gambia	Thailand

CULTURAL TIES: STUDENTS ABROAD

The final tie for which external linkages are examined is represented by figures on students attending foreign universities. Table 7.4 includes the most important relationships expressed in a matrix identifying students at the university level who are studying in foreign countries; the matrix relates all seventy LDCs to the fifty countries host to the largest number of foreign students. A country is listed with a partner if more than half of its students abroad are studying in that country; otherwise the countries in which its students are enrolled are listed as "diversified."

What can we say about these ties? Once again, the general pattern governing all linkages described so far is in evidence, but there are some nuances. The most important is that certain regionally prominent LDCs serve as important centers of higher education for less de-

United Kingdom
| Malawi | Zambia |
| Mauritius | Sri Lanka |

Argentina
| Bolivia | Paraguay |
| Uruguay | |

| *Belgium* | *India* |
| Zaire | Mauritania |

| *Ivory Coast* | *Italy* |
| Niger | Somalia |

Diversified
Lebanon	France, U.S.A.
Peru	Argentina, U.S.A.
Afghanistan	U.S.A., W. Germany, France
Turkey	U.S.A., W. Germany, France
Ghana	U.S.A., U.K.
Syria	Lebanon, Spain, Turkey
Singapore	U.K., U.S.A.
Greece	W. Germany, U.S.A.
Kenya	India, U.K.
Rwanda	Zaire, Belgium
Sudan	U.K., Czech., Yugoslavia
Tanzania	India, Kenya, Uganda
Togo	France, Ivory Coast
Uganda	India, U.S.A.
Upper Volta	Ivory Coast, France
Jordan	Syria, Yugoslavia, U.S.A.
Haiti	U.S.A., France
Malaysia	U.K., U.S.A., Canada

SOURCE: see appendix IV.

veloped LDCs of their region. The most important of these are the Ivory Coast, Argentina, Mexico, India, Kenya and Tanzania; we may assume that in many cases teachers in these countries have in turn received their training in France, the United States, the Soviet Union or Britain, thus confirming the "semiperiphery" concept discussed in the last chapter.

Aside from these characteristics, the pattern of linkages for this mode of external dependence is similar to that for previously discussed modes and serves to reinforce the picture of a powerful, if not all-pervasive, feudal interaction structure governing the relationship between developed and less developed countries.

THE DIVERSIFIED PARTNERS GROUPING:
A CLOSER LOOK

To this point much has been said about the "satellites" in a North-South feudal interaction structure, and much less about countries that have escaped close incorporation into such a structure. But the latter are certainly as interesting as the former, and it should be useful briefly to explore some of the features that distinguish countries with "diversified" external ties from those more closely integrated into a world "metropolitan-satellite" structure.

One interesting exercise is to focus directly on what appeared in this chapter to be one of the most important factors shaping the nature and degree of LDCs' participation in feudal interaction structures, a legacy of formal colonialism. A series of analyses of covariance was performed, with former colonial status as the dichotomous dummy variable, the usual metric controls (GNP per capita and natural resource endowment) as covariates, and each of the indicators of external dependence, one at a time, as dependent variables. The question asked was, quite simply, whether countries that escaped formal colonialism in recent times do indeed differ from former colonies in the nature, extent and concentration of their external ties.

The dichotomous factor was coded as follows: former colonies of France, Britain, the Netherlands, Belgium, Italy, Japan and the United States were coded 0; and all LDCs that have not recently been colonies of any of these powers were coded 1. Latin American former Spanish and Portuguese colonies were not included in the analysis because their long and intensive, but historically remote, history of formal colonialism, and the special semicolonial relationship of some of these countries with the United States in the nineteenth and early twentieth centuries, seemed to render them a special case.[15]

The principal findings are presented in table 7.5. Relationships between modes of external dependence and the controls are not reported, although the controls were included in every equation.

As can be seen, there are some definite differences between LDCs that were once colonies and those that escaped formal colonialism. We find, for example, that countries "never a colony" are significantly lower in trade dependence than are countries with a legacy of formal colonialism; this seems to reflect a holdover from colonial trade policies that attempted to ensure that colonial production would be closely geared to supplying the mother country with raw materials. We find also that countries that escaped formal colonialism maintain

Table 7.5 Analysis of Covariance Relating Former Status as a Colony, Along with Metric Controls, to Indicators of External Dependence

Dependent Variable	*Beta Weight*	
Trade	−.29 (.01)	"Never a colony" lower
Concentration	−.33 (.01)	"Never a colony" lower
Arms Transfers	+.44 (.01)	"Never a colony" higher
Finance	Not signif.	
Aid-Trade Terms	Not signif.	
Students Abroad	Not signif.	
Investment	Not signif.	

ties that are less concentrated by partner than do former colonies; this relationship has been evident throughout this chapter. Countries "never a colony" tend, on the other hand, to receive higher levels of arms transfers than former colonies, perhaps indicating that they, more than former colonies, view themselves as isolated actors in a hostile world.

For *investment, finance, students abroad* and *aid-trade terms* linkages, on the other hand, there is no significant difference between the two groups of LDCs. This may be a reflection of the fact that many of these ties are of relatively recent origin, having become major North-South linkages only after most colonies were already independent. If this is the case, we may have an example of the newer and even more insidious "neocolonial" ties so often cited by dependency theorists.

CONCLUSION

What can we say about the external linkages of LDCs when examined from a core-periphery perspective? The clear conclusion is that there do indeed exist strong networks linking dominant DCs to groups of LDCs which tend to interact intensively with them and only to a limited degree with alternative DC partners or other LDCs. Moreover, these patterns hold for all but a few of the LDCs included in this study.

But we must go further than simply affirming the existence of a feudal interaction structure; we must outline its general characteristics. Several patterns seem to persist from one mode of external dependence to another. One is the very close relationship between France and her former African colonies: only in a few cases does

France maintain secondary linkages with countries other than these, while the former French colonies of Black Africa in turn rarely maintain significant ties to any country but France. The only exception to this generality is in the area of arms transfers, in which France is an important secondary supplier of arms to a large and diverse group of LDCs.

The United States is the center of a second, somewhat looser, grouping. In most cases we find an inner circle of countries from Central America and the Caribbean, which interact almost exclusively with the United States, and outside of this a series of concentric rings consisting of South American countries, Liberia and, in some cases, large countries of Asia. But the influence of the United States often goes beyond its principal partners: it serves as an important secondary partner to LDCs in almost every area of the world (except francophone Africa), especially in the field of private direct investment.

A third and looser grouping of former colonies, particularly those in Africa, forms around the United Kingdom. It is strongest in the area of investment ties. The members of this group tend to have important secondary ties to other LDCs, but only in the case of private direct investment ties is Britain itself an important partner of countries outside its primary sphere of influence.

The position of Japan varies most by mode of external dependence: while it is an important actor in the trade matrix, its position in other matrices ranges from moderate to very limited. The Federal Republic of Germany, too, plays an important secondary role in the trade matrix, and is also an important secondary donor in the matrix dealing with development assistance. In only a few cases, however, is it the principal partner of any LDC.

Belgium, the Soviet Union and the People's Republic of China play some role in various matrices, but their role is only in a few cases of major importance.

Another group consists of the countries whose external ties, whatever their principal partner or partners, are limited in extent; these are the countries designated with an asterisk in the tables. We might view these countries as on the fringes of the various networks in which they are involved.

Finally, there is the group of LDCs whose partners are listed as "diversified." These countries might be viewed as deeply enmeshed in a given network, but beyond the dominant influence of a single DC partner. The identity of this group varies somewhat from one mode of external dependence to another, but it most frequently consists of countries with little or no experience of formal colonialism. These countries tend to be located in Southern Europe, the Middle East and Southeast Asia, although they occasionally count among their members the African countries with the weakest legacy of colonial ties and certain large countries of South America.

CHAPTER EIGHT

Future Directions

THE RESEARCH REPORTED HERE has been essentially exploratory and, while it has answered some questions, it has (as was, indeed, one of its purposes) raised many others. Here are a few of the areas in which I feel this study might most fruitfully be expanded upon.

A first issue that demands greater attention is the matter of relations *among* less developed countries, especially between those at intermediate levels of development (Wallerstein's "semiperiphery") and those at lower levels.[1] One promising strategy in this area might be simply to identify a group of potentially semiperipheral countries (say, Hong Kong, Taiwan, the Republic of Korea, Brazil, Argentina, Mexico, Nigeria, India, Kenya, the Ivory Coast and a few others) and then directly to examine these countries' ties with less developed LDCs. A perspective on the actual nature of the network of semi-periphery-periphery ties might be achieved by the analysis of a series of data matrices as was done in chapter 7; the only difference would be that the matrices would focus directly upon the relationship of regionally prominent LDCs with smaller and poorer countries of a region. Further research might construct a series of regressions based on ties of less developed LDCs with an identified group of "semi-peripheral" countries; analysis might parallel the more general regression model of this study, but might, in addition, examine such factors as physical distance, differences in levels of development, product complementarities and incompatibilities and so on.[2]

Both of these modes of analysis would, unfortunately, be rather seriously limited by data deficiencies: while, for example, it has been suggested that semiperipheral countries dominate capital formation in and serve as a magnet for low-wage labor from less developed satellites, systematic data on inter-LDC investment ties and labor migrations are scarce.[3] Moreover, it would be difficult, given available

data, to trace a good or capital flow that is channeled from developed
market economy countries *through* semiperipheral countries to less
developed LDCs.[4] Nevertheless, a limited analysis of inter-LDC ties
does seem possible, especially in such areas as trade and educational
ties.

A second direction for future research is to work toward increasing
the *specificity* of the indicators typically used in studying dependency
relations. More effort seems most clearly to be called for in the areas
of trade ties and ties of private direct investment. While I maintain
that the fairly general indicators used in this study have meaning,
especially since controls have been introduced for GNP per capita
and natural resource endowment, it is obviously desirable to disaggregate these indicators into sectoral components based on such distinctions as between tropical product agriculture, mining and manufacturing. An effort in this direction would be no easy task, but
would, I think, move us toward a more sophisticated appreciation of
distinctions among dependency theorists and of the possibility that
very different processes may be subsumed not only under the broad
rubric "dependency," but also within such narrower notions as
"trade dependence" or "investment dependence."

A third item on an agenda for future research would be to tap directly the dynamic aspect of dependency theory by means of longitudinal analysis. While the possibilities for longitudinal analysis of a
large number of countries are severely limited by lack of data (this is
especially true for data on private direct investment stocks and income distribution), it seems possible that a series of regressions could
be constructed for a much smaller sample than that examined here,
say a dozen LDCs, ranging in time to the late 1940s or even earlier.[5]
Analysis in this mode would constitute a very different study from
this one, and would create a whole series of ambiguities of its own,
but might usefully complement if not supersede the findings of this
study.

But perhaps the most effective strategy for time series analysis
would involve not an effort to analyze as many countries for as long a
period as possible, but instead a carefully paired comparison of tem-
poral trends in only two countries—preferably countries that have a
great deal in common, but nevertheless vary widely on characteristics
that are of most direct interest (i.e., levels of external dependence). A
paired comparison of this sort, were it conducted for countries for
which available data are relatively extensive, would not only allow

attention to dynamic trends but would also allow descent to the sub-national level, something that is most difficult to do for more than a few countries whose data coverage is unusually extensive.

SUMMARY AND A FEW FINAL WORDS

In the introductory chapter it was suggested that this study would address three basic sets of questions. In this chapter the questions are repeated along with a brief summary of some of the principal findings relevant to each.

Question I Does external dependence constitute a syndrome which, while it may consist of distinct subsyndromes, contains no serious inconsistencies? What are some of the broad mechanisms through which external dependence operates?

These questions were addressed in chapter 3. In chapter 3, thirteen indicators of *external dependence,* as the term is usually used in the literature, were proposed and discussed. These represented an attempt to measure the relative extent and partner concentration of the external ties of seventy less developed countries in the areas of trade, private direct investment, economic assistance, debt, arms transfers and higher education.

The evidence of correlational and R-factor analysis suggested that the first question could be answered affirmatively: no strong negative correlations were found among indicators which would cast doubt upon the coherence of external dependence as an internally consistent condition. With regard to the second question the R-factor analysis indicated that it was indeed possible to construct several relatively clear composite dimensions from a number of narrow indicators of North-South interaction: a composite indicator of *trade dependence* was constructed from indicators of the extent, commodity concentration and relative degree of processing of trade ties; a composite indicator of *finance dependence* was constructed from indicators of debt service ties and reserves holdings; a composite indicator of *partner concentration dependence* was constructed from indicators of the partner concentration of trade, aid and investment ties; and a composite indicator of *aid-trade terms dependence* was constructed from an indicator of the extent of economic assistance ties and an indicator of relative terms of trade. These four composite indicators, together with indicators of private direct foreign investment stocks, arms transfers and higher education ties, constituted the seven indicators of external dependence used in the study.

Question II   Are high levels of external dependence in less developed countries related to basic internal structural distortions in these countries, resulting in a relatively disadvantaged position for nonelites? Are they related to economic stagnation? Do relationships continue to hold when important outside variables are taken into account?

Chapter 4 examined a number of contributions to the dependency literature relevant to these questions. Chapter 5 then tested, by means of a series of multiple regression equations, the relationship of the seven modes of external dependence already described to a series of dependent variables, including indicators of income distribution, social welfare, social insurance coverage, primary and secondary educational enrollment, tax progressivity, unemployment rates, and resources devoted to the maintenance of coercive apparatus. The basic hypothesis was that in highly dependent LDCs an "internationalized" elite, its position reinforced by external contacts, would pursue a development strategy to improve its own standing and that of the transnational class to which it belonged, but which would result in an overall decline in the standing of nonelites.

Included in each multiple regression, for purposes of control, were indicators of economic development level and natural resource endowment. An additional measure of control was achieved by dividing the sample into more homogenous subsamples based on such characteristics as absolute population and GNP, region and former colonial metropolis.

For the series of regressions based on the whole sample it was found that 15 of 20 significant relationships were in the direction predicted by dependency theorists. For the series of regressions based on subsamples of the general sample, 53 of 69 significant relationships confirmed dependency hypotheses.

With regard to the narrow issue of the relationship of modes of external dependence to aggregate economic growth in LDCs, it was found that for LDCs at lower levels of development external dependence was not strongly related to economic growth rates, but that for countries at higher levels the relationship of trade and concentration dependence to economic growth was negative while that of investment dependence was positive.

Question III   What is the regional dimension of the external interactions of LDCs? Do there exist regional subgroupings of countries that share a common pattern of external linkages? Are these interactions structured according to a "feudal interaction structure" linking groups of LDC "satellites" with major DC partners?

Chapters 6 and 7 explored the regional configuration of some of the most important interactions of less developed countries.

In chapter 6 a Q-factor analysis was done for each geographical region included in the study. From this analysis were derived clusters of LDCs that were similar in the nature, extent and partner concentration of their external contacts. For the African countries these clusters were compared to a historically based classification scheme proposed by Samir Amin; his categories were more or less reflected in the findings, but such variables as colonial heritage and general export composition appeared to play a larger role in the formulation of regional subgroupings than was attributed to them by Amin. For the Latin American countries clusters tended to be based on geographical subregion: fairly distinct clusters emerged for the Central American countries, the Andean countries, the ABC countries of South America and the former British colonies of Guyana and Jamaica. For the Asian countries the clustering pattern, while demonstrating some interesting configurations, was on the whole less distinct, suggesting that for this region there does not seem to exist a clear-cut subregional dimension to the pattern of external ties.

In chapter 7 the question was explored whether North-South political-economic relations are patterned according to a feudal interaction structure in which LDCs' external ties are largely confined to a single DC "metropolis" of which they are "satellites." Large matrices were constructed representing relationships between LDCs and individual DC partners in the areas of trade, private direct investment, economic assistance, arms transfers and educational ties.

The overall finding was that feudal interaction structures are indeed in evidence for each of the ties examined, but that actual patterns of interaction differ in many details depending upon the particular partner or mode of interaction in question and the size and colonial heritage of the LDCs whose ties are being examined. For example, it was found that France maintained the most tightly exclusive interaction structure of any major DC, the United States the most diverse and far-flung and the United Kingdom a structure that was surprisingly weak given its imperial history; that trade ties tended to be the most widely dispersed by partner of any major mode of interaction, investment ties the most dominated by one DC partner (the United States) and arms transfers the most clearly delineated on an East-West basis; and that LDCs whose external ties were most diversified were most frequently among those whose colonial heritage was weak or nonexistent or which were unusually large or remote.

This study has purported to offer a cross-national test of certain hypotheses of dependency theory. The questions at this point can only be, have dependency hypotheses withstood the test? Have they successfully resisted systematic attempts at falsification? The answer, in a word, can only be yes: "dependency" does appear to represent a coherent condition (although one capable of operating through distinct modes), the consequences of which tend to be more or less as dependency theorists have hypothesized. There are, to be sure, exceptions, but on the whole the findings fairly strongly confirm the hypotheses tested. Dependency theorists do seem to have a point that merits serious consideration.

But to conclude that the most general dependency hypotheses were or were not borne out was not the sole or even the main goal of this study. What was attempted was not so much to assess the validity of the dependency approach as a rather amorphous whole as to specify some of the actual processes that are subsumed within the broad, overarching dependency structures that are said to characterize North-South relations. It is one thing to say that "external dependence" causes "structural distortions" in less developed countries; but one goes a great deal further to say that coherent modes of "investment" or "trade" dependence demonstrate particular patterns of relationship with social welfare or the income share of the top 20 percent of the population in LDCs or that ties of economic assistance have the weakest effect on the internal distribution of power and wealth of any presumed mode of external dependence. Similarly, it is useful to suggest that the nature, extent and partner concentration of LDCs' external ties are "important" (or, in the most extreme formulation, "all-important") in explaining variance among LDCs in certain structural characteristics; but it is much more useful to determine that a certain proportion of the variance in these characteristics is accounted for by these factors, that another proportion is accounted for by certain key control variables and that a third residual proportion cannot be accounted for and is presumably attributable to factors outside the model (including, of course, measurement error).[6] Finally, it is one thing to propose that North-South relations are structured according to a feudal interaction structure, but it is quite another to examine specific similarities and differences among the relationships of individual developed countries to Third World nations in a number of important areas.

The purpose of this study, then, has been not so much to determine whether the very broad generalizations of dependency theory represent a more or less valid approach to North-South relations as to specify the actual operation of North-South contacts in as subtle and detailed a manner as possible. In doing this it has probably raised as many questions as it has answered, but that is true of almost any research effort, and is, indeed, one of the reasons that research is undertaken in the first place.

APPENDIX ONE

"Rigorous Empiricism" and Dependency Theory: Mismatched Language Traditions? Arguments of Duvall

RECENTLY, A NUMBER OF SCHOL-
ars from both within and outside the dependency tradition have expressed concern that the burgeoning literature purporting cross-nationally to test dependency theory (or certain hypotheses thereof) has in a fundamental sense missed the point. A particularly comprehensive and thoughtful expression of such misgivings is offered in an article by Raymond Duvall in the Winter, 1978, issue of *International Organization;* Duvall's arguments are, in fact, so cogent and so relevant to some of the central assumptions of this study that they demand and will receive a rather detailed discussion.[1]

For Duvall the term *dependency* is used in a manner most consistent with the contribution of dependency theorists when it is restricted to the discussion of a particular historical phenomenon, the progressive integration during the last three centuries of ever more of the world into an international capitalist order thoroughly dominated by a transnational leading class based in the developed market economy countries. The dynamic of interaction between this core and peripheral groups has been such that the peripheral groups have come to be integrated into a unified global structure in which their subordinate position has been progressively reinforced. The overall logic of interaction has been, in short, the logic of capitalism writ large: in Duvall's composite definition *dependence* refers to no less than "a context of differentially or asymmetrically structured reflections of the processes of capitalist production and reproduction at the international level."[2]

In accordance with this definition Duvall concludes that when dependency theorists speak of dependency they are referring to "a 'frame' . . . of reference, . . . a general cue [or] 'script,' " the central purpose of which is to "demarcate the general context of . . . inquiry."[3] For him dependency is a qualitatively distinct form of relationship and its claims can be fully addressed only by the "wholistic [sic] descriptive analysis of historical processes of social-structural transformation";[4] in his estimation any attempt to test dependency theory by "measuring dependence as the central concept within that theory" is doomed to prove a "misdirected and . . . nonsensical enterprise" that is not even "relevant" to dependency theory.[5]

The key difficulty for Duvall is that the formulators and the testers of dependency theory have worked from fundamentally different "language traditions." Dependency theory, in his estimation, operates within a language tradition which "places primary emphasis on 'concrete analysis,' and detailed, historical, descriptive, contextually-bound knowledge claims about processes and conditions of the structural transformation of peripheral capitalist states."[6] Scholars who attempt to test dependency hypotheses, on the other hand, have almost always worked within the very different tradition of "rigorous empiricism," which has led them toward "attempts to increase the analytical scope and precise empirical content of the term dependence by developing measurement models for it."[7] These attempts have failed, in words of Cardoso and Faletto cited by Duvall, to "describe [a] social process in terms of a 'complex whole,' . . . whose structural movement derives from the contradictory forces which sustain it,"[8] and have instead, in "scientific" (positivistic? bourgeois ? First Worldist?) fashion created elaborate structures of bloodless abstractions that have been drained of all of the "muscles and meat" that "give . . . life and movement to social structures."[9] When language traditions so different meet, the almost inevitable result is that the practitioners "literally speak . . . past one another."[10]

Is the only alternative to mindless empiricism, then, the strict "dialectical analysis of concrete situations of dependence,"[11] presumably by total immersion in the analysis of a single situation in a single country? Must we fully accept the "historical uniqueness argument of the contextual specificity of causal relations" that has led some dependency theorists to "reject explicitly the notion of theory in favor of (descriptive) 'analysis of concrete situations of dependence' "?[12] Duvall would not go this far: "If dialogue with rigorous empiricists is to occur, the *extreme* form of this epistemology must be rejected."[13] But he does deem it absolutely essential that any test of dependency theory place in a central position the idea of *context,* and he decries "totalizing" measurement strategies in which a concept is assumed to mean the same thing regardless of the context in which it occurs. Indeed, he doubts that such "commonsense" notions as the extent and concentration of physical transactions of countries tap the underlying concept of "the forms and extent of metropole capitalist penetration" at all: he allows that, at best, they can only tap the *"media* or mechanisms of contingency and / or the *potential* for subordination or support."[14]

Duvall's central point is that of context. And, indeed, it is true that most cross-national analyses of dependency hypotheses have studiously avoided issues of context; we would almost think that many of these studies were reporting findings about anonymous respondents to a survey rather than a collection of individual countries, each with a distinct regional, subregional and individual identity about which our previous knowledge is considerable. In several studies, in fact, the countries analyzed are not even named.

This failure to consider context is very damaging, and in this study every effort has been made to keep such matters as fully as possible in sight. Along these lines I have examined regression residuals and speculated on reasons why they may not have fit regression-based generalizations; have explored the possibility that contextual factors might have resulted in qualitative discontinuities within the data set that would make whole-sample findings misleading, but would be revealed if regressions were constructed for parallel subsamples delineated by various contextual criteria; have allowed for a number of distinct (and empirically derived) *forms* of external contacts of LDCs and several broad modes of internal "structural distortions," any or all of the former of which may or may not relate to any or all of the latter in either direction; have directed attention to the inclusion of certain basic metric controls at every level of analysis; have assessed first-order multiplicative interaction effects and explored several nonlinear functions in the multiple regression exercise; and finally, have explicitly and in some detail focused on the regional context of LDCs' external ties (in the Q-factor analysis), and examined directly the network of ties between LDCs and their principal individual partners (in the dyadic analysis of chapter 7).

In short I have tried to keep always in sight the actual countries, subregions and regions with which I was dealing.[15] Limitations of time and energy, the necessity for parsimony of analysis and the exigencies imposed by data unavailability have ensured that this study remains a long way from the level of attention to contextual factors that Duvall (and I) would prefer, but the study does, I think, make useful progress in the right direction.

Duvall's argument for attention to context is clearly justified, and I accept it in principle and have tried to implement it. But he goes further than I would prefer when he seems to express doubt about the ability of *any* indicators based ultimately on the extent and concentration of physical transactions to tap effectively the central concepts of dependency theory, arguing that such indicators can at best address only the *"media* or mechanisms of contingency and / or the *potential* for subordination or support.''[16] I agree fully that there is a pressing need for more discerning indicators in this area; while I think the indicators used here are better in some specific ways than those of previous studies, there is still much room for improvement, and I have suggested several directions in which I intend to proceed in this effort in chapter 8. Still, I am not at all sure what even moderately generalizable indicators could be used to tap directly, without recourse to data on physical transactions, the broad but vague notion of the "forms and extent of metropole capitalist penetration." Certainly, the indicators proposed in the Duvall et al. study that Duvall describes at some length, although very well chosen, hardly provide the basis for a "precise test model" as he suggests.[17] Take only one variable, the "coercive authoritarianism of the peripheral state." Duvall and his associates have elsewhere described the precise indicators they will use to measure this concept: an indicator of the relative size of the coercive apparatus of the state (i.e., the size of the military and paramilitary establishments); an indicator of the extent to which cabinet-level and above positions in the government are held by active members of the armed forces; a judgmental indicator of the political influence of the armed forces; a media-based indicator of the "frequency and severity of coercive negative sanctions targeted at social collectivities"; and a "very imperfectly estimated" indicator of the number of political prisoners.[18] These indicators are excellent, given data availability, but they hardly *fully* measure the underlying abstract concept of "coercive authoritarianism"; for one thing many would doubt that the body counts on which most of these indicators

are based can be interpreted literally. The point is not that these indicators are not good ones (they are), but that they too are ultimately
grounded in "commonsense" considerations and fail fully to tap the
underlying abstract condition that they are intended to measure.

But that the indicators used in this study (as well as that of Duvall
et al.) are not perfect does not necessarily mean that they are useless.
At the very least it is evident that countries *do* vary widely in the extent and concentration of their external ties, and (as this study has
shown) this variance *is* related to certain internal structural characteristics in these countries, generally in the direction that dependency
theorists have predicted. Are these facts irrelevant to "dependency
theory"? Perhaps so, if dependency theory is strictly confined to the
"descriptive analysis of historical processes of social-structural transformation."[19] But even if these findings represent something
narrower than a test of dependency theory as a whole, this hardly
means that they are not relevant to at least *some* of the concerns of
dependency theorists, of which private direct investment, arms
transfers and trade ties, as well as matters of economic and social distribution, are among the most prominent.

I would take the matter a step further by suggesting that I have
some doubts that dependency theorists actually operate as firmly and
universally within an orientation to knowledge that is "holistic and
particularistic" as Duvall would maintain. For one thing, as Duvall
himself admits, "there are exceptions of some importance" to this
tradition among dependency theorists, as when they speak of "cultural dependence of the Ivory Coast on France, or of the technological dependence of Brazil or Mexico."[20] He argues that, while this
"secondary usage" creates "a real ambiguity" it "does not justify
the position that the [notion of] measured dependence is central to
dependencia theory. It is not!"[21] Perhaps not. But even accepting
this assessment (for which no evidence is offered—does this issue
call for the late unlamented art of content analysis?) does the examination of a secondary, but still important, usage inevitably result in a
"misdirected and nonsensical enterprise"? I would, of course, argue
that it does not.

But the matter goes deeper. While Duvall emphasizes the concrete,
historical and descriptive side of dependency theory, it can hardly be
denied that among its most striking characteristics is the extremely
broad (totalistic?) nature of its *claims*, which often go far beyond the
unique and contextually bound situations on which they are based. In

fact one of the reasons I have tried in this study to include a larger number of countries than is typical even in cross-national analyses in this area is to provide an antidote to the strong tendency of dependency theorists to select for intensive analysis cases which, even on the face of it, seem to represent extreme examples of "dependency," however defined.

I maintain, then, that this study does have relevance to *some* of the concerns of dependency theorists. I need hardly repeat that I do not pretend that analysis in this mode can *replace* intensive descriptive analysis, or that this study has provided an unambiguous and final "test" of dependency theory as a whole, but only that it *complements* other modes of analysis, to the benefit, I would hope, of both.

APPENDIX TWO

Marxist Responses to Dependency Theory and Their Place in This Study: Arguments of Brenner

AS WAS SEEN IN CHAPTER 5, THE series of regressions on which an important part of this study was based generally confirmed dependency hypotheses: countries with relatively extensive and concentrated external ties *did* tend to exhibit the serious internal "structural distortions" (although not necessarily the slower economic growth) that dependency theorists predicted. It is important to repeat that this finding is not at all a product of the manner in which the problem was set up, and is not at all self-evident. On the one hand, it was entirely possible that in the regressions all of the independent variables together would have explained little of the variance in the dependent variables, that relationships would be few and weak; if this were the case, we would begin to doubt the explanatory power of the modes of external dependence and begin to look to other factors in explaining patterns of distribution in LDCs. On the other hand, it was just as possible that a pattern would have emerged in which relationships were frequent and strong, but were consistently in the direction predicted not by the dependency approach, but by the economic liberal-sociological modernization approaches discussed in chapter 4; if this were the case, we might begin to look more favorably upon these approaches.

But this is *not* what happened. As was indicated, most of the regressions revealed that "externally dependent" countries did demonstrate relatively inequitable patterns of distribution, and that this finding held up even when a number of controls were introduced and account was taken of potential contextually based discontinuities in the overall sample. Matters did not have to work out this way, but they did.

Of course, an essentially correlational exercise of the sort reported here does not definitively "prove" that a given mode of external dependence has a given effect. One way of putting the problem is that certain fundamental variables may not have been introduced into the analysis which, had they been included, would have caused the relationships reported here to "wash out." The range of potential variables of this sort is virtually unlimited, but attention is in practice probably best directed toward variables that previous scholars have proposed as relevant to the problems being explored.

Several such variables, those most often discussed in the mainstream economic development literature, have already been included in the model. But other variables, not so easily operationalized, have been proposed by a number of scholars of the left who operate within a framework of analysis that I will call *neotraditional Marxism*. These scholars reject the extreme optimism of the early Marx about the inevitable spread of capitalism and its ability to break down the "Chinese Walls" around prefeudal forms.[1] But they fully accept what they consider the more fundamental Marxist argument that the ultimate locus of development in any country is to be found not in its position in the world political economy, but in the unique pattern of class relations *within* that country. These scholars explicitly and emphatically reject the revision of Marx by Wallerstein and others that in their view redefines the class struggle between bourgeoisie and proletariat within every society as a struggle between a *world* bourgeoisie and a *world* proletariat. Neotraditional Marxists feel that, even aside from the practical implications such a redefinition has for workers' movements in developed countries, it is not at all true to Marx's main message that the fundamental dynamic of a country's history is ultimately to be found nowhere but in the history of class relations within that country.

An excellent example of this line of argument is found in a recent article by Robert Brenner in the *New Left Review* entitled "The Origins of Capitalist Development: A Critique of Neo-Smithian Marxism."[2] In this long article Brenner directly disputes what he views as the assumption of Wallerstein that "the growth in the world division of labour *is* the development of capitalism."[3] For Brenner this assumption is fundamentally misconceived; he would seek the locus of capitalist development not in global relations (Wallerstein's "trade-based division of labour") but instead precisely where Marx has proposed, in the "origin of the property/surplus extraction system (class system) of free wage labour, the historical process by which labour power and the means of production become commodities."[4] In Brenner's view Wallerstein confuses "production for exchange" with true capitalism; the latter, he maintains, operates only when and if large-scale wage labor emerges, and not before.[5] Did now-developed countries receive the impetus for their development when they began, in the "long" sixteenth century, to extract resources from peripheral areas? In Brenner's view they did not: capitalist development began only when there occurred in the now-industrialized countries "an *historically-evolved* correspondence between, on the one hand, the methods which the ruling class of landlords and tenants were required to use in order best to increase their surplus and, on the other hand, the requirements of the development of productive forces."[6] Similarly, for LDCs today: the only way to examine the dynamic of development is to "focus centrally on the productivity of labour as the essence and key to economic development."[7]

How does this debate relate to the analysis of this study? In one sense the application is straightforward and the predictions of neo-traditional Marxists can be placed in direct contrast to the predictions of other approaches. Dependency theorists, for example, would predict that high levels of external dependence would be associated with maldistribution and (except in certain cases such as Cardoso's "associated-dependent development") with economic stagnation in LDCs; adherents to the liberal economic-sociological modernization model would predict that external ties would be related to rapid economic growth as well as, at least in the long run, more equitable distribution in LDCs; literal adherents to the arguments of the early Marx would predict that external ties would be related to intensified class polarization in LDCs, but that rapid economic growth would flow from capitalist penetration into a precapitalist environment; and, finally, neotraditional Marxists like Brenner would predict little relationship in either direction between external ties and either growth or distribution in LDCs and would argue instead that development in LDCs, as was historically the case for now-developed countries, is the product not of external forces but of the unique pattern of class relations within each country.

The competing predictions are clear enough, and are quite easily incorporated into the structure of this study: if indicators of the development of "wage labor as a commodity" were somehow derived and introduced into the model, Brenner's approach would lead us to expect a substantial proportion of previously unexplained variance successfully to be explained.

But when we move beyond Brenner's arguments (perhaps beyond a point that Brenner himself would accept) the picture becomes muddied. For is it not possible that the issue may not be *whether* historically determined patterns of internal class relations within an LDC *or* its position in relation to a dominant capitalist world economy is the critical factor in explaining patterns of politics in LDCs, but that the two factors *interact* in some complex fashion? Is it not possible, for example, that a country's underlying pattern of class relations structures *both* the extent, concentration and form of external ties *and* the internal "structural distortions" that presumably reflect it?

These questions impel us toward the historical specificity that Duvall considers central to the language tradition within which dependency theorists have worked.[8] But in a fundamental way attention to underlying patterns of class relations transcends dependency approaches, for global relations are no longer conceived as the ultimate factor in explaining development and underdevelopment: primary importance is instead attributed to patterns of class formation that are essentially internal in nature, and to the extent that external factors enter the picture at all they are considered to be thoroughly conditioned by these internal factors.

How one might in practice explore neotraditional Marxists' hypotheses is a most difficult problem, for in most LDCs a wage-labor sector exists alongside a subsistence sector, and the boundary is rarely distinct. But even if such problems were successfully confronted, the argument that the emergence of wage labor as a commodity is the most fundamental impetus to capitalist development in LDCs is itself open to dispute, not only in a general sense by dependency theorists but much more directly by scholars like Arghiri Emmanuel, who argues in *Unequal Exchange* that the level of wages in LDCs is ultimately determined not by internal but by global forces. Emmanuel suggests that the power of developed countries to structure their exchanges with LDCs has resulted in a situation in which wages in the latter have been kept artificially low, with wage laborers quite simply receiving less value for an hour's work than do their counterparts in developed countries *even given* differences in productivity. For him Brenner's "fundamental" factor—the emergence and character of wage labor in LDCs—is in turn thoroughly conditioned by yet more fundamental global factors.[9]

And so it goes. The problem faced by social scientists is that at some point they must slice into the complex chain of causation that constitutes social reality and select factors which are inevitably, in some sense, epiphenomenal reflections of a "deeper" reality, but which are nevertheless interesting and important in their own right. After all, the findings reported here do have relevance to at least some of the hypotheses dependency theorists have typically proposed and some of the short- and medium-term policy prescriptions they have forwarded. Alternative explanations invoking more "fundamental" factors, especially those predicting relationships in the opposite direction from these findings, must confront not only dependency theorists and scholars like Emmanuel but also these findings. This study is, then, hardly the last word on the subject, but it does, I maintain, make a contribution to the debate.

APPENDIX THREE

Methods

THIS APPENDIX OFFERS A MORE DE-
tailed discussion of some of the methods employed in this study than
could be provided in the body of the text. The first part deals with the
multiple regression analysis of chapter 5, and the second with the Q-
factor analysis of chapter 6.

Techniques not explicitly discussed follow standard procedures, as
outlined in works by Blalock, Kerlinger and Pedhazur, Ferguson,
Kmenta, Hilton, Draper and Smith and others.[1]

With a few exceptions the statistical programs used in the study are
those described in Norman Nie et al., *Statistical Package for the
Social Sciences;* version 7.0 of SPSS was used for most runs.[2] The
data analysis was done on the IBM 360/370 installation of the Columbia University Center for Computing Activities.

THE MULTIPLE REGRESSION ANALYSIS

Significance Statistics

Since this study deals with a group of countries chosen for their interest, which is not a random sample of any larger population, significance statistics are employed only as a customary and useful means
of eliminating from consideration findings so weak that they might
easily have occurred even if values had been randomly assigned to
cases or so unstable that they might be expected to change dra-
matically even if a small number of additional cases were added to
the sample. No implication is made that nonsignificant relationships
do not really exist; all that is suggested is that they are weak enough
to be not worth reporting. Similarly, no implication is made that findings reported here have validity beyond the particular cases examined, a data set which does, however, encompass a relatively large

proportion of all non-oil-producing LDCs with populations greater than one million.

Clearly, inferential statistics are a mixed blessing in cross-national analysis, where "samples" are inevitably small and fixed. I suggest that readers take general note of significance statistics, but that attention be more closely focused on the magnitude of regression coefficients than on their significance level.[3]

Collinearity

As is well known, serious problems can arise when multiple regression analysis is attempted with independent variables that are highly intercorrelated. In this study, however, the use of R-factor analysis on most independent variables prior to the multiple regression analysis has allowed indicators that might have been highly intercorrelated in their raw state to be melded into composite factor scores. Of the 36 bivariate correlations among the seven independent variables and two controls used in the multiple regressions, no intercorrelation is greater than ±.55, and most are much less; since it is generally agreed that collinearity becomes a serious problem only when correlations among independent variables are greater than ±.80, we would not expect it to be a problem here.

Issues of Control

Of central importance in a study of this sort is the matter of control. In this section a somewhat more detailed discussion than could be provided in the text will be offered of the methods used in the multiple regression model to control for GNP per capita and natural resource endowment.

No problem arises when we focus on the proportion of variance in the dependent variable that is *uniquely* accounted for by each explanatory variable in the multiple regressions. But a decision is called for when we deal with variance whose explanation is *shared* by more than one variable, especially when one is a variable of substantive interest and the other a control variable. Which variable should get "credit" for shared variance, the indicator of external dependence or the control? The decision made can have important implications for the findings that are reported.

In this study the problem is not as serious as it might have been since variables of substantive interest and controls do not tend to be highly intercorrelated; table A3.1 reproduces the intercorrelations.

Table A3.1 Correlations between Controls and Independent Variables

Independent Variables	Controls	
	GNP per Capita	Natural Resource Endowment
Trade	−.04	.43
Finance	−.16	.08
Concentration	−.12	−.15
Aid-Trade Terms	−.51	−.06
Investment	.26	.40
Arms Transfers	.01	−.06
Students Abroad	−.41	−.16

Still, as can be seen, there are some moderate intercorrelations (were there not, control would have been unnecessary in the first place), and a decision on apportioning variance is called for.

We must first consider how previous scholars have addressed this issue. One study in which the matter is explicitly discussed is Verba and Nie's *Participation in America*. In this study the authors adjust physically for the effects of control variables by constructing a linear regression relating each control to the dependent variables, and then using the residuals from this analysis as dependent variables in further regressions.

When this technique is used, variance whose explanation is shared by a control and an independent variable is attributed *exclusively* to the control. Verba and Nie suggest some of the implications of such a procedure:

> If one or more of the control variables is associated with the independent variable . . . we are likely to be taking out too much by taking out all the linear effects of this control variable. In fact, whenever there is association we will be taking out some of the effects for which the control variables and the independent variable are jointly·responsible. Therefore, the strategy of analysis implied by the use of linear adjustment is a conservative one.[4]

For Verba and Nie's analysis such a conservative strategy makes a good deal of sense, since their "controls" (principally indicators of socioeconomic status) are among the variables most central to their explanatory model. For a cross-national study of the sort done here, on the other hand, we might well decide that differences among LDCs in GNP per capita and natural resource endowment, while they must be accounted for, are not of as central importance to the topic at hand as was the case in Verba and Nie's study: we would prefer in this study to focus as much as possible on the modes of external dependence.

Should, then, a method be used that allows jointly explained variance to be attributed exclusively to the variable of interest rather than to the control? This could easily be accomplished by entering control variables as the last step in a stepwise regression employing a hierarchical F-test.

In some ways this method would seem a useful way of testing dependency hypotheses. But, although it was experimented with, the decision in the end was not to employ it because, quite simply, just as Verba and Nie's method would provide too conservative a test of explanatory variables other than the controls, so this method would provide too liberal a test of dependency hypotheses.[5] A critic of dependency approaches might respond to the use of such a technique by suggesting that one of the most important goals of science is theoretical elegance or parsimony, and that if shared variance is substantial, it might rather be attributed to more basic and traditional variables like GNP per capita and natural resource endowment than to less "fundamental" variables like modes of external dependence. A dependency theorist would, of course, say just the opposite.

In this study the problem is addressed by using a simultaneous inclusion model with a standard F-test, a technique whereby each independent variable receives credit for its *unique* share of variance explained in the dependent variable, and shared variance is ignored in the computation of significance statistics for individual predictors (although not in the computation of R^2 for the entire equation). This traditional approach seemed best under the circumstances, but it should be remembered that it does result in a rather conservative test of both dependency hypotheses and the alternate hypothesis that most of the variance in the dependent variables is attributable to GNP per capita and natural resource endowment.[6]

Interaction

The multiple regression techniques used in this study require the assumption that the effects of explanatory variables are additive. In this section an examination will be made of the degree to which this assumption is violated in the basic regression analyses of the study.

An analysis was done for all first-order multiplicative interaction effects. (There are 36 for each regression.) First, all variables were converted to standard scores; this was to ensure that multiplicative interaction terms were not based on the particular units in which variables were measured, which could in some cases result in highly skewed interaction terms. Then all first-order interactions were entered into the equations and Kmenta's test for interaction employed: [7]

$$ F_{Q-K,\ n-Q} = \frac{SSR_Q - SSR_K / Q - K}{SSE_Q / n - Q} $$

where K = original variables
Q = original + new variables
n = number of cases

For the two dependent variables, *welfare* and *education budget,* the 36 interaction terms did not add significantly to the sum of squares explained. But for the dependent variable, *coercive potential,* the interaction terms did together add significantly to variance explained: the R^2 increased from .66 to .94 and the F-ratio derived from Kmenta's formula was significant at the .01 level.

Where do we go from here? The most desirable course of action would be to identify the particular interactions that accounted for most of the additional .28 of variance explained by the interaction effects and to include these in further regressions; we could simply say that when a pair of variables so identified varied *together,* their explanatory power received a boost above and beyond the explanatory power of each. This possibility was experimented with, but it was finally decided not to follow through on it. The reasons were these: first, an increase in R^2 from .66 to .94 did not really seem to indicate an equation *dominated* by interaction; and, second, the strongest individual interactions did not in this instance appear to be of great substantive interest, and their inclusion did not seem likely to add much to our overall understanding of the process of dependency. In sum the increased adherence to regression assumptions that would derive from the inclusion of interaction terms did not seem to justify the complication of the explanatory model that their inclusion would entail.

For *top 20 income share, bottom 40 income share* and *unemployment* an interaction test of the type proposed by Kmenta could not be done because of a paucity of cases. The 36 individual interaction terms were thus examined individually and it was found that, although a few were significantly related to dependent variables if entered as the last variable in the equation, none represented a really dominant interaction effect. Thus individual interaction terms were again not included in the general model. Further attention to interaction effects is no doubt in order, including attention to higher-order interactions, but I would propose that this await the development of a pared-down regression model, with fewer independent variables, that might be derived from this study.

Residuals and Regression Assumptions

In chapter 5 of this study regression residuals were discussed in an effort to identify individual countries that strayed from the generalizations expressed in the regression equations. In addition to this exercise a more systematic analysis of residuals was done in order to explore the extent to which the regressions violate assumptions necessary to their effective application and, especially, to the interpretation of significance statistics.[8]

The first and most important task was to examine the relationship between regression residuals and y-predict values for each equation. Scatterplots were constructed for each standardized y-predict-standardized residual pair and regression statistics computed to determine whether: (1) y-predicts and residuals were linearly related, which would imply that an important predictor had been omitted from the regressions on which they were based; (2) y-predicts and residuals were curvilinearly related, suggesting that nonlinear relationships were present that had not been accounted for; or (3) residual variance itself varied by level of y-predict, indicating that the homoscedasticity assumption of ordinary least squares regression had not been met.

The findings were as follows: (1) of the bivariate regressions relating each y-predict-residual pair, none was significant at the .10 level; (2) visual inspection of the scatterplots and an *F*-test for linearity (for a three-way breakdown of y-predict) provided no strong evidence of unincluded curvilinear relationships; and (3) visual inspection of scatterplots and examination of variance statistics for thirds of the general sample demarcated by level of y-predict suggested that heteroscedasticity was not a problem.

The next task was to examine the relationship between each *independent* variable and the regression residuals associated with it; evidence of any but a random relationship would suggest violations of regression assumptions traceable to an independent variable. Again, bivariate regression statistics were computed and scatterplots examined and again no bivariate regression was significant at the .10 level and no curvilinear relationship was in evidence.

The third and final task was to consider the distribution of residuals around the y-predict line; the assumption behind inferential regression statistics is, of course, that the distribution is normal. A good notion of how error is distributed can be achieved simply by examining the third and fourth moments of the dispersion of residuals about their mean. These statistics were calculated and it was found that the distribution of no residual indicated skewness or kurtosis greater than ± 1.00 except that associated with the regression attempting to explain variance in countries' *coercive potential*. As will be remembered, this problem, owing largely to the presence of semioutlier Jordan, was discussed in the text and an alternative regression without Jordan was constructed that differed only moderately from the whole-sample regression.[9]

In conclusion residuals analysis indicates that necessary assumptions about error do not appear to have been seriously violated by the multiple regression analyses of this study. For any minor violations of regression assumptions that may have remained undetected in this rather broad-based residuals analysis, it seems entirely reasonable to invoke regression analysis' famous "robustness," its relative imperviousness to minor violations of assumptions.

THE Q-FACTOR ANALYSIS

Q-factor analysis is rarely used in political science or sociological research, so it is useful briefly to list the techniques employed:

1. After some experimentation it was decided to use the thirteen indicators of external dependence rather than the composite dimensions derived from the R-factor analysis of chapter 3. The reason for this is that the larger number of "cases" that the former allowed for seemed to result in a more finely discriminated factor analysis solution.

2. These thirteen variables were standardized and the case-variable matrix transposed separately for the 29 countries of Black Africa, the 20 of Latin America and the Caribbean, the 11 of Asia, the 6 of the Middle East and the 4 of Southern Europe included in the study.

3. The transposed matrices were submitted to principal component

factor analysis with oblique rotation; 1.0 was used in the principal diagonal and Delta was set at 0.0.

4. The large number of variables (i.e., individual LDCs) in the factor analyses generally resulted in the extraction of a large number of factors, the last few of which tended to be weak and difficult to interpret, when the Kaiser criterion for factor rotation was employed. Accordingly, other criteria to determine the number of factors to be rotated were employed if their use made the findings more readily interpretable. For example, use of the Kaiser criterion resulted in the rotation of nine factors for the African subfile, with the last few factors weak and encompassing mostly secondary loadings; when the number of factors rotated was limited to five, the results were clearer and easier to interpret. (When a reduced number of factors was rotated, the eigenvalue of the last factor extracted was 2.40 and the five factors that remained still explained 80.6 percent of the total variance in the African cases.) Similarly, for the Latin American and Caribbean cases use of the Kaiser criterion resulted in the rotation of seven factors, but the results were most meaningful when their number was reduced to six. (The eigenvalue of the sixth factor was 1.46 and the six factors still explained 87.4 percent of the variance of these cases.) For the Southern European countries the problem was somewhat different. Here it was necessary to reduce the minimum eigenvalue cutoff from the Kaiser criterion value of 1.00 to 0.95; without this slight adjustment rotation could not have taken place, since only one factor would have been extracted.

Since the Kaiser criterion is an entirely arbitrary (if often useful) tool, there seems no difficulty in using slightly different criteria for selecting the number of factors to be rotated if this results in more meaningful findings.

5. The pattern loadings for each factor were coded and used as dependent variables in a series of multiple regression analyses in which the original indicators of external dependence were the independent variables.[10] The intention was to determine which variables produced the loadings on particular factors and the degree and direction of the relationship. The regression equations were constructed as follows:

Pattern loading on factor k =
b_1 (export concentration)
$+ b_2$ (exports)
$+ b_3$ (commodity concentration)

$+b_4$ (level of processing)
$+b_5$ (trade terms)
$+b_6$ (investment)
$+b_7$ (investment concentration)
$+b_8$ (reserves)
$+b_9$ (debt service)
$+b_{10}$ (arms transfers)
$+b_{11}$ (students abroad)
$+b_{12}$ (aid)
$+b_{13}$ (aid concentration)
$+$ error term

While this may seem a large number of variables relative to the number of cases available for this study, it should be remembered that the regression analysis only completes a closed circle that began when the original variables were converted to "cases" prior to the Q-factor analysis. Since the purpose of this exercise is only to recover variables already introduced, the F-ratios and other significance statistics tend to be very high despite the high ratio of cases to variables, and R^2s adjusted for the number of cases are similar to raw R^2s.

APPENDIX FOUR

Sources of Indicators

A COMMENT ABOUT THESE DATA

IN READING DRAFTS OF THIS study many people have expressed concern about the reliability of data from and about Third World countries. I share these concerns, and have been very careful to examine physically data for all variables, to construct frequency plots and to compute summary statistics in order to determine whether particular variables or values on them seemed improbable. Any random measurement error, either on my part or on the part of the original compilers, that may have crept into these data, would, of course, serve only to reduce correlations and add to unexplained variance.

But I think the unreliability of data for Third World countries can be exaggerated. Surely such data are improving very rapidly, thanks to the growing involvement since the late 1960s of the IBRD and the OECD in compiling data for LDCs and to the increasing sophistication of the United Nations and its specialized agencies and regional commissions in collecting and interpreting data. The result of this activity is that statistical data (aside from South American countries, for which data coverage has long been quite good) is incomparably better than was the case even in the mid-1960s. The prospects for meaningful cross-national research concerning Third World countries are, in my view, quite bright, and can only improve in the future.

THE INDICATORS OF THIS STUDY:
SOURCES AND COMMENTS

This appendix offers more detailed information about the indicators used in this study than could be provided in the text. The reader who desires still more detailed information is advised to consult the sources listed here, almost all of which devote considerable attention to definitions and methods. Full citations to sources are provided in the bibliography.

Exports Exports as a proportion of GNP, 1970

Source: United Nations Conference on Trade and Development (UNCTAD), *Handbook of Trade and Development Statistics,* 1972, table 1.1.

Missing: None.

Comments: Exports are in current prices F.O.B. Trade statistics vary somewhat among countries, especially in matters of transshipments; see the source for detailed comments.

Many previous studies have related imports plus exports to GNP in tapping the extent of trade dominance and dependence. This approach has much to recommend it, but in this study exports alone are related to GNP in order to remain consistent with other indicators of trade dependence (e.g., *commodity concentration*) which are of theoretical interest only when measured for exports. Import figures are not, however, ignored; they form the basis of the DC-LDC matrix for trade ties discussed in chapter 7. The data used in that chapter are derived from the same source.

Export Concentration Proportion of exports directed toward
the two principal export receiving countries, 1970

Source: United Nations, *Yearbook of International Trade Statistics,* 1974 and other issues.

Missing: None.

Comments: Although in all other instances partner concentration was formulated as a ratio of ties with a single partner to total ties, in the case of trade ties data for the two principal partners were employed. Upon examining the data for both formulations, I deemed the latter more appropriate since the range of partners was so much wider for trade ties than for any of the other linkages.

Commodity Concentration Modified Hirschman index of
export commodity concentration, 1972

Source: UNCTAD, *Handbook,* 1976, table 4.5.

Missing: None.

Comments: Commodities were defined at the three-digit SITC level. The modified Hirschman index is constructed according to the following formula:

$$H_j = \frac{m}{m-100} - \frac{100}{m-100} \sqrt{\sum_{i=1}^{n} \left(\frac{x_i}{X}\right)^2}$$

Where j = country index
n = number of commodities
m = minimum Hirschman index $\left(\frac{100}{\sqrt{n}}\right)$
x_i = value of commodity i
$$X = \sum_{i=1}^{n} x_i$$

(The standard Hirschman index is thus modified to run from zero to 1.0, with the latter representing the most extreme concentration.)

Level of Processing   Galtung's Trade Composition Index, 1970

Source: United Nations, *Yearbook of International Trade Statistics,* 1974 and other issues.

Missing: None.

Comments: The construction of an index of this sort requires an operational distinction between "processed goods" and "primary products." The operational definition of the former is derived from UNCTAD, *Trade in Manufactures of Developing Countries and Territories,* 1973, and includes SITC sections 5 through 8 less 68 (nonferrous metals) and also less 667 (gemstones), "exports of which from developing countries consist mainly of the raw products of mining"; 711 (power-generating machinery, nonelectric), "exports of which from developing countries consist largely of aircraft and other engines being returned to the country of origin for repairs and modifications"; and 735 (ships and boats), "exports of which from developing countries except Yugoslavia consist mostly of secondhand ships." "Primary products" are defined as SITC sections 0–4, 667 and 68, although it is acknowledged that these categories include certain semiprocessed goods, particularly foodstuffs. SITC sections 711, 735 and 9 are not included in the calculations. It should be noted that considerable rounding went into the calculation of this index.

As was noted in the text, the direction of this index has been reversed.

Terms of Trade   Terms of trade, unweighted average,
1968–1971

Source: IBRD, *World Tables 1976,* table 11.

Missing: None.

Comments: In the words of the source

> . . . terms of trade are a measure of the relative level of export prices as compared with import prices. Also called "net barter terms of trade," they are calculated as a ratio of the export price index to the import price index—or, alternatively, of the export unit value index to the import unit value index. The terms of trade therefore show changes over time in the relative level of export prices as a percentage of import prices.

As was noted in the text, the direction of this scale has been reversed.

Investment   Estimate of private direct investment owned by firms based
in OECD-DAC countries, end-1971, as a proportion of 1971 GNP

Source: OECD, *Development Co-operation,* 1972, table IV-4.

Missing: Mauritius.

Comments: Distinguishing direct investments from portfolio investments and determining the nationality of ownership of investment holdings are among the central questions in measuring this variable; detailed explanations of the criteria used and an extensive discussion of sources are provided in OECD-DAC, *Stock of Private Direct Investments.* These figures have been updated from the end-1967 figures given in this source; supplementary data and the assumptions made are described in the first source cited above.

Investment Concentration   Proportion of total private direct investment
from firms based in OECD-DAC countries from firms based
in the principal investor country, end-1967.

Source: OECD-DAC, *Stock of Private Direct Investments.*
Missing: Mauritius, Yugoslavia.

Aid   Official Development Assistance receipts of LDCs, 1969–1971
average, as a proportion of 1970 GNP

Source: OECD, *Development Co-operation,* 1972, table 23.
Missing: None.
Comments: In formulating this indicator, multilateral flows (about 16 percent of total
ODA in 1971) were included along with bilateral flows; this seemed the best way to
reflect the arguments of critics of economic assistance programs such as Theresa
Hayter (*Aid As Imperialism*) that many multilateral programs are no less damaging to
LDCs' sovereignty than are bilateral programs.

Aid Concentration   Proportion of Official Development Assistance supplied
by the principal donor, 1969–1971

Source: OECD, *Development Co-operation,* 1973, table 26. For Congo, Gambia,
Guyana and Mauritius the source is OECD, *Development Co-operation,* 1974, and
the indicator is based on 1969–1972 averages.
Missing: While data are available for this indicator for all cases, it was decided not to
include in any computations data for Spain, Yugoslavia or Greece. The reason is that
these countries in 1969–1971 received so little ODA (less than .2 percent of GNP)
that concentration figures are misleading.

Debt Service   Adjusted annual 1–15 year debt service as
a proportion of current exports, 1970

Source: OECD, *Development Co-operation,* 1973, table IV-4.
Missing: None.
Comments: This debt service ratio is constructed, in the words of the source, to
express

> . . . debt service due in the next 15 years, less the difference between end-1971
> gross reserves and two months' imports (1968–1970 average) as a percentage of
> 15 years' export earnings at the present annual rate (1968–1970 average). The
> . . . data . . . are based on amounts outstanding, including undisbursed, since
> future debt service payments are only available on this basis.

Reserves   International reserves at the end of 1970 as a
proportion of imports in the preceding year

Source: United Nations, *World Economic Survey,* part 2, 1974, table IV-16. Certain
data are derived from United Nations, *Statistical Yearbook,* 1974, tables 148 and
192.
Missing: None.
Comments: The Liberian government maintains no official reserves; see IMF, *Surveys of African Economies,* vol. 6, p. 278.

As was noted in the text, the direction of this scale has been reversed.

Arms Transfers   Value of arms transfers from major suppliers,
1965–1974, as a proportion of 1970 GNP

Source: United States Arms Control and Disarmament Agency, *World Military Expenditures and Arms Transfers, 1965–1974,* table II.
Missing: None.
Comments: The following is the definition of *arms transfers* used in the source:

> Arms transfers represent the international transfer under grant, credit or commercial sales terms of military equipment usually referred to as "conventional." . . . Excluded are foodstuffs, medical equipment, and other material potentially useful for the military but with alternative civilian uses. . . . The data represent arms transfers to governments and do not include the value of arms obtained by subnational groups. (p. 7)

Students Abroad   University students studying abroad in fifty selected
countries as a proportion of total university enrollments, c.1970

Source: UNESCO, *Statistical Yearbook,* 1972, table 4.8 (for students abroad) and tables 5.1 and 5.2 (for total university students). Data for the Gambia and Mauretania refer to 1968 and derive from UNESCO, *Statistical Yearbook,* 1970 and United Nations Economic Commission for Africa, *Survey of Economic Conditions in Africa,* 1970, part 1; these figures refer to forty host countries rather than fifty.
Missing: None.
Comments: Students enrolled in the fifty host countries represent about 95 percent of the known total. For full definitions see the source.

Educational Enrollment   Gross educational enrollment ratio for the
first and second levels of schooling, c.1970

Source: UNESCO, *Statistical Yearbook,* 1974, table 3.2.
Missing: None.
Comments: For exact definitions of the components of this indicator see the source; for a more general discussion see Taylor and Hudson, *World Handbook of Political and Social Indicators,* p. 203. Data for Haiti, Pakistan, India and Lebanon are for 1965; data for Chad and Mauritania cover only primary education.

Social Insurance Programs   Extent of social insurance
coverage, early 1971

Source: United States Department of Health, Education, and Welfare, *Social Security Programs Throughout the World, 1971.*
Missing: No data are missing, but data for the fourteen former French African colonies are not included in the analysis. The reason is that these data describe almost identical programs that seem unrealistically extensive in terms of coverage. To avoid including data for programs that exist mostly on paper, these countries are excluded.
Comments: Many programs applied only to employed persons (and sometimes their families), and domestic or family laborers are often explicitly excluded. Programs were coded as present even if it was indicated that they applied only to certain regions and were in effect in other regions only "within the limits of facilities available." Certain other programs were coded as present if they were mandated or supervised by government authority even if the government did not directly contribute to

them. Certain sickness and maternity programs were coded as present even if they included only maternity benefits.

Programs were not coded as present if they consisted only of mandatory severance pay or if they applied only to public employees.

Social Welfare　Composite indicator of infant mortality, life expectancy, literacy and caloric consumption, 1970

Sources: For the first three, James Howe, ed., *The U.S. and the Developing World: An Agenda for Action,* 1974. For the last, United Nations Food and Agricultural Organization, *Production Yearbook,* 1972.

Missing: None.

Comments: Various gaps in the data were filled by reference to the United Nations *Demographical Yearbook* and other standard sources. The direction of the infant mortality indicator was, of course, reversed.

Education Budget　Educational expenditures as a proportion of total public expenditures, c. 1970

Sources: The principal source was UNESCO, *Statistical Yearbook,* 1974, table 6.1. Supplementary sources were UN, Economic Commission for Africa, *Survey of African Economies,* part 1; Ruddle and Odermann, eds., *Statistical Abstract for Latin America,* 1972; and United Nations, *Statistical Yearbook,* 1972, 1973 and 1974.

Missing: None.

Comments: In a few cases data on capital expenditures were not available, and current educational expenditures were related to total current expenditures.

Direct Taxes　Direct taxes as a proportion of total government revenue, 1970

Source: IBRD, *World Tables, 1976.*

Missing: None.

Top 20 Income Share, Bottom 40 Income Share　Shares in the distribution of household income, as near as possible to 1970

Sources: Chenery and Syrquin; Chenery et al.; and Paukert. Also consulted was Adelman and Morris, *Economic Growth and Social Equity.* For income share of the top 5 and bottom 20 percent of the population the source was IBRD, *World Tables, 1976.*

Missing: Cameroun, Central African Empire, Congo, Ethiopia, Gambia, Ghana, Liberia, Malawi, Mali, Mauritania, Mauritius, Rwanda, Somalia, Togo, Upper Volta, Zaire, Egypt, Jordan, Syria, Guatemala, Haiti, Paraguay, Afghanistan, Indonesia, Singapore.

Unemployment　Unemployed as a proportion of the total labor force, c, 1970

Source: IBRD, *World Tables, 1976,* table 3.

Missing: Benin, Burma, Chad, Ethiopia, Malawi, Rwanda, Niger, Nigeria, Sudan, Tanzania, Zaire, Cameroun, Gambia, Haiti, India, Kenya, Madagascar, Mauretania, Thailand, Togo, Ecuador, Guatemala, Paraguay, Indonesia, Pakistan, Central African Empire and Mali.

Comments: In the words of the source "the unemployed are usually defined as persons who are able and willing to take a job, who are out of a job on a given day, have remained out of a job, and were seeking work during the enumeration period."

Military Expenditures Total military expenditures as a proportion of GNP, 1970

Sources: United States Arms Control and Disarmament Agency, *World Military Expenditures.* For Mauritius, Stockholm International Peace Research Institute, *World Armaments and Disarmament,* 1974. For Nigeria, Costa Rica, Indonesia and Ecuador, Robert C. Sellers, *Armed Forces of the World: A Reference Handbook,* 3d ed.
Missing: None.

Military Manpower Manpower in military service per 1,000 population

Sources: Same as for *Military Expenditures.*
Missing: None.
Comments: Gambia has no army; security duties are carried out by 150 men within the Gambian police establishment. Costa Rica has no formal army, but it maintains a 1,200-man Civil Guard that serves as a virtual army.

Internal Security Forces Internal security forces per 1,000 population

Sources: Primary source: Sellers, *Armed Forces of the World.* Secondary source: T. N. Dupuy, *The Almanac of World Military Power.* For Republic of Korea, a 1965 estimate from Taylor and Hudson, *World Handbook of Political and Social Indicators.*
Missing: None.
Comments: A general discussion of data on internal security forces is offered in Taylor and Hudson p. 20.

GDP Growth Rate Average annual growth rate of gross domestic product at market prices, 1970–1974

Source: UNCTAD, *Handbook of International Trade and Development Statistics,* 1976, table 6.2.
Missing: Data are missing for Jordan; data for Nigeria, Indonesia, Ecuador and Tunisia are not included in the analysis because they were or became major oil producers during this period.
Comments: These figures "have in general been calculated from an exponential trend . . . from data at constant market prices." See the source for more detailed comments.

GNP Per Capita Gross national product in 1970, in market prices in United States dollars, divided by mid-1970 population estimate

Source: OECD, *Development Co-operation,* 1973, table IV-4.
Missing: None.
Comment: GNP at market prices differs from GNP at factor cost in that it includes indirect taxes. Many studies, especially early studies, focus on the latter; for those interested in comparison, it is noted that estimates of GNP at market prices are generally about 20 percent higher than estimates of GNP at factor cost. See Delacroix, "The Export of Raw Materials," p. 800, footnote 1.

Natural Resource Endowment   Index of natural resource endowment,
c.1970

Sources: Principal source: John P. Albers et al., *Summary of Petroleum and Selected Mineral Statistics.* Supplementary source: United Nations, *Yearbook of International Trade Statistics,* 1974.

Missing: None.

Absolute Population, Absolute GNP   Absolute population and
gross national product, 1970

Source: IBRD, *World Bank Atlas,* 1973.

Missing: None.

Notes

1. WHAT THIS BOOK IS ABOUT

1. William G. Tyler and J. Peter Wogart, "Economic Dependence and Marginalization: Some Empirical Evidence," p. 36.

2. James A. Caporaso, "Introduction: Dependence and Dependency in the Global System," *International Organization* (Winter 1978), 32:5. Caporaso refers to an article by Raymond Duvall in the same issue of *International Organization*. Duvall's arguments can only be done justice in a fairly extensive discussion, which is offered in appendix I of this study, " 'Rigorous Empiricism' and Dependency Theory: Mismatched Language Traditions?"

3. Douglas A. Hibbs, *Mass Political Violence*, pp. 201, 202. The studies referred to are Edwin Kuh and John R. Meyer, "How Extraneous Are Extraneous Estimates?" p. 381; and Kuh, "The Validity of Cross-Sectionally Estimated Behavior Equations in Time Series Applications," pp. 207–8.

4. Richard Rubinson, "Reply to Bach and Irwin," p. 820.

5. *Ibid.*, p. 819. Rubinson refers to Morris Zelditch, "Intelligible Comparisons," p. 282.

6. Although careful attention has been given to indicators of distribution and the pervasiveness of social welfare, this study remains at the whole-nation aggregate level. A useful discussion of difficulties in interpreting such data is offered in Guillermo O'Donnell, *Modernization and Bureaucratic-Authoritarianism*, pp. 22–26. But a case for nation-level aggregate analysis is made by Morris Zelditch in "Intelligible Comparisons"; Zelditch argues that "the state is the unit of investigations of economic development because it is the largest permanent source of the kinds of decisions that determine the conditions of economic growth" (p. 282). Whatever the merits of these arguments any large-scale study of Third World countries is, of course, in practice limited by data unavailability to whole-nation aggregate analysis.

7. McGowan and Smith, for example, repeated Walleri's analysis (which included both developed and less developed countries) for the LDCs only and discovered that many of his findings were considerably altered. Rubinson, on the other hand, did find similar patterns for developed and underdeveloped countries, although many of his coefficients were reduced. See Patrick J. McGowan and Dale L. Smith, "Economic Dependency in Black Africa," p. 199; and Richard Rubinson, "Dependence, Government Revenue and Economic Growth, 1955–1970," p. 17. The study referred to by McGowan and Smith is R. Dan Walleri, "The Political Economy of International Inequality,"

8. Susanne Bodenheimer, "Dependency and Imperialism," p. 347.

9. Guy J. Gilbert, "Socialism and Dependency," p. 108.

10. George Lichtheim, *Imperialism,* p. 39.

11. David Ray, "The Dependency Model of Latin American Underdevelopment," p. 8.

12. A useful contribution along these lines is provided in Uwe Stehr, "Unequal Development and Dependency Structures in COMECON."

13. I have not mentioned the last category, relations among LDCs. Here one thinks particularly of relations between semideveloped and less developed countries, which have excited considerable interest among dependency theorists. For a discussion of this literature see chapter 6; some suggestions as to how research into inter-LDC relations might be conducted are offered in chapter 8.

14. Philip J. O'Brien, "A Critique of Latin American Theories of Dependency," p. 24.

15. *Ibid.* McGowan and Smith discuss these issues and review a number of works in these areas; see *passim.*

16. John S. Odell, "Correlates of U.S. Military Assistance and Military Intervention," p. 145.

2. SOME PREVIOUS CROSS-NATIONAL QUANTATIVE TESTS OF DEPENDENCY THEORY

1. A list of studies in this mode, aside from the seven discussed in this chapter, would include the following articles as of early 1979: Richard Vengroff, "Dependency and Underdevelopment in Black Africa" and "Neo-Colonialism and Policy Outputs in Africa"; Albert Szymanski, "Dependence, Exploitation, and Economic Growth"; Richard Rubinson, "The World-Economy and the Distribution of Income Within States" and "Dependence, Government Revenue, and Economic Growth, 1955–1970"; R. Dan Walleri, "Trade Dependence and Underdevelopment"; Neil R. Richardson, "Political Compliance and U.S. Trade Dominance"; Elisabeth L. Gidengil, "Centres and Peripheries"; W. Ladd Hollist and Thomas H. Johnson, "Modelling United States / Latin American Cooperation and Conflict"; James L. Ray and T. Webster, "Dependency and Economic Growth in Latin America"; and David Snyder and Edward L. Kick, "Structural Position in the World System and Economic Growth, 1955–1970." The ongoing work of the Yale Dependence Project, under the direction of Bruce Russett, should also be mentioned; see Steven Jackson et al., "Conflict and Coercion in Dependent States"; Raymond Duvall et al., "A Formal Model of 'Dependencia' Theory: Structure and Measurement"; and Duvall and Russett, "Some Proposals to Guide Research in Contemporary Imperialism."

2. Tyler and Wogart, "Economic Dependence and Marginalization."

3. *Ibid.,* p. 38.

4. *Ibid.,* p. 42.

5. *Ibid.,* p. 43.

6. *Ibid.,* p. 42.

7. Chase-Dunn, "The Effects of International Economic Dependence on Development and Inequality."

8. The three indicators are GNP per capita, 1950 and 1970; kilowatt hours of electricity consumed per capita, 1950 and 1965; and the percentage of the male labor

force employed in agriculture, 1950 and 1960. The former two indicators are transformed according to a logarithmic function.

9. Economic development level is also essentially controlled in the first set of equations, since this variable at an earlier point in time is included as an independent variable in the panel regression model.

10. Chase-Dunn, p. 726.

11. In an earlier study Chase-Dunn did include trade indicators in his analysis, with similar results. See his "International Economic Dependence in the World System."

12. Alschuler, "Satellization and Stagnation in Latin America."

13. *Ibid.*, p. 77.

14. As described by Osvaldo Sunkel, "the great concentration in one or two main cities of each country . . . poses a striking disequilibrium. . . . It is perhaps precisely in the ecological characterization of the main cities of Latin America that the phenomenon of internal polarization becomes most dramatic and explicit." Osvaldo Sunkel, "Transnational Capitalism and National Disintegration in Latin America."

15. Alschuler, p. 63.

16. Particularly the following works: Organisation for Economic Co-operation and Development (OECD), *Stock of Private Direct Investment by D.A.C. Countries in Developing Countries, End-1967* and its annual updates; and OECD, *Development Co-operation*. Much more will be said about these and other data sources in the next chapter.

17. In Alschuler's analysis Venezuela measures almost three standard deviations below the mean in both "satellization" and "development," while no other case is much more than one standard deviation from the mean in either direction. The extreme scores seem to result from the facts that Venezuela, already at a high level of GNP per capita and the educational indicator in 1960, did not change as much relative to this high level as did some of the other members of the sample and that Venezuela is, of course, *much* more heavily penetrated by foreign investment (in oil) than any other Latin American country. Leaving aside the obvious fact that Venezuela's situation today is very different from that in 1960–1965, two questions are in order: (1) Would the findings change substantially if GNP per capita were entered as a control? (2) Would the findings change substantially if the single case of Venezuela had been omitted? The answer to each of these questions, even from cursory examination of Alschuler's data and the plot of his first canonical variate, seems to be an unequivocal yes.

18. McGowan, "Economic Dependence and Economic Performance in Black Africa"; and McGowan and Smith, "Economic Dependency in Black Africa: An Analysis of Competing Theories."

19. McGowan, p. 35.

20. McGowan and Smith, p. 233. McGowan and Smith have in mind Marx's predictions of the inevitable spread of capitalism and its ability to break down the "Chinese Walls" around less developed areas of the world. In appendix II I distinguish this approach from both dependency theory and from what I call "neotraditional" Marxist approaches, which focus on the development of wage labor as a commodity as the key factor in capitalist development and express skepticism about a central role in this process of global forces.

21. See table 3.1 of this study for a listing of the authors' indicators of external ties. The source of their trade verticality indicator is Irma Adelmen and Cynthia Taft Morris, *Society, Politics, and Economic Development.*
22. West, "Economic Dependence and Policy in Developing Countries."
23. *Ibid.*, p. 167. A final indicator, "technical assistance received," was marginally significant on a Spearman ranking but was excluded from the general test. It was experimentally included in the main series of equations with similar, but weaker, results.
24. It should be noted that only one of these variables is at an interval level of measurement; the others are dichotomous or trichotomous.
25. Kaufman et al., "A Preliminary Test of the Theory of Dependency," *Comparative Politics* 7 (April 1975).
26. See *ibid.*, p. 311, for a complete description of these indicators.
27. *Ibid.*
28. See *ibid.*, pp. 314–15, for a statement of the formal hypotheses the authors are testing.
29. *Ibid.*, p. 329.
30. As can be seen, in the West and Kaufman et al. articles "external dependence" serves as a dependent variable in a slightly different model.
31. One of the few attempts to collect data on a number of noneconomic North–South linkages is that of Marshall Singer in *Weak States in a World of Powers.*

3. OPERATIONALIZING EXTERNAL DEPENDENCE

1. Johan Galtung, "A Structural Theory of Imperialism," pp. 87–91.
2. Karl Deutsch, "Theories of Imperialism and Neocolonialism," pp. 25–26.
3. Reginald H. Green and Ann Seidman, *Unity or Poverty?* pp. 37–51.
4. Matters have not always worked out quite so badly: recent Brazilian coffee crop failures have not only resulted in higher coffee prices, but have so encouraged diversification that Brazil is now one of the world's leading exporters of soybeans.
5. It should be noted that two arguments were not discussed in this section. A first is the contention that the domestic well-being and strategic security of *DCs* rests in large measure on their trade relationship with LDCs, which provide them with essential raw materials. Critics of this argument suggest that, on the contrary, LDC trade is becoming ever *less* essential to the well-being of industrial nations, a fact attested to by the continual decline in non-oil-producing LDCs' already small share in world trade. These competing arguments are not directly addressed in this study, since they would require analysis of the trade relations of *developed* countries rather than LDCs.

A second argument is that of H. W. Singer and (from a different point of view) Arghiri Emmanuel that vertical trade is not so much a matter of the nature of products exchanged as of the conditions under which they are produced: Singer stresses differences in the level of technological development of DCs and LDCs, Emmanuel differences in wage rates. For these scholars the indicator of trade verticality used in this study (based on the relative level of processing of goods exchanged) is, if not wholly misleading, not the most direct indicator of trade dependence (although they would probably accept the other three trade indicators used in this study); they would prefer indicators based more directly on differences in technological resources or man-hours that went into the production of goods exchanged. I am not aware of any cross-national studies of dependency hypotheses that have attempted to develop such indicators, and I think any effort in this area would require a study of its own, probably a case study or a comparison of a small number of countries. I would suggest that this study touches on Singer's and Emmanuel's points in a general way, but does not offer a specific or detailed test of their hypotheses. See Arghiri Emmanuel, *Unequal Exchange;* and H. W. Singer, "The Distribution of Gains from Trade—Revisited."

6. These arguments have been often and persuasively criticized. A principal criticism is that simply comparing investment earnings and capital flows for a single year is misleading, since capital outflows represent earnings on *past* investments. For examples of this counterargument see Benjamin Cohen, *The Question of Imperialism;* David Ray, "The Dependency Model of Latin American Underdevelopment"; and Charles Nisbet, "Transferring Wealth from Underdeveloped to Developed Countries Via Private Direct Investment."

7. Stephen Hymer, "The Multinational Corporation and the Law of Uneven Development," p. 114.

8. Citation from Celso Furtado in Osvaldo Sunkel, "Big Business and 'Dependencia,' " p. 527.

9. Jack Woddis, *An Introduction to Neocolonialism,* p. 97. See also Judith Hart, *Aid and Liberation;* Theresa Hayter, *Aid As Imperialism;* Tibor Mende, *From Aid to Recolonization;* Denis Goulet and Michael Hudson, *The Myth of Aid;* and Susanne Bodenheimer, "Dependency and Imperialism." For a novel and striking fictional treatment see John Updike, *The Coup* (New York: Knopf, 1978).

10. Bodenheimer, pp. 352–53. Bear in mind the assessment of one commentator, generally sympathetic to dependency arguments, that "aid does indeed accelerate infuence, but it is not a prime candidate for the role of neocolonialist villain assigned to it by some commentators." Henry Bretton, *Power and Politics in Africa,* p. 69.

11. One case study in this mode is Andrzej Krassowski, *Development and the Debt Trap.* See also Cheryl Payer, *The Debt Trap.*

12. The contagion effect is examined in Jerry Weaver, "Arms Transfers to Latin America."

13. Thomas John Bossert, "Dependency and Disintegration of the State," p. 15. See also Steven Jackson et al. "Conflict and Coercion in Dependent States."

14. The high cost of military expenditures in LDCs and its impact on other policy initiatives is discussed in Milton Leitenberg, "Notes on the Diversion of Resources for Military Purposes in Developing Nations."

15. See, for example, Juan E. Corradi, "Cultural Dependence and the Sociology of Knowledge"; Karl P. Sauvant, "Multinational Enterprises and the Transmission of Culture"; *Latin American Perspectives* 5 (Winter 1978), special issue on "Culture in the Age of Mass Media"; and Jacques Delacroix, "Permeability of Informational Boundaries and Economic Growth."

16. A useful survey of media ties is offered in UNESCO, *World Communications.* Peter B. Evans makes the striking estimate that in Brazil, expenditures of American manufacturing affiliates on advertising are a third as large as recurring public expenditures on all forms of education; see Evans, "National Autonomy and Economic Development."

17. Eugene Wittkopf, *Western Bilateral Aid Allocations,* p. 31.

18. Another is the problem of thresholds. This concerns the possibility that ratio indicators will be misleading if there are limits above or below which the factor of interest is unlikely to go. It is possible, to cite an example, that even for very small countries economic assistance grants will not fall below a certain minimum: an expensive project like a dam or road is either built or not built and is of no use if half-finished.

For most of the variables used here this is not, however, a serious problem. One reason is that countries with very small populations are excluded: only three LDCs studied had populations of less than one million in 1970. Another is that GNP rather than population is usually used as the standardization term, which means that very large populations in the subsistence sector will have some effect on aggregates (as they should) but will not have an undue effect.

19. Wittkopf himself suggests that such standardization is "defensible" (p. 31), and the serious problems that he experiences in his regressions as a result of outliers might have been ameliorated if standardization for country size had been done.

20. As will be seen, the regressions will also include GNP per capita and an index of natural resource endowment as control variables.

Some scholars have expressed misgivings about the uninformed use of ratio variables and have advised that regression residualizing is often a preferred alternative. They agree, however, that when concern is indeed with relative and not absolute amounts, correlation among ratios is entirely acceptable—provided that inference is not extended to relationships among absolute (unstandardized) variables. Indeed, regression residualizing itself has drawbacks, especially when degrees of freedom are at a premium or when extensive transformations of very abnormally distributed raw variables would be required. On the topic of ratio variables see Karl Schuessler, "Analysis of Ratio Variables: Opportunities and Pitfalls," p. 395; and on the topic of residualizing for control purposes see Fred N. Kerlinger and Elazar J. Pedhazur, *Multiple Regression in Behavioral Research*, pp. 415–18.

21. Or, in some cases, the proportion of total transactions with OECD countries. For trade ties two principal partners are focused upon; see appendix IV for a discussion.

22. This indicator is described in some detail in Galtung, pp. 101–3.

23. IMF, *Balance of Payments Yearbook;* United Nations, *External Financing of Economic Development;* United States, Department of Commerce, *Survey of Current Business.* Stefan Robock and Kenneth Simmonds, in *International Business and Multinational Enterprises,* p. 45, cite a number of sources for major Western countries.

24. OECD, *Stock of Private Direct Investment.* The figures cover investments from firms based in the United States, the United Kingdom, France, Belgium, the Federal Republic of Germany, Canada, the Netherlands, Austria, Denmark, Australia, Italy, Japan, Norway, Portugal, Sweden and Switzerland.

Although the OECD has annually revised summary investment stocks figures, an updated study incorporating the detailed sectoral and source breakdown offered in the 1972 study has not been undertaken and is not now underway. Personal communication from Iman Wilkins, Private Investment Section, Development Co-operation Directorate, OECD, May 31, 1979.

25. Public investments are, however, included in the totals when they are deemed to have been motivated by "business-type considerations." *Ibid.,* p. 138.

26. The report cautions that these figures probably underrepresent the true extent of private direct investment in LDCs, but there is no reason to suspect that this introduces bias in comparing one LDC to another. *Ibid.*, p. 135. See also Robock and Simmonds, p. 44.

27. One study of direct investments by LDC firms in the U.K. indicated that they amounted to less than one hundredth of the amount of private direct investments by U.K. firms in LDCs. See OECD, *Stock of Private Direct Investments*, p. 158.

28. OECD, *Development Co-operation*, 1972, p. 45.

29. Tibor Mende, in *From Aid to Recolonization*, likens the term *foreign aid* to an artichoke, whose leaves "have to be plucked one by one. Many have to be discarded as worthless. Others contain the nutritive substance responsible for its reputation" (p. 42). The definition employed here comes close to including only the "heart" of the artichoke as defined in some detail by Mende.

30. It is recognized that substantial increases have recently occurred in the debt burden of many LDCs, especially since 1972 (although some analysts express doubt that, given the rate of economic growth and world inflation, these increases have been as large as they might seem from the absolute figures). These increases are not included in these figures which, to remain consistent with the other indicators of the study, are based on the situation in 1970. Future analysis might focus more closely on debt trends; the basic figures are published regularly in the World Bank's *World Debt Tables*. Another useful survey of basic debt and reserves figures is Irving S. Friedman, *The Emerging Role of Private Banks in the Developing World*.

31. OECD, *Development Co-operation*, 1973, p. 77 (note to Table IV.4).

32. Reginald H. Green, "Political Independence and the National Economy," p. 290. For an analysis of monetary ties from a dependency perspective see S. R. Dixon-Fyle, "Monetary Dependence in Africa: The Case of Sierra Leone."

33. The term *comprador* derives from early Portuguese trade with China. It originally referred only to native employees of foreign trading companies, but in the dependency literature it often takes on the broader connotations of "bridgehead" or "internationalized" elite.

34. West, p. 67.

35. Kaufman et al., p. 313.

36. Like Kaufman et al., McGowan and Smith performed an *R*-factor analysis on their indicators of external dependence and found some interesting patterns, but returned to their original variables for subsequent analysis. See McGowan and Smith, p. 216.

37. The correlation matrix discussed in this paragraph includes all of the independent variables of the study, including those that were excluded from subsequent *R*-factor analysis for reasons already cited.

38. Delta was set at 0.0, and 1.0 was placed in the principal diagonal.

4. THE DOMESTIC CONSEQUENCES OF EXTERNAL DEPENDENCE
I. A Survey of the Literature

1. Lichtheim, *Imperialism*, p. 12.
2. *Ibid.*
3. Karl Deutsch, "Theories of Imperialism and Neocolonialism," pp. 15–17, 21–24; and Joseph Schumpeter, *Imperialism and Social Classes*.
4. Tom Kemp, "The Marxist Theory of Imperialism," p. 17.

5. J. A. Hobson, *Imperialism: A Study;* and V. I. Lenin, *Imperialism: The Highest Stage of Capitalism* (the standard International Publishers text.) Although Lenin's *Imperialism* has certainly had an important influence on world history, opinion on its merit as a scholarly work has often been negative. As put by Alexander Erlich, "the use of *Imperialism* as a basic text has probably had more to do with Lenin's stature as the leader of a victorious revolution than with his prominence as a theorist." John Kenneth Galbraith concurs, remarking that "not even a committed disciple could think it an impressive work, although many have risen to the occasion. It is assertive and contentious, and although very short, it is very tedious." Alexander Erlich, "A Hamlet without the Prince of Denmark," p. 36; John Kenneth Galbraith, *The Age of Uncertainty,* p. 147.

6. Hobson's underconsumptionist thesis has been often and persuasively attacked. See, for example, D. K. Fieldhouse, "Imperialism: An Historiographical Revision."

7. Lenin, p. 216.

8. *Ibid.,* p. 217.

9. Alfred Meyer, *Leninism,* p. 263.

10. As late as the spring of 1917 (a year after *Imperialism* was written), Lenin maintained that the Revolution would occur first in highly developed countries, and that the Russian Revolution then underway was an "accident of history." In April 1917, he expressed his astonishment at events in Russia: "Marx said that France would start and Germany would finish the job. And now, what do you know?—the Russian proletariat has achieved more than anyone else!" Quoted in Meyer, p. 253.

11. This is not to say that many particular elements of Lenin's approach have not been very influential in the formulation of later dependency approaches. For example, his ideas on informal means of control sound very modern: he suggests that there is "a variety of forms of dependence," one of which occurs when "countries which, formally, are politically independent are, in fact, enmeshed in the net of financial and diplomatic dependence" (p. 234). He also stresses the notion of "comprador elite" when he says that "it is not difficult to imagine the solid bonds that are . . . created between British finance capital . . . and the Argentine bourgeoisie, the leading businessmen and politicians of that country" (pp. 234–235).

12. Ronald Robinson, "Non-European Foundations of European Imperialism," p. 118.

13. For classic statements of the structuralist viewpoint see Gunnar Myrdal, *Rich Lands and Poor;* H. W. Singer, "The Distribution of Gains between Investing and Borrowing Countries"; and United Nations [Raul Prebisch], *Towards a New Trade Policy for Development.* Good discussions of the evolution of the thought of several early structuralists later prominent in the development of dependency theory are offered in Harold Brookfield, *Interdependent Development,* pp. 133–51; and Joseph A. Kahl, *Modernization, Exploitation and Dependency in Latin America.*

14. The argument that LDCs' terms of trade have deteriorated is very controversial among economists, but there is little doubt that it is widely accepted among Third World policymakers, so much so that one economist has termed this argument the "new orthodoxy" of North-South trade, as opposed to the old orthodoxy of comparative advantage. See James Ingram, *International Economic Relations,* pp. 84–94.

15. With, of course, varying success. For a good review of efforts in this area see

H. Jon Rosenbaum and William G. Tyler, "South-South Relations: The Economic and Political Content of Interactions Among Developing Countries."

16. There are some exceptions among dependency theorists; see, for example, Michael Barratt Brown, *The Economics of Imperialism,* in which the argument is made that terms of trade for LDCs have alternately improved and deteriorated over the last century.

17. Arghiri Emmanuel, *Unequal Exchange,* pp. 145–46, 148. Emmanuel is hardly a typical dependency theorist, but on this, I think, he expresses the mainstream view.

18. Proposed alternatives to the present system are almost invariably vague, often invoking such notions as "World Socialism." This all-or-nothing approach is criticized by I. William Zartman in "Europe and Africa: Recolonization or Dependency?" A very pessimistic prognosis for alternatives to the present order, at least in the near future, is offered in Immanuel Wallerstein, "Dependence in an Interdependent World: The Limited Possibilities of Transformation within the Capitalist World-Economy."

19. Galtung, "A Structural Theory of Imperialism."

20. *Ibid.,* p. 83.

21. Deutsch, p. 27.

22. Lucian Pye, *Aspects of Political Development,* pp. 8, 10.

23. The quotation is from Chase-Dunn, p. 725. He cites Wilbert Moore and David Feldman, *Labor Commitment and Social Change in Developing Areas* (New York: Social Science Research Council, 1960).

24. Mende, p. 6.

25. Julio Cotler, "The Mechanics of Internal Domination and Social Change in Peru," pp. 409–10. He cites Andrew G. Frank, "La participación popular en lo relativo a algunos objetivos económicos rurales," unpublished manuscript.

26. Eric Wolf, *Peasant Wars of the Twentieth Century,* ch. 1.

27. Rodolfo Stavenhagen, "Seven Fallacies about Latin America," p. 19.

28. A more extended discussion of these issues, making a distinction between traditional Marxists and what I will call "neotraditional" Marxists, is offered in appendix II. A good introduction to Marx's thought on the subject is offered in Owen and Sutcliffe, eds., *Studies in the Theory of Imperialism,* especially the essays by Kemp and Barratt Brown. This useful collection also contains an extensive annotated bibliography of primary and secondary sources.

29. Shlomo Avineri, ed., *Karl Marx on Colonialism and Modernization,* p. 3.

30. Raul A. Fernandez and Jose F. Ocampo, "The Latin American Revolution," p. 36.

31. Paul A. Baran, *The Political Economy of Growth,* p. 221.

32. *Ibid.,* pp. 221–22.

33. Fernando Henrique Cardoso, "Associated-Dependent Development," p. 160.

34. *Ibid.,* p. 163. One is reminded, by the co-optation of potentially destabilizing elements described by Cardoso, of Barrington Moore's description of the Indian caste system: "Any attempt at innovation . . . simply became the basis of another caste. . . . Thus, [even] opposition to society and preying on society became a part of society in the form of bandit castes." Barrington Moore, Jr., *Social Origins of Dictatorship and Democracy,* p. 458.

Could something similar be said about academic political scientists' and sociologists' scramble to embrace "dependency theory" as an established subfield within their disciplines? Dependency has, for example, become a regularly represented—indeed, quite fashionable—topic at annual meetings of the American Political Science Association and the American Sociological Association, much as was the case ten or fifteen years ago with modernization theory. An interesting reaction to such developments from a prominent Latin American dependency theorist is offered in Fernando Henrique Cardoso, "The Consumption of Dependency Theory in the United States."

35. Green, p. 275.

36. Brookfield, p. 157.

37. Richard Sklar, *Corporate Power in an African State*, p. 8.

38. *Ibid.*, p. 199.

39. *Ibid.*, p. 208.

40. James Petras and Thomas Cook, "Dependency and the Industrial Bourgeoisie," p. 163.

41. Colin Leys, *Underdevelopment in Kenya;* and Theodore H. Moran, *Multinational Corporations and the Politics of Development.*

42. Cardoso, p. 149.

43. *Social and Economic Studies* 22 (March 1973). An earlier and more optimistic version of Sunkel's thesis is offered in "National Development Policy and External Dependence in Latin America."

44. Sunkel, p. 143.

45. *Ibid.*, pp. 147–148.

46. *Ibid.*, p. 163.

47. *Ibid.*, pp. 145–146.

48. Jose Serra, "The Brazilian 'Economic Miracle,' " p. 120. An earlier study by Frank draws similar conclusions; see Andre Gunder Frank, "On the Mechanisms of Imperialism."

49. Serra, p. 121.

50. Thomas Weisskopf, "Capitalism, Underdevelopment, and the Future of the Poor Countries," p. 59.

51. Jackson et al., p. 628.

52. Andre G. Frank, "The Development of Underdevelopment," pp. 9–13.

53. *Ibid.* Many would argue that commercial contact of this sort is actually precapitalist. For a summary of such arguments and a refutation see Luis Vitale, "Latin America: Feudal or Capitalist?"

54. Sunkel, "Big Business," p. 520; Sunkel, "National Development Policy"; Bodenheimer, pp. 332, 339; Weisskopf, pp. 44, 54ff.; Walter Rodney, *How Europe Underdeveloped Africa;* Kwame Nkrumah, *Neo-Colonialism;* James O'Connor, "International Corporations and Economic Underdevelopment," pp. 56–57; and Samir Amin, "Development and Structural Change: The African Experience," p. 330. Dos Santos suggests that dependent countries can expand only as a reflection of the developed countries and, while he admits that this can have either a positive or a negative effect on economic growth, the implication is that the effect will almost always be negative. See Theotonio dos Santos, "The Structure of Dependence."

55. Rubinson, "Dependence, Government Revenue and Economic Growth." Rubinson suggests that Brazil, South Korea and other fast-growing LDCs have experi-

enced rapid economic growth because they have "autonomous and authoritarian political regimes which provide the political conditions necessary for development" (p.
23).

56. Bill Warren, "Imperialism and Capitalist Industrialization."

57. *Ibid.*, p. 12.

58. *Ibid.*, pp. 4, 44.

59. A rather expansive definition of "development" as opposed to "growth" is
offered in Ronald Chilcote and Joel C. Edelstein, "Introduction: Alternative Perspectives on Development and Underdevelopment in Latin America," p. 28.

60. Arghiri Emmanuel, "Myths of Development Versus Myths of Underdevelopment," p. 63. See also Andre G. Frank, "Dependence Is Dead, Long Live the
Theory of Dependency and the Class Struggle," p. 100.

61. Philip McMichael, James Petras, and Robert Rhodes, "Imperialism and the
Contradictions of Development," p. 87.

62. Cardoso, "Associated-Dependent," p. 156.

63. *Ibid.*, p. 149.

64. This is what dependency theorists focus on when they speak of exploitation. It
is even possible, one would think, that a particular DC-LDC relationship which was
definitely to the detriment of an LDC would not confer any advantage at all on the
DC partner: it may have been so incompetently handled by DC interests that potential
benefits did not accrue, or it may have been motivated by benevolent but misguided
considerations. I think most dependency theorists would consider such a relationship
exploitative nonetheless if the LDC partner were the worse for it, whatever the DC
intentions or gains. Most dependency theorists, however, suggest that the usual mo-
tive behind DC contact with LDCs is profit, and that they (or the leading sectors in
them) usually profit from dependency relations.

5. THE DOMESTIC CONSEQUENCES OF EXTERNAL DEPENDENCE
II. The Basic Regression Model

1. Phillips Cutright, "Political Structure, Economic Development, and National
Social Security Programs." The indicator used here differs from the Cutright index
in that it is not multiplied by the number of years (over a given time period) that programs were in effect.

2. Many scholars question the validity of using ordinal-level measurements in statistical techniques that strictly require measurement at the interval level. See, for example, Thomas Wilson, "A Critique of Ordinal Measurement"; and Lawrence
Mayer, "A Note on Treating Ordinal Data as Interval Data." This practice is
avoided in this study, but in a few cases it seemed justified. For arguments and evidence supporting the practice see Sidney Verba and Norman Nie, *Participation in
America*, appendix G; Edward Tufte, "Improving Data Analysis in Political
Science"; and Sanford Labovitz, "The Assignment of Numbers to Rank-Order
Categories."

3. Hibbs, *Mass Political Violence*, pp. 54ff.; Jackman, *Politics and Social Equality*, pp. 21–25. The individual variables were scaled in this manner instead of being
entered separately into the factor analysis because it was judged that all four *together*
were about as important in the explanatory model as any of the other individual
variables—it is clear that caloric consumption, literacy and so on are in themselves

further removed from theoretical concerns than are the other dependent variables. If all four were individually entered into the factor analysis, they would tend to dominate it by sheer weight of numbers in a manner unfavorable to the overall concerns of the study.

4. Hibbs, p. 57.

5. Jackman, p. 164. The quotation is from Richard A. Musgrave, *Fiscal Systems*, p. 173.

6. As the result of a recent OECD study, comparable income distribution data are now available for most OECD members; see Malcom Sawyer, "Income Distribution in OECD Countries."

7. Robert Jackman, in *Politics and Social Equality*, was forced to rely exclusively on sectoral income distribution figures for data on the central dimension of his study. He indicates that Paukert's data "came to my attention only as the book was going to press." The book was published in 1975. See his "The Need for Reader Access to Measures of Variables Used in Quantitative Cross-National Studies." Even some very recent cross-national tests of dependency hypotheses have employed data on sectoral income distributions, including Walleri's and Gidengil's studies, both published in 1978.

8. Irma Adelman and Cynthia Taft Morris, *Economic Growth and Social Equity in Developing Countries;* Chenery and Moises Syrquin, *Patterns of Development, 1950–1970;* Chenery et al., *Redistribution with Growth;* Felix Paukert, "Income Distribution at Different Levels of Development"; and IBRD, *World Tables 1976.*

9. Since data are unavailable for so many cases on so important a variable, it is worthwhile to do an analysis of variance relating availability of data on this indicator to each of the other variables in the study in order to determine how representative are the cases for which data are available. The analysis was done for three variables with significant amounts of missing data: *top 20 income share* and *bottom 40 income share,* each with 25 missing data points, and *unemployment* with 27. For all of these variables data availability was significantly related to GNP per capita, the control; this is not at all surprising, since the ability to collect data is itself an important characteristic of economic development. For *top 20 income share* and *bottom 40 income share* there was also a significant relationship with *students abroad.* (Countries with missing data had higher scores on *top 20 income share* and lower scores on *bottom 40 income share.*) No other mode of external dependence demonstrated a significant relationship to the availability of data on these variables, and it thus seems that the cases for which data are available on these variables are more or less typical of those for which they are unavailable, at least in terms of the level of external dependence.

Nevertheless, data were *not* replaced by any formula, weighted or otherwise, for these or any other dependent variables in the study, and all significance tests employed utilize only as many cases as are available on the dependent variable in a given equation.

10. United States, Arms Control and Disarmament Agency, *World Military Expenditures and Arms Transfers, 1965–1974,* pp. 6–7.

11. Gidengil and Alschuler employ "deviational change" indicators to measure GDP growth rates: they simply use as their economic growth indicator residuals from a regression that uses time $t - 1$ GDP per capita to explain time t GDP per capita.

Such a strategy causes serious difficulties: any least squares regression used to relate variables as abnormally distributed as GDP per capita estimates is almost sure to involve error that is *highly* heteroscedastic and thus to cause concern about violation of the assumptions of even so robust a technique as ordinary least squares regression. See Gidengil, p. 54 and Alschuler, p. 66.

12. Arghiri Emmanuel, in "Myths of Development Versus Myths of Underdevelopment," p. 71, disagrees. His point is that population increases represent increases not only in consumers but also in potential producers. This point was taken into consideration, but the considerations cited above prevailed; populations, after all, tend to increase most at the top and bottom end of the age scale, where productive potential is most limited.

13. While all other indicators in this study are based on gross *national* product, the economic growth indicator is based on gross *domestic* product. This is in deference to the argument of Szymanski and others that, by excluding most income generated in the foreign-owned sector, use of GNP growth rates unfairly biases findings against the hypothesis that foreign contact fosters growth. I recognize that there is another side to this argument, but upon consideration I decided that a GDP-based indicator was preferable. See Szymanski, p. 64, footnote 10.

14. We must assume that other differences among LDCs are largely embodied in the broad variables explicitly chosen for control, that they are not relevant to the issues at hand or that they have individually minor effects that are not mutually reinforcing, but tend to cancel one another out.

15. Chenery and Syrquin, *Patterns of Development;* Grant Reuber, *Private Foreign Investment in Development*.

16. Carlos F. Diaz-Alejandro, "North-South Relations," p. 214.

17. See appendix III for a detailed discussion of statistical control in relation to this study.

18. Chenery and Syrquin, p. 152.

19. By John P. Albers et al.

20. The *b*'s and beta weights are not identical since this is not true of all independent variables and since the control variables are not in standardized form. The regressions are, of course, based on ordinary least squares principles.

21. For readers whose background in regression may be rusty, the following explanations should be helpful: a *beta weight* expresses the predicted change in a dependent variable for each one-unit change in an independent variable when both are measured in standard deviation units; a *significance level* gives the liklihood that demonstrated relationships have occurred solely by chance; and R^2 (the coefficient of determination) expresses the proportion of variance in the dependent variable attributed to all of the independent variables and controls together.

22. Cardoso, "Associated-Dependent Development," p. 149.

23. Sunkel, "Transnational Capitalism," p. 143.

24. Weisskopf, "Capitalism," p. 52.

25. Analysis of parallel subsamples of the general sample based on region reveals that this relationship is strongest for African LDCs. In sub-Saharan Africa, where class structures are not as rigid as in many other parts of the underdeveloped world, higher education abroad appears most likely to serve as a vehicle of social mobility.

26. Taylor and Hudson, p. 124.

27. For a similar use of this transformation see Donald Morrison et al., *Black Africa: A Comparative Handbook.*

28. A "communality analysis" was done to determine the contribution to variance in *Coercive Potential* uniquely explained by "external interventions." For a discussion of this technique see Fred N. Kerlinger and Elazar J. Pedhazur, *Multiple Regression in Behavioral Research,* pp. 297–305.

29. See chapter 2 of this study for a summary of these authors' findings.

30. Cardoso, p. 156; Emmanuel, p. 77.

31. There is also a close relationship with *arms transfers,* but this is not discussed because it is not directly relevant to dependency predictions.

32. Judith Hart, *Aid and Liberation;* Theresa Hayter, *Aid As Imperialism;* and Denis Goulet and Michael Hudson, *The Myth of Aid.* It must be noted that *Aid-Trade Terms* also has a terms of trade component that helps to account for its variance.

6. A REGIONAL PERSPECTIVE OF EXTERNAL DEPENDENCE
I. A Q-Factor Analysis

1. Immanuel Wallerstein, "Class Formation in the Capitalist World-Economy."

2. Samir Amin, *L'Afrique de l'Ouest Bloquée,* cited in Immanuel Wallerstein, "Dependence in an Interdependent World," pp. 13–14.

3. Stephen Hymer, "The Multinational Corporation," p. 114. For a more specific application in the African context see Kenneth W. Grundy, "Intermediary Power and Global Dependence."

A related use of a center-periphery framework involves applications to relations not among nations but among geographical regions within a single country. A good example is a study by Julio Cotler of the "structural dualism" between the dominant coast and the subordinate sierra in Peru. Another very interesting article, by Michael Hechter, applies center-periphery imagery to interethnic relations in a more general way. See Julio Cotler, "The Mechanics of Internal Domination and Social Change in Peru"; and Michael Hechter, "Towards a Theory of Ethnic Change."

4. Richard Rubinson, "Dependence, Government Revenue and Economic Growth," pp. 23–24, does discuss these matters in general terms, but he does not introduce them into his statistical analysis.

5. Examples of other techniques used in similar research are: R. D. McKinlay and A. S. Cohan, "A Comparative Analysis of the Political and Economic Performance of Military and Civilian Regimes"; and sociometric choice methods in William Minter, *Imperial Network and External Dependency.* Some previous uses of *Q*-factor analysis include Arthur S. Banks and Phillip Gregg, "Grouping Political Systems: A *Q*-Factor Analysis of *A Cross-Polity Survey*"; and Bruce M. Russett, *International Regions and the International System.*

6. Actually on pattern loadings from an oblique factor solution. Appendix III discusses the *Q*-factor analysis in more technical detail.

7. Samir Amin, "Underdevelopment and Dependence in Black Africa." Note that this article is available in three slightly different versions; all references are to the *Journal of Peace Research* text.

8. Only countries among the twenty-nine Black African countries covered in this study are listed in the discussion of Amin's groups.

9. Amin, p. 115. A good description of both of these practices can be found in Geoffrey Gorer, "Taxation and Labor Practices in French West Africa."

10. Amin, p. 117.

11. *Ibid.*

12. *Ibid.*, p. 114.

13. *Ibid.*, p. 106.

14. *Ibid.*, p. 115. A discussion of African migration from a dependency perspective is offered in Joel W. Gregory and Victor Piché, "African Migration and Peripheral Capitalism."

15. Amin, p. 106.

16. The factors for this region are discussed out of sequence for reasons of clarity of presentation.

17. All figures here and elsewhere in this chapter are, unless otherwise noted, from the main data bank.

18. To avoid the ennui that often sets in when a reader is confronted with reams of undigested figures, the findings of the regression equations are presented verbally in the next sections. A finding is reported only if it is statistically significant at the .01 level.

19. Of Zambia's exports 95.3 percent are devoted to copper; for Zaire the figure is 66.0 percent. Of Mauritius' exports, 90.7 percent are sugar cane, while 84.0 percent of Gambia's exports are groundnuts or groundnut oil. Figures are for 1970.

20. As has been indicated, Chile also clusters with the "Andean" group.

21. Kaufman et al., p. 329.

22. *Ibid.*

23. Figures are from the general data bank and also from United Nations, Economic and Social Commission for Asia and the Pacific, *Statistical,* various issues.

24. Very few dependency theorists have emerged from the milieu of Asian studies. It seems that this is not a coincidence, but is reflective of the fact that Asian countries tend simply to be *less* dependent than the countries of Latin America and Africa that dependency theorists have most emphasized. To explore this possibility, an analysis of variance was conducted for the indicators of external dependence, and it was found that four (*investment, concentration, trade* and *students abroad*) were indeed significantly lower for South and East Asian countries than for Latin American, African or Middle Eastern countries; only one (*arms transfers*) was significantly higher. Thus it appears that Asian countries *do* tend to be on the whole less dependent than are LDCs of other regions, except in the political-strategic arena represented by statistics on arms transfers.

25. In this spirit a series of analyses of covariance was conducted relating membership in the subgroups identified in this chapter, along with the metric controls, to the dependent variables identified in chapter 5. The findings were, however, disappointingly unilluminating, owing largely to the limited number of cases that regional analysis of this sort allows.

7. A REGIONAL PERSPECTIVE ON EXTERNAL DEPENDENCE
II. Linking LDCs to Their Principal Partners

1. See Galtung, "A Structural Theory of Imperialism"; Klaus Jürgen Gantzel, "Dependency Structures as the Dominant Pattern in World Society"; Bruce J. Ber-

man, "Clientelism and Neocolonialism"; Jorge Dominguez, "Mice that Roared"; Jon A. Christopherson, "Structural Analysis of Transaction Systems"; Minter, *Imperial Network;* and Russett, *International Regions.*

2. See, for example, Gantzel, p. 204.

3. Underlying concentration is, of course, the relative *extent* of LDCs' external ties; as will be seen, this dimension will also enter the analysis of this chapter, although rather roughly.

4. Of the modes of external dependence dealt with in this study, only ties of external finance (the debt service and reserves holdings indicators) are not represented in this chapter.

5. The method used in this chapter is simple categorization. After some consideration it was decided that the application of data reductive statistical techniques would in this instance sacrifice more in clarity than it offered in power, and that the most instructive approach was the relatively simple one used here.

6. The eighteen partners are the United States, the Soviet Union, France, the United Kingdom, Japan, the Federal Republic of Germany, India, Pakistan, Italy, Switzerland, Brazil, Canada, Belgium-Luxembourg, Chile, the Netherlands, Spain, Uruguay, and Singapore. Several other countries, important in the trade of only one or two LDCs, were also listed where necessary.

7. In this section imports rather than exports are used as an indicator of trade dependence. This was thought to be a useful corrective to previous chapters, which focus largely on exports.

8. These particular criteria were chosen because they seemed to result in an illuminating division of the raw data. They are, however, arbitrary, and different criteria might have resulted in somewhat different findings.

As will be seen, the criteria employed differ from one mode of external dependence to another, and the analyses are thus not strictly comparable. It does, however, seem reasonable to compare broad patterns across modes of external dependence, and it is in this spirit that such comparisons are made.

9. The reasons for the limited outside presence that does occur are evident: the two North African states established American contact during the Second World War and have maintained it since; Togo was a League of Nations mandate and was thus perhaps less closely administered than other French colonies and was, moreover, administered in part by Britain; and Mali was long dominated by radical officers with ties to the Soviet Union.

10. Belgium and Luxembourg constitute a fully integrated trade bloc and data on trade are collected jointly.

11. There are many sources on this subject. Among the most interesting are Gerard and Victoria Curzon, "Neo-Colonialism and the European Community"; Negosava Petrovic, "Relations between the European Community and the 18 Associated African Countries"; and I. William Zartman, *The Politics of Trade Negotiations between Africa and the European Economic Community.*

12. Commonwealth preferences, as well as the trade preferences offered by France to her colonies or by the EC to its associates, should not be confused with the "Generalized System of Preferences" proposed by the United Nations Conference on Trade and Development (UNCTAD). In fact the two are diametrically opposed: the first three are selective, while the last would apply equally to all LDCs.

It should also be noted that the French actually subsidized certain of their colonies' exports—the so-called *suprix* that these products received on the French market.

13. As has been indicated, data in this detail are available only for end-1967. Data on investment concentration are not available for Yugoslavia or Mauritius. Only investment from OECD-DAC members is considered.

14. But note that Britain has a long history of portfolio investment overseas, the amounts of which are not included in these figures.

15. There might be some disagreement over the exact composition of the "never a colony" grouping. Ethiopia was, of course, occupied by Italy in this century and Haiti a French colony until the early nineteenth century; Greece and parts of Yugoslavia were once Turkish colonies; and Egypt and Jordan were for some time British protectorates, although both were formally independent by the 1920s. All were coded 1.

8. FUTURE DIRECTIONS

1. See especially Immanuel Wallerstein, "Class Formation in the Capitalist World-Economy," and "Dependence in an Interdependent World." Although this study has included data on such ties where available and appropriate, the data have often tended to become lost in the overall figures for LDCs' external ties, which are, of course, dominated by ties with developed market economy countries.

2. A good example of how the second strategy might be enacted is found in Alice H. Amsden, "Trade in Manufactures between Developing Countries."

3. Data on labor migrations are especially difficult to interpret, since migrants from neighboring countries into, say, Nigeria or Venezuela, are often of less-than-legal status.

4. Or, to cite an even more complex possibility, how would we categorize portfolio investment by wealthy Brazilians in American multinationals that then invest heavily in Bolivia? Untangling such flows would be most difficult.

5. See chapter 1 for a fuller discussion of longitudinal analysis as related to this study.

6. Obviously, I do not mean to imply that any such determination is exact.

APPENDIX ONE: "RIGOROUS EMPIRICISM"

1. Duvall, "Dependence and Dependencia Theory." It is very important to note that this section does *not* discuss Duvall's argument that tests of dependency hypotheses must carefully focus on dynamic elements by means of time series analysis. This issue has already been discussed in chapter 1.

2. Duvall, p. 57.

3. *Ibid.*, pp. 52, 54, 60.

4. *Ibid.*, p. 60.

5. *Ibid.*, pp. 60, 68.

6. *Ibid.*, p. 56.

7. *Ibid.*, p. 59.

8. *Ibid.*, p. 55. The quotation is from Fernando Henrique Cardoso and Enzo Faletto, "Preface to the American Edition," *Dependency and Development in Latin America.*

9. *Ibid.*

10. Duvall, p. 53.
11. *Ibid.*, p. 56, quotation from Cardoso and Faletto.
12. Duvall, p. 74.
13. *Ibid.*
14. *Ibid.*, p. 68.
15. Duvall criticizes the practice of "rigorous empiricists" of focusing on discrete countries rather than transnational classes. But he does not follow up on this suggestion, and his proposals for improving dialogue, as expressed in his example of how a better specified model would look, uses individual nations as units. I think I have in part addressed this objection by focusing on economic and social distribution in LDCs, but much more must be done in this area. Some suggestions were made in chapter 8; the reader might also consult chapter 1, note 6, in which this matter was briefly discussed.
16. *Ibid.*, p. 68.
17. *Ibid.*, p. 77.
18. Raymond Duvall et al., "A Formal Model of 'Dependencia' Theory;" pp. 47ff. of the typescript version. The measurement strategies Duvall describes have been further elaborated in Steven Jackson et al., "Conflict and Coercion in Dependent States."
19. Duvall, p. 60.
20. *Ibid.*, p. 58, footnote 16.
21. *Ibid.*, p. 59, footnote 20.

APPENDIX TWO: MARXIST RESPONSES

1. A good discussion of the traditional Marxist view is provided in McGowan and Smith. Marx's own views on the subject are clear, well expressed in his frequently cited comments in a New York *Herald Tribune* article: "England has to fulfill a double mission in India: one destructive, the other regenerating—the annihilation of the old Asiatic society and the laying of the material foundations of Western society in Asia." Quoted in Barratt Brown, "A Critique of Marxist Theories of Imperialism," p. 46.
2. *New Left Review* no. 104 (May–June 1977).
3. *Ibid.*, p. 54.
4. *Ibid.*, p. 53.
5. *Ibid.*, p. 50.
6. *Ibid.*, p. 78.
7. *Ibid.*, p. 91.
8. Duvall's notion of dependency seems closely identified with that of Wallerstein. See Appendix I.
9. Five appendixes offer an interesting series of exchanges between Arghiri Emmanuel and Charles Bettelheim, who argues from a position in many respects not unlike that of Brenner.

APPENDIX THREE: METHODS

1. Hubert M. Blalock, *Social Statistics;* Kerlinger and Pedhazur, *Multiple Regression;* George A. Ferguson, *Statistical Analysis in Psychology and Education;* Jan

Kmenta, *Elements of Econometrics;* Gordon Hilton, *Intermediate Politometrics;* and N. R. Draper and H. Smith, *Applied Regression Analysis.*

2. Norman Nie et al., *Statistical Package for the Social Sciences.*

3. See on this point Bruce M. Russett, "Some Decisions in Regression Analysis of Time-Series Data," p. 34; and Blalock, *Social Statistics,* pp. 162–63.

Unless otherwise noted, one-tailed tests were performed, on the assumption that dependency theory offers a clear expectation of the direction of relationships. A useful discussion of the interpretation of one-tailed tests, and an argument that they are underused in social and behavioral research, is offered in Ferguson, *Statistical Analysis,* pp. 150–51. For the application of one-tailed tests to regression coefficients see Hilton, *Intermediate Politometrics,* pp. 64–69. Finally, for a classic justification of the use of one-tailed tests in the kinds of research reported here, see Henry F. Kaiser, "Directional Statistical Decisions."

4. Sidney Verba and Norman H. Nie, *Participation in America: Political Democracy and Social Equality,* p. 408.

5. Some misgivings about the indiscriminate use of stepwise regression are offered in Michael Lewis-Beck, "Stepwise Regression: A Caution."

6. A communality analysis was done, which decomposed unique effects of individual variables as well as joint effects of each control-independent variable combination. The results were, however, not very instructive since the communalities (i.e., the proportions of variance shared by more than one variable) tended to be very small: there are 511 unique and joint effects in all (including higher-order joint effects) for each multiple regression in this study. For a discussion of communality analysis see Kerlinger and Pedhazur, *Multiple Regression,* pp. 297–305.

7. Kmenta, pp. 456–57.

8. The analysis followed closely that suggested in Draper and Smith.

9. The assumption that regression residuals be uncorrelated with one another is not examined; since the data of this study are cross-sectional and were arranged alphabetically there is no reason to suspect autocorrelation.

10. This technique was suggested by Professor Gerald Finch of Columbia University. I later came across a similar application in J. Barry Riddell, *The Spatial Dynamics of Modernization in Sierra Leone.*

Selected Bibliography

Adelman, Irma and Cynthia Taft Morris. *Economic Growth and Social Equity in Developing Countries*. Stanford: Stanford University Press, 1973.
—— *Society, Politics, and Economic Development: A Quantitative Approach*. Baltimore: Johns Hopkins University Press, 1967.
Albers, John P., M. Devereux Carter, Allen C. Clark, Anny B. Coury, and Stanley P. Scheinfurth. *Summary of Petroleum and Selected Mineral Statistics for 120 Countries and Offshore Areas*. United States Geological Survey Professional Paper Number 817. Washington, D.C.: Government Printing Office, 1973.
Alschuler, Lawrence R. "Satellization and Stagnation in Latin America." *International Studies Quarterly* (March 1976), 20:39–82.
Amin, Samir. *Accumulation on a World Scale*. 2 vols. New York: Monthly Review Press, 1974.
—— "Development and Structural Change: The African Experience." In Barbara Ward, J. D. Runnals, and Lenore D'Anjou, eds., *The Widening Gap: Development in the 1970s*, pp. 312–33. New York: Columbia University Press, 1971.
—— "Underdevelopment and Dependence in Black Africa: Historical Origin." *Journal of Peace Research* (1972), 9:105–19.
Amsden, Alice H. "Trade in Manufactures between Developing Countries." *Economic Journal* (December 1976), 86:778–90.
Arrighi, Giovanni and John S. Saul. *Essays on the Political Economy of Africa*. New York: Monthly Review Press, 1973.
Avineri, Shlomo. *Karl Marx on Colonialism and Modernization*. Garden City, N.Y.: Doubleday, 1969.
Banks, Arthur. *Cross-Polity Time Series Data*. Cambridge: M.I.T. Press, 1970.
Banks, Arthur and Phillip Gregg. "Grouping Political Systems: A Q-Factor Analysis of *A Cross-Polity Survey*." *American Behavioral Scientist* (November 1965), 9:3–6.
Baran, Paul A. *The Political Economy of Growth*. New York: Monthly Review Press, 1957.

Barratt Brown, Michael. "A Critique of Marxist Theories of Imperialism." In Roger Owen and Bob Sutcliffe, eds., *Studies in the Theory of Imperialism*, pp. 35–70. London: Longman, 1972.

Berman, Bruce J. "Clientelism and Neocolonialism: Center-Periphery Relations and Political Development in African States." *Studies in Comparative International Development* (Summer 1974), 9:3–25.

Blalock, Hubert M., Jr. *Social Statistics*, 2d ed. New York: McGraw-Hill, 1972.

Bodenheimer, Susanne. "Dependency and Imperialism: The Roots of Latin American Underdevelopment." *Politics and Society* (May 1971), 1:327–57.

Bossert, Thomas John. "Dependency and the Disintegration of the State: Lessons from Allende's Chile." Paper prepared for delivery at the 1977 annual meeting of American Political Science Association, Washington, D.C.

Brenner, Robert. "The Origins of Capitalist Development: A Critique of Neo-Smithian Marxism." *New Left Review* (May–June 1977), no. 104, pp. 25–92.

Bretton, Henry. *Power and Politics in Africa*. Chicago: Aldine, 1973.

Brookfield, Harold. *Interdependent Development*. London: Methuen, 1975.

Caporaso, James A. "Dependence and Dependency in the Global System: A Structural and Behavioral Analysis." *International Organization* (Winter 1978), 32:13–44.

—— "Introduction: Dependence and Dependency in the Global System." *International Organization* (Winter 1978), 32:1–12.

—— Methodological Issues in the Measurement of Inequality, Dependence, and Exploitation." In Steven Rosen and James Kurth, eds., *Testing Theories of Economic Imperialism*, pp. 87–114. Lexington, Mass.: D. C. Heath, 1974.

Cardoso, Fernando Henrique. "Associated-Dependent Development: Theoretical and Practical Implications." In Alfred Stepan, ed., *Authoritarian Brazil: Origins, Policies, and Future*, pp. 142–78. New Haven: Yale University Press, 1973.

—— "The Consumption of Dependency Theory in the United States." *Latin American Research Review* (1977), 12:7–24.

Cardoso, Fernando Henrique and Enzo Faletto. *Dependency and Development in Latin America*. Berkeley: University of California Press, 1979.

Chalmers, Douglas A. "Developing on the Periphery." In James Rosenau, ed., *Linkage Politics: Essays on the Convergence of National and International Systems*, pp. 67–93. New York: Free Press, 1969.

Chase-Dunn, Christopher. "The Effects of International Economic Dependence on Development and Inequality: A Cross-National Study." *American Sociological Review* (December 1975), 40:720–38.

—— "International Economic Dependence in the World System." Ph.D. dissertation, Stanford University, 1975.

Chenery, Hollis and Moises Syrquin. *Patterns of Development, 1950–1970.* London: Oxford University Press for IBRD, 1975.

Chenery, Hollis, Montek S. Ahluwalia, C. L. G. Bell, John H. Duloy, and Richard Jolly. *Redistribution with Growth: Policies to Improve Income Distribution in the Context of Economic Growth—A Joint Study by the World Bank's Development Research Center and the Institute of Development Studies, University of Sussex.* London: Oxford University Press, 1974.

Chilcote, Ronald and Joel Edelstein. "Introduction: Alternative Perspectives of Development and Underdevelopment in Latin America." In Chilcote and Edelstein, eds., *Latin America: The Struggle with Dependency and Beyond,* pp. 4–29. New York: Halsted Press, 1974.

Christopherson, Jon A. "Structural Analysis of Transaction Systems: Vertical Fusion or Network Complexity?" *Journal of Conflict Resolution* (December 1976), 20:637–62.

Cohen, Benjamin. *The Question of Imperialism: The Political Economy of Dominance and Dependence.* New York: Basic Books, 1973.

Corradi, Juan Eugenio. "Cultural Dependence and the Sociology of Knowledge: The Latin American Case." In Corradi, June Nash, and Hobart Spalding, Jr., eds., *Ideology and Social Change in Latin America,* pp. 7–30. New York: Gordan and Breach, 1977.

Cotler, Julio. "The Mechanics of Internal Domination and Social Change in Peru." In Irving Louis Horowitz, ed., *Masses in Latin America,* pp. 407–45. New York: Oxford University Press, 1970.

Cotler, Julio and Richard Fagen, eds. *Latin America and the United States: The Changing Political Realities.* Stanford: Stanford University Press, 1974.

Curzon, Gerard and Victoria Curzon. "Neo-Colonialism and the European Community." In George W. Keeton and Georg Schwarzenberger, eds., *Yearbook of World Affairs,* 25:118–41. New York: Praeger, 1971.

Cutright, Phillips. "Political Structure, Economic Development and National Social Security Programs." In John V. Gillespie and Betty Nesvold, eds., *Macro-Quantitative Analysis: Conflict, Development and Democratization,* pp. 539–55. Beverly Hills: Sage Publications, 1971.

Delacroix, Jacques. "The Export of Raw Materials and Economic Growth: A Cross-National Study." *American Sociological Review* (October 1977), 42:795–808.

—— "Permeability of Informational Boundaries and Economic Growth." *Studies in Comparative International Development* (Spring 1977), 12:3–28.

Deutsch, Karl W. "Theories of Imperialism and Neocolonialism." In Steven Rosen and James Kurth, eds., *Testing Theories of Economic Imperialism*, pp. 15–33. Lexington, Mass.: D. C. Heath, 1974.

Diaz-Alejandro, Carlos F. "North-South Relations: The Economic Component." In C. Fred Bergsten and Lawrence B. Krause, eds., *World Politics and International Economics*, pp. 213–242. Washington, D.C.: The Brookings Institution, 1975.

Dixon-Fyle, S. R. "Monetary Dependence in Africa: The Case of Sierra Leone." *The Journal of Modern African Studies* (June 1978), 16:273–94.

Dominguez, Jorge. "Mice that Roared: Some Aspects of International Politics on the World's Peripheries." *International Organization* (Spring 1971), 25:175–208.

Draper, N. R. and H. Smith. *Applied Regression Analysis.* New York: Wiley, 1966.

Dupuy, T. N. *The Almanac of World Military Power.* Harrisburg, Pa.: Stackpole Books, 1970.

Duvall, Raymond. "Dependence and Dependencia Theory: Notes toward Precision of Concept and Argument." *International Organization* (Winter 1978), 32:51–78.

Duvall, Raymond, Steven Jackson, Bruce Russett, Duncan Snidal, and David Sylvan. "A Formal Model of 'Dependencia' Theory: Structure and Measurement." In Bruce Russett and Richard Merritt, eds., *From National Development to Global Community.* Forthcoming.

Duvall, Raymond and Bruce Russett. "Some Proposals to Guide Research on Contemporary Imperialism." *Jerusalem Journal of International Relations* (Fall 1976), 2:1–27.

Emmanuel, Arghiri. "Myths of Development Versus Myths of Underdevelopment." *New Left Review* (May–June, 1974), no. 85, pp. 61–82.

—— *Unequal Exchange: A Study of the Imperialism of Trade.* New York: Monthly Review Press, 1972.

Erlich, Alexander. "A Hamlet without the Prince of Denmark." *Politics and Society* (Fall 1973), 4:35–53.

Evans, Peter B. "National Autonomy and Economic Development: Critical Perspectives on Multinational Corporations in Poor Countries." *International Organization* (Summer 1971), 25:675–92.

Fagen, Richard. "Studying Latin American Politics: Some Implications of a Dependencia Approach." *Latin American Research Review* (1977), 12:13–26.

Ferguson, George A. *Statistical Analysis in Psychology and Education* 3d ed. New York: McGraw-Hill, 1971.

Fernandez, Raul A. and Jose F. Ocampo. "The Latin American Revolution: A Theory of Imperialism, Not Dependency." *Latin American Perspectives* (Spring 1974), 1:30–61.

Fieldhouse, D. K. " 'Imperialism': An Historiographical Revision." In

Kenneth Boulding and Tapan Mukerjee, eds., *Economic Imperialism: A Book of Readings*, pp. 95–123. Ann Arbor: University of Michigan Press, 1972.

Foxley, Alejandro. *Income Distribution in Latin America*. Cambridge: Cambridge University Press, 1976.

Frank, Andre Gunder. *Capitalism and Underdevelopment in Latin America*. New York: Monthly Review Press, 1967.

—— "Dependence Is Dead, Long Live Dependence and the Class Struggle." *Latin American Perspectives* (Spring 1974), 1:75–87.

—— "The Development of Underdevelopment." In Robert I. Rhodes, ed., *Imperialism and Underdevelopment: A Reader*, pp. 4–17. New York: Monthly Review Press, 1970.

—— "On the Mechanisms of Imperialism: The Case of Brazil." In Robert I. Rhodes, ed., *Imperialism and Underdevelopment: A Reader*, pp. 89–100. New York: Monthly Review Press, 1970.

Friedman, Irving S. *The Emerging Role of Private Banks in the Developing World*. New York: Citicorp, 1977.

Furtado, Celso. *Economic Development of Latin America: A Survey from Colonial Times to the Cuban Revolution*. Cambridge: Cambridge University Press, 1970.

Galbraith, John Kenneth. *The Age of Uncertainty*. Boston: Houghton-Mifflin, 1977.

Galtung, Johan. "A Structural Theory of Imperialism." *Journal of Peace Research* (1971), 8:81–117.

Gantzel, Klaus Jürgen. "Dependency Structures as the Dominant Pattern in World Society." *Journal of Peace Research* (1973), 10:203–15.

Ghai, Dharam P. "The Concept and Strategy of Economic Independence." In Ghai, ed., *Economic Independence in Africa*, pp. 9–34. Nairobi and Dar es Salaam: East African Literature Bureau, 1973.

Gidengil, Elisabeth. "Centres and Peripheries: An Empirical Test of Galtung's Theory of Imperialism." *Journal of Peace Research* (1978), 15:51–66.

Gilbert, Guy J. "Socialism and Dependency." *Latin American Perspectives* (Spring 1974), 1:107–23.

González Casanova, Pablo. "Internal Colonialism and National Development." *Studies in Comparative International Development* (December 1965), 1:27–37.

Gorer, Geoffrey. "Taxation and Labor Practices in French West Africa in the 1930s." In Wilfred Carty and Martin Kilson, eds., *The Africa Reader: Colonial Africa*, pp. 101–7. New York: Vintage, 1970.

Goulet, Denis and Michael Hudson. *The Myth of Aid*. New York: Orbis, 1971.

Green, Reginald H. "Political Independence and the National Economy: An

Essay on the Political Economy of Decolonisation." In *African Perspectives: Papers in the History, Politics, and Economics of Africa Presented to Thomas Hodgkin*, pp. 273–324. Cambridge: Cambridge University Press, 1970.

Green, Reginald H. and Ann Seidman. *Unity or Poverty?: The Economics of Pan-Africanism*. Baltimore: Penguin Books, 1968.

Gregory, Joel W. and Victor Piché. "African Migration and Peripheral Capitalism." *African Perspectives* (1978), pp. 37–50.

Griffin, Keith. "The International Transmission of Inequality." *World Development* (March 1974), 2:3–15.

Grundy, Kenneth W. "Intermediary Power and Global Dependency: The Case of South Africa." *International Studies Quarterly* (December 1976), 20:553–80.

Hart, Judith. *Aid and Liberation: A Socialist Study of Aid Policies*. London: Victor Gollancz, 1973.

Hayter, Theresa. *Aid As Imperialism*. Harmondsworth, Middlesex, England: Penguin Books, 1971.

Hechter, Michael. "Lineages of the Capitalist State." *American Journal of Sociology* (March 1977), 82:1057–1074.

—— "Towards a Theory of Ethnic Change." *Politics and Society* (Fall 1971), 2:21–47.

Hibbs, Douglas A., Jr. *Mass Political Violence: A Cross-National Causal Analysis*. New York: Wiley-Interscience, 1973.

Hilton, Gordon. *Intermediate Politometrics*. New York: Columbia University Press, 1976.

Hobson, J. A. *Imperialism: A Study*. Ann Arbor: University of Michigan Press, 1965.

Hollist, W. Ladd and Thomas H. Johnson. "Modelling United States/Latin American Cooperation and Conflict: Dependencia Arguments." Paper prepared for delivery at the 1977 annual meeting of the Americal Political Science Association, Washington, D.C.

Howe, James, ed. *The U.S. and the Developing World: An Agenda for Action*. New York: Praeger, for Overseas Development Council, 1974.

Hveem, Helge. "The Global Dominance System: Notes on a Theory of Global Political Economy." *Journal of Peace Research* (1973), 10:319–40.

Hymer, Stephen. "The Multinational Corporation and the Law of Uneven Development." In Jagdish Bhagwati, ed., *Economics and World Order from the 1970's to the 1990's*, pp. 113–40. New York: Macmillan, 1972.

Ingram, James. *International Economic Relations*. Englewood Cliffs, N.J.: Prentice-Hall, 1966.

International Bank for Reconstruction and Development (IBRD). *World Bank Atlas*. Washington, D.C.: IBRD, annual.

—— *World Debt Tables: External Public Debt of LDCs.* Washington, D.C.: IBRD, annual with supplements.

—— *World Tables 1976.* Baltimore: John Hopkins University Press, 1976.

International Monetary Fund (IMF). *Balance of Payments Yearbook.* Washington, D.C.: IMF, annual.

—— *Surveys of African Economies,* vol. 6. Washington, D.C.: IMF, 1975.

Jackman, Robert W. "The Need for Reader Access to Measures of Variables Used in Quantitative Cross-National Studies: A Reply." *The American Sociological Review* (August 1976), 41:752–54.

—— *Politics and Social Equality.* New York: Wiley-Interscience, 1975.

Jackson, Steven, Bruce Russett, Duncan Snidal, and David Sylvan. "Conflict and Coercion in Dependent States." *The Journal of Conflict Resolution* (December 1978), 12:627–58.

Jain, Shail. *Size Distribution of Income: A Compilation of Data.* Washington, D.C.: IBRD, 1975.

Jalee, Pierre. *The Third World in World Economy.* New York: Monthly Review Press, 1968.

Kahl, Joseph. *Modernization, Exploitation and Dependency in Latin America: Germani, González Casanova, and Cardoso.* New Brunswick, N.J.: Transaction Books, 1976.

Kaiser, Henry F. "Directional Statistical Decisions." *Psychological Review* (May 1960), 67:160–67.

Kaufman, Robert R., Harry I. Chernotsky and Daniel S. Geller. "A Preliminary Test of the Theory of Dependency." *Comparative Politics* (April 1975), 7:303–30.

Kemp, Tom. "The Marxist Theory of Imperialism." In Roger Owen and Bob Sutcliffe, eds., *Studies in the Theory of Imperialism,* pp. 15–34. London: Longman, 1972.

Kerlinger, Fred N. and Elazar J. Pedhazur. *Multiple Regression in Behavioral Research.* New York: Holt, Rinehart and Winston, 1973.

Kmenta, Jan. *Elements of Econometrics.* New York: Macmillan, 1971.

Knorr, Klaus. *Power and Wealth: The Political Economy of International Power.* New York: Basic Books, 1973.

Krassowski, Andrzej. *Development and the Debt Trap: Planning and External Borrowing in Ghana.* London: Croom Helm, 1974.

Kuh, Edwin. "The Validity of Cross-Sectionally Estimated Behavior Equations in Time Series Applications." *Econometrica* (April 1959), 27:197–214.

Kuh, Edwin and John R. Meyer. "How Extraneous Are Extraneous Estimates?" *The Review of Economics and Statistics* (December 1957), 39:380–93.

Labovitz, Sanford. "The Assignment of Numbers to Rank-Order Categories." *The American Sociological Review* (June 1970), 35:514–24.

Leitenberg, Milton. "Notes on the Diversion of Resources for Military Purposes in Developing Nations." *Journal of Peace Research* (1976), 13:111–16.

Lenin, V. I. *Imperialism: The Highest Stage of Capitalism.* In Henry M. Christman, ed., *Essential Works of Lenin,* pp. 177–270. New York: Bantam Books, 1966.

Lewis-Beck, Michael. "Stepwise Regression: A Caution." *Political Methodology* (1978), 5:213–40.

Leys, Colin. *Underdevelopment in Kenya: The Political Economy of Neocolonialism.* Berkeley: University of California Press, 1974.

Lichtheim, George. *Imperialism.* New York: Praeger, 1971.

Mack, Andrew. "Comparing Theories of Economic Imperialism." In Steven Rosen and James Kurth, eds., *Testing Theories of Economic Imperialism,* pp. 35–55. Lexington, Mass.: D. C. Heath, 1974.

McGowan, Patrick J. "Economic Dependence and Economic Performance in Black Africa." *The Journal of Modern African Studies* (March 1976), 14:25–40.

McGowan, Patrick J. and Dale L. Smith. "Economic Dependency in Black Africa: An Analysis of Competing Theories." *International Organization* (Winter 1978), 32:179–235.

McKinlay, R. D. and A. S. Cohan. "A Comparative Analysis of the Political and Economic Performance of Military and Civilian Regimes: A Cross-National Aggregate Study." *Comparative Politics* (October 1975), 8:1–30.

McMichael, Philip, James Petras, and Robert Rhodes. "Imperialism and the Contradictions of Development." *New Left Review* (May–June 1974), no. 85, pp. 83–104.

Magdoff, Harry. *The Age of Imperialism.* New York: Monthly Review Press, 1969.

Mayer, Lawrence. "A Note on Treating Ordinal Data as Interval Data." *The American Sociological Review* (June 1971), 36:519–520.

Mende, Tibor. *From Aid to Recolonization: Lessons of a Failure.* New York: Pantheon Books, 1973.

Meyer, Alfred. *Leninism.* Cambridge: Harvard University Press, 1957.

Minter, William. *Imperial Network and External Dependency: The Case of Angola.* Beverly Hills: Sage Professional Papers in International Studies, 02–011, 1972.

Moore, Barrington, Jr. *Social Origins of Dictatorship and Democracy: Lord and Peasant in the Making of the Modern World.* Boston: Beacon Press, 1966.

Moran, Theodore. *Multinational Corporations and the Politics of Development: Copper in Chile.* Princeton: Princeton University Press, 1974.

Morrison, Donald, Robert C. Mitchell, John N. Paden, and Hugh M. Stevens, eds. *Black Africa: A Comparative Handbook.* New York: Free Press, 1972.

Myrdal, Gunnar. *Rich Lands and Poor: The Road to World Prosperity.* New York: Harper & Row, 1957.

Nie, Norman H., C. Hadlai Hull, Jean G. Jenkins, Karin Steinbrenner, and Dale H. Bent. *Statistical Package for the Social Sciences.* 2d ed. New York: McGraw-Hill, 1975.

Nisbet, Charles. "Transferring Wealth from Underdeveloped to Developed Countries Via Direct Foreign Investment: A Marxist Claim Reconsidered." *Southern Economic Journal* (July 1970), 37:93–96.

Nkrumah, Kwame. *Neo-Colonialism: The Last Stage of Imperialism.* New York: International Publishers, 1966.

Øberg, Jan. "Arms Trade with the Third World as an Aspect of Imperialism." *Journal of Peace Research* (1975), 12:213–34.

O'Brien, Philip J. "A Critique of Latin American Theories of Dependency." In Ivor Oxaal, T. Barnett, and D. Booth, eds., *Beyond the Sociology of Development,* pp. 7–27. London: Routledge and Kegan Paul, 1975.

O'Connor, James. "International Corporations and Economic Underdevelopment." *Science and Society* (Spring 1970), 34:42–60.

Odell, John S. "Correlates of U.S. Military Assistance and Military Intervention." In Steven Rosen and James Kurth, eds., *Testing Theories of Economic Imperialism,* pp. 143–61. Lexington, Mass.: D. C. Heath, 1974.

O'Donnell, Guillermo. *Modernization and Bureaucratic-Authoritarianism: Studies in South American Politics.* Politics of Modernization Series, no. 9. Berkeley: Institute of International Studies, University of California, 1973.

Organisation for Economic Co-operation and Development (OECD). *Development Co-operation: Efforts and Policies of the Members of the Development Assistance Committee.* Paris: OECD, annual.

——*Geographical Distribution of Financial Flows to Developing Countries: Data on Disbursements and Commitments in 1974.* Paris: OECD, 1976.

——Development Assistance Directorate. *Stock of Private Direct Investments by D.A.C. Countries in Developing Countries, End-1967.* Paris: OECD, 1972.

Owen, Roger and Bob Sutcliffe, eds. *Studies in the Theory of Imperialism.* London: Longman, 1972.

Paukert, Felix. "Income Distribution at Different Levels of Development." *International Labour Review* (August–September 1973), 108:97–125.

Payer, Cheryl. *The Debt Trap: The IMF and the Third World.* New York: Monthly Review Press, 1975.

Petras, James and Thomas Cook. "Dependency and the Industrial Bourgeoisie: Attitudes of Argentine Executives toward Foreign Economic Investment and U.S. Policy." In Petras, ed., *Latin America: From Dependence to Revolution,* pp. 143–63. New York: Wiley, 1973.

Petrovic, Negosava. "Relations between the European Economic Community and the 18 Associated African Countries." *International Problems* (Belgrade) (1971),127–43.

Poulantzas, Nicos. "Internationalisation of Capitalist Relations and the Nation-State." *Economy and Society* (May 1974), 3:145–79.

Pye, Lucian W. *Aspects of Political Development.* Boston: Little, Brown, 1966.

Ray, David. "The Dependency Model of Latin American Underdevelopment: Three Basic Fallacies." *Journal of Interamerican Studies and World Affairs* (January 1973), 15:4–20.

Reuber, Grant. *Private Foreign Investment in Development.* Oxford: Clarendon Press, 1973.

Richardson, Neil R. "Political Compliance and U.S. Trade Dominance." *The American Political Science Review* (December 1976), 70:1098–1109.

Riddell, J. Barry. *The Spatial Dynamics of Modernization in Sierra Leone: Structure, Diffusion, and Response.* Evanston: Northwestern University Press, 1970.

Robinson, Ronald. "Non-European Foundations of European Imperialism: Sketch for a Theory of Collaboration." In Roger Owen and Bob Sutcliffe, eds., *Studies in the Theory of Imperialism,* pp. 117–42. London: Longman, 1972.

Robock, Stefan H. and Kenneth Simmonds. *International Business and Multinational Enterprises.* Homewood, Ill.: Richard D. Irwin, 1973.

Rodney, Walter. *How Europe Underdeveloped Africa.* London: Bogle-L'Ouverture Publications and Dar es Salaam: Tanzania Publishing House, 1972.

Rosenbaum, H. Jon and William G. Tyler. "South-South Relations: The Political and Economic Content of Interactions Among Developing Countries." In C. Fred Bergsten and Lawrence B. Krause, eds., *World Politics and International Economics,* pp. 243–74. Washington, D.C.: The Brookings Institution, 1975.

Rubinson, Richard. "Dependence, Government Revenue, and Economic Growth, 1955–1970." *Studies in Comparative International Development* (Summer 1977), 12:3–28.

——"Reply to Bach and Irwin." *American Sociological Review* (October, 1977), 42:817–21.

——"The World-Economy and the Distribution of Income Within States: A Cross-National Study." *American Sociological Review* (August 1976), 41:638–59.

Ruddle, Kenneth and Donald Odermann, eds. *Statistical Abstract of Latin America 15*. Los Angeles: UCLA Latin American Center Publications, University of California, 1973.

Russett, Bruce M. *International Regions and the International System: A Study in Political Ecology*. Chicago: Rand McNally, 1967.

——"Some Decisions in the Regression Analysis of Time-Series Data." In James F. Herndon and Joseph L. Bernd, eds., *Mathematical Applications in Political Science*, 5:31–50. Charlottesville: The University Press of Virginia, 1971.

Santos, Theotonio dos. "The Structure of Dependence." In K. T. Fann and Donald Hodges, eds., *Readings in U.S. Imperialism*, pp. 225–36. Boston: Porter-Sargent, 1971.

Sauvant, Karl P. "Multinational Enterprises and the Transmission of Culture: The International Supply of Advertising and Business Education." *Journal of Peace Research* (1976), 13:49–65.

Sawyer, Malcom. "Income Distribution in OECD Countries." *OECD Economic Outlook, Occasional Studies* (July 1976), pp. 3–36.

Schuessler, Karl. "Analysis of Ratio Variables: Opportunities and Pitfalls." *American Journal of Sociology* (September 1974), 80:379–95.

Schumpeter, Joseph. *Imperialism and Social Classes: Two Essays*. New York: Meridian Books, 1955.

Sellers, Robert C. *Armed Forces of the World: A Reference Handbook*, 3d ed. New York: Praeger, 1971.

Serra, Jose. "The Brazilian 'Economic Miracle.'" In James Petras, ed., *Latin America: From Dependence to Revolution*, pp. 100–40. New York: Wiley, 1973.

Singer, H. W. "The Distribution of Gains between Borrowing and Investing Countries." *American Economic Review* (May 1950), 40:473–85.

Singer, Marshall. *Weak States in a World of Powers*. New York: Free Press, 1972.

Sklar, Richard. *Corporate Power in an African State: The Political Impact of Multinational Mining Companies in Zambia*. Berkeley: University of California Press, 1975.

Snyder, David and Edward L. Kick. "Structural Position in the World System and Economic Growth, 1955–1970: A Multiple-Network Analysis of Transnational Interactions." *American Journal of Sociology* (March 1979), 84:1097–1126.

——"The Distribution of Gains from Trade and Investment—Revisited." *Journal of Development Studies* (July 1975), 11:376–82.

Stallings, Barbara. *Economic Dependency in Africa and Latin America*. Beverly Hills: Sage Professional Papers in Comparative Politics, 01–031, 1972.

Stauffer, Robert B. *Nation Building in a Global Economy: The Role of the Multinational Corporation.* Beverly Hills: Sage Professional Papers in Comparative Politics, 01–039, 1973.

Stavenhagen, Rodolfo. "Seven Fallacies About Latin America." In James Petras and Maurice Zeitlin, eds., *Latin America: Reform or Revolution?* pp. 13–31. Greenwich, Conn.: Fawcett Publications, 1968.

Stehr, Uwe. "Unequal Development and Dependency Structures in COME-CON." *Journal of Peace Research* (1977), 14:115–28.

Stevenson, Paul. "External Economic Variables Influencing the Economic Growth Rate of Seven Major Latin American Nations." *Canadian Review of Sociology and Anthropology* (November 1972), 9:347–57.

Stockholm International Peace Research Institute (SIPRI). *World Armaments and Disarmament: SIPRI Yearbook.* Cambridge: M.I.T. Press, annual.

Sunkel, Osvaldo. "Big Business and 'Dependencia': A Latin American View." *Foreign Affairs* (April 1972), 50:517–33.

——"National Development Policy and External Dependence in Latin America." In Yale H. Ferguson, ed., *Contemporary Inter-American Relations: A Reader in Theory and Issues,* pp. 465–92. Englewood Cliffs, N.J.: Prentice-Hall, 1972.

—— "Transnational Capitalism and National Disintegration in Latin America." *Social and Economic Studies* (March 1973), 22:132–76.

Szentes, Tamás. *The Political Economy of Underdevelopment.* Budapest: Akadémiai Kiadó, 1976.

Szymanski, Albert. "Dependence, Exploitation, and Economic Growth." *Journal of Political and Military Sociology* (Spring 1976), 4:53–65.

Taylor, Charles Lewis and Michael C. Hudson, eds. *World Handbook of Political and Social Indicators.* 2d ed. New Haven: Yale University Press, 1972.

Tufte, Edward. "Improving Data Analysis in Political Science." *World Politics* (July 1969), 21:641–654.

Tyler, William G. and J. Peter Wogart. "Economic Dependence and Marginalization: Some Empirical Evidence." *Journal of Interamerican Studies and World Affairs* (February 1973), 15:36–45.

United Nations. Conference on Trade and Development. *Handbook of International Trade and Development Statistics.* New York: United Nations, quadrennial with supplements.

—— Department of Economic and Social Affairs. *Demographic Yearbook.* New York: United Nations, annual.

—— Economic Commission for Africa. *African Statistical Yearbook.* Addis Ababa: United Nations, ECA, annual.

—— Economic Commission for Europe. *Economic Survey of Europe.* Geneva: United Nations, annual.

—— Economic Commission for Latin America. *Economic Survey of Latin America*. New York: United Nations, annual.

—— Economic and Social Commission for Asia and the Pacific. *Statistical Yearbook for Asia and the Pacific*. Bangkok: ESCAP, annual.

—— Educational, Scientific, and Cultural Organization. *Statistical Yearbook*. Paris: The UNESCO Press, annual.

—— Food and Agricultural Organization. *Production Yearbook*. Rome: FAO, annual.

—— *The External Financing of Economic Development: The International Flow of Long-Term Capital and Official Donations, 1964–1968*. New York: United Nations, 1970.

—— *Multinational Corporations in World Development*. New York: United Nations, 1973.

—— *Statistical Yearbook*. New York: United Nations, annual.

—— *Survey of Economic Conditions in Africa*. New York: United Nations, 1973.

—— [Raul Prebisch]. *Towards a New Trade Policy for Development: Report by the Secretary-General of the United Nations Conference on Trade and Development*. New York: United Nations, 1964.

—— *Trade in Manufactures of Developing Countries and Territories, 1973 Review*. New York: United Nations, 1974.

—— *World Communications: A 200-Country Survey of Press, Radio, Television and Film*. New York: Unipub, 1975.

—— *World Economic Survey*. New York: United Nations, annual.

—— *Yearbook of International Trade Statistics*. New York: United Nations, annual.

United States. Arms Control and Disarmament Agency. *World Military Expenditures and Arms Transfers, 1965–1974*. Washington, D.C.: Government Printing Office, 1976.

—— Department of Commerce. *Survey of Current Business*. Washington, D.C.: Government Printing Office, monthly.

—— Department of Health, Education, and Welfare. *Social Security Programs Throughout the World, 1971*. Washington, D.C.: Government Printing Office, 1971.

Vaitsos, Constantine V. *Intercountry Income Distribution and Transnational Enterprises*. Oxford: Clarendon Press, 1974.

Vengroff, Richard. "Dependency and Underdevelopment in Black Africa: An Empirical Test." *The Journal of Modern African Studies* (December 1977), 15:613–30.

—— "Neo-Colonialism and Policy Outputs in Africa." *Comparative Political Studies* (July 1975), 8:234–50.

Verba, Sidney, and Norman H. Nie. *Participation in America: Political Democracy and Social Equality*. New York: Harper & Row, 1972.

Vitale, Luis. "Latin America: Feudal or Capitalist?" In James Petras and Maurice Zeitlin, eds., *Latin America: Reform or Revolution?*, pp. 32–43. Greenwich, Conn.: Fawcett Publications, 1968.

Walleri, R. Dan. "The Political Economy of International Inequality: A Test of Dependency Theory." Ph.D. dissertation, University of Hawaii, 1976.

—— "Trade Dependence and Underdevelopment: A Causal-Chain Analysis." *Comparative Political Studies* (April 1978), 11:94–127.

Wallerstein, Immanuel. "Class Formation in the Capitalist World-Economy." *Politics and Society* (May 1975), 5:367–76.

—— "Dependence in an Interdependent World: The Limited Possibilities of Transformation within the Capitalist World-Economy." *African Studies Review* (April 1974), 17:1–26.

—— *The Modern World System: Capitalist Agriculture and the Origins of the European World-Economy in the Sixteenth Century.* New York: Academic Press, 1974.

—— "The Rise and Future Demise of the World Capitalist System: Concepts for Comparative Analysis." *Comparative Studies in Society and History* (September 1974), 16:387–415.

Warren, Bill. "Imperialism and Capitalist Industrialization." *New Left Review* (September–October 1973), no. 81, pp. 3–44.

Weaver, Jerry. "Arms Transfers to Latin America: A Note on the Contagion Effect." *Journal of Peace Research* (1974), 11:213–28.

Weisskopf, Thomas E. "Capitalism, Underdevelopment, and the Future of the Poor Countries." In Jagdish Bhagwati, ed., *Economics and World Order from the 1970's to the 1990's*, pp. 43–77. New York: Macmillan, 1972.

West, Robert LeRoy. "Economic Dependence and Policy in Developing Countries." In C. Fred Bergsten and William G. Tyler, eds., *Leading Issues in International Economic Policy*, pp. 157–83. Lexington, Mass.: D. C. Heath, 1973.

Wilson, Thomas P. "A Critique of Ordinal Variables." *Social Forces* (March 1971), 49:432–44.

Wittkopf, Eugene R. *Western Bilateral Aid Allocations: A Comparative Study of Recipient State Attributes and Aid Received.* Beverly Hills: Sage Professional Papers in International Studies, 02-005, 1972.

Woddis, Jack. *An Introduction to Neocolonialism.* New York: International Publishers, 1967.

Wolf, Eric R. *Peasant Wars of the Twentieth Century.* New York: Harper & Row, 1969.

Zartman, I. William. "Europe and Africa: Decolonization or Dependency?" *Foreign Affairs* (January 1976), 54:325–43.

—— *The Politics of Trade Negotiations between Africa and the European Economic Community: The Weak Confront the Strong.* Princeton: Princeton University Press, 1971.

Zeitlin, Irving R. *Capitalism and Imperialism: An Introduction to Neo-Marxian Concepts.* Chicago: Markham, 1972.

Zelditch, Morris, Jr. "Intelligible Comparisons." In Ivan Vallier, ed., *Comparative Methods in Sociology: Essays on Trends and Applications,* pp. 267–307. Berkeley: University of California Press, 1971.

Index

ABC countries (Argentina, Brazil, Chile), 111
Absolute GNP, indicator: discussion of, 78,
  176; used in analysis, 86-87
Absolute population, indicator: discussion of,
  78, 176; used in analysis, 86-87
Adelman, Irma, 73
Afghanistan, 128
Africa, North, 192n9
Africa, sub-Saharan, 99-108
"Africa of the Colonial Economy," see Amin,
  Samir
"Africa of the Concession-Owning
  Companies," see Amin, Samir
"Africa of the Labour Reserves," see Amin,
  Samir
Aid, indicator: discussion of, 39, 172; used in
  analysis, 42-46
Aid, international economic, 32-33, 131-32;
  tied to purchases in donor country, 45; see
  also "Official Development Assistance"
Aid concentration, indicator: discussion of, 39,
  172; used in analysis, 42-46
Aid-trade terms, indicator: discussion of, 45;
  used in analysis, 84
Alschuler, Lawrence R., 19-21, 65, 74, 87,
  179n17
America, Central, 25, 110, 122, 127
America, South, 25, 122, 127
Amin, Samir, 65, 97, 99-108; "Africa of the
  Colonial Economy," 99, 102, 104, 107-8;
  "Africa of the Concession-Owning Com-
  panies," 100, 108; "Africa of the Labour
  Reserves," 100, 108
Analysis of covariance, 139, 191n25
Analysis of variance, 191n24
Andean countries, 110-11
Argentina, 40, 54, 137, 142
Arms transfers, indicator: discussion of, 40,
  173; used in analysis, 80-81, 84, 133-35

Asia, 113-16; as a relatively less dependent
  region, 191n24
"Associated-dependent development," see
  Cardoso, Fernando Henrique
Australia, 11

Baran, Paul A., 58
Belgium, 103, 106, 129
Belgium-Luxembourg (trade bloc), 123-24
Benin (Dahomey), 100, 102, 106
Blalock, Hubert M., 160
Bodenheimer, Susanne, 33, 64
Bolivia, 193n4
Bottom 40 income share, indicator: discussion
  of, 72-73, 174; used in analysis, 84
Bourgeoisie, national, 56-62; see also Elite,
  internationalized
Brazil, 54, 62, 64-65, 74, 130, 142, 153,
  180n4, 193n4
Brenner, Robert, 155-59
Britain, see United Kingdom
Brookfield, Harold, 59
Burma, 93, 115

Cameroun, 105
Canada, 10, 111, 128, 130
Caporaso, James A., 6
Cardoso, Fernando Henrique, 58-59, 61,
  66-67, 81, 87-90, 150
Caribbean, 110, 122, 127
Center-periphery imagery, 53-64, 119-21
Central African Empire (Republic), 100, 102
CEPAL (Economic Commission for Latin
  America), 51
Chad, 100
Chase-Dunn, Christopher, 18-19, 65, 74, 87
Chenery, Hollis B., 73, 76, 77
Chernotsky, Harry I., see Kaufman, Robert R.
  et al.